MW00635657

Praise for *Measuring What Matters*

"A great book for motivated managers who want to take control of their environment. Offers strategies to improve the effectiveness of senior management teams that must collaborate to plan and implement operational initiatives."
—JAY MORLEY, PRESIDENT, NATIONAL ASSOCIATION OF COLLEGE AND UNIVERSITY BUSINESS OFFICERS

"Moves measurement to the next level by equipping work teams with commonsense tools to measure the connections that bind them to their core stakeholders. It may be common sense, but it most assuredly is not common practice. Therein lies the opportunity!"
—WILLIAM P. SIMPSON, PRESIDENT, UNIVERSITY OF CONNECTICUT COOPERATIVE CORPORATION

"Using this book to build and execute strategy is almost certain to lead to success—whether you work in the bottom-line drive or not-for-profit world."
—GARY F. SHAPIRO, SENIOR VICE PRESIDENT, INTELLECTUAL PROPERTY, FOLLETT HIGHER EDUCATION GROUP

"Hits the core of executing business strategy every day. Napier and McDaniel have created a work that is for anyone starting a business, operating a business, or just in a business. It is applicable to all business owners, operators, and managers."
—BRITT HINTON, PRESIDENT, ACADEMIC BOOK SERVICES, INC.; PRESIDENT, KUDZU BOOK TRADERS

"Provides a simple way to measure, communicate, train, and implement objectives to meet the needs of stakeholders—not at the 30,000-foot level, but at the team level. At Cornell University, we are doing this and it really works!"
—THOMAS ROMANTIC, DIRECTOR, CORNELL BUSINESS SERVICES

MEASURING WHAT MATTERS

MEASURING
WHAT
MATTERS

SIMPLIFIED TOOLS FOR ALIGNING TEAMS
AND THEIR STAKEHOLDERS

ROD NAPIER & RICH McDANIEL

Mountain View, California

Published by Davies-Black Publishing, a division of CPP, Inc., 1055 Joaquin Road, 2nd Floor, Mountain View, CA 94043; 800-624-1765.

Special discounts on bulk quantities of Davies-Black books are available to corporations, professional associations, and other organizations. For details, contact the Director of Marketing and Sales at Davies-Black Publishing; 650-691-9123; fax 650-623-9271.

Visit the Davies-Black Publishing Web site at www.daviesblack.com.

10 09 08 07 06 10 9 8 7 6 5 4 3 2 1
Printed in the United States of America

Library of Congress Cataloging-in-Publication Data
Measuring what matters : simplified tools for aligning teams and their stakeholders / Rod Napier & Rich McDaniel.— 1st ed.
    p. cm.
Includes bibliographical references and index.
ISBN 13: 978-0-89106-211-0
ISBN 10: 0-89106-211-4
1. Teams in the workplace. 2. Organizational change. 3. Management.
I. McDaniel, Rich. II Title.
HD66.N35 2006
658.4′022—dc22
                                                                      2005030671
FIRST EDITION
First printing 2006

Contents

List of Exercises   viii
Preface   ix
Acknowledgments   xv
About the Authors   xvii

Part One: A Framework for Measurement

1 **Measuring What Matters** Exchanging Value with Stakeholders 3

2 **Owners Come First** Exchanging Value with Owners 27

3 **Customers Come First** Exchanging Value with Customers 79

4 **Employees Come First** Exchanging Value with Employees 129

5 **Stakeholders Come First** The Winning Exchange of Value 171

Part Two: Power Tools for Management

6 **Trust Matters** The Key to Organizational Change 187

7 **Leadership Matters** A Case Study of a Manager 213

8 **Teamwork Matters** The Group Management Questionnaire 261

9 **Performance Matters** Developmental Supervision 307

10 **Profit Matters** The PEI-Genesis Story 345

Appendix   361
Notes   375
Index   379

Exercises

1. Who Are Our Owners?   29
2. Owners Value Purpose Alignment: How Are We Doing?   38
3. Owners Value "Process Performance": How Are We Doing?   48
4. Who Are Our Customers?   85
5. What Do Our Customers Value and Expect?   90
6. How Are We Doing at Meeting or Exceeding Customers' Expectations?   96
7. Who Are Our Employees?   134
8. What Do Our Employees Value and Expect?   138
9. How Is the Company Doing at Meeting or Exceeding Employee Expectations?   140
10. The Trust Survey   202
11. Follow-Up to the Trust Survey   208
12. The Group Management Questionnaire (GMQ)   279
13. The Supervisory Dialogue   319
14. The Supervisory Review   339
15. The Leadership Effectiveness Survey   340

Preface

Successful managers understand that giving and receiving are inseparably linked and that the exchange of value among core stakeholders lies at the center of all organizational purpose. One well-circulated story to make the point describes a manager who died and went to heaven. There he found all former managers separated into two groups—the failures in one hall and the successful ones in the other. Around mealtime he entered the hall of those who had failed and was surprised to find the occupants thin and hungry looking. When the angels began to serve dinner, large platters of delicious foods were placed at the tables, but before anyone was seated, another angel came along and strapped a long iron spoon to each manager's arm. The long handles of the spoons were fastened to the managers' wrists and biceps, making it impossible for them to bend their arms. As a result, no one was able to lift the spoon to his mouth.

Walking over to the hall of those who had succeeded, the newly arrived manager was surprised to find this group well fed and healthy. Dinner was already on the table, and an angel had just finished strapping the long iron spoons to the arms of the diners. Each manager then dipped his spoon into the food and fed the person seated across from him.

Successful managers covet loyal customers, productive employees, and supportive owners, and they are keenly aware of the interdependencies that bind them to the company. In effect, value is being delivered in return for value received. The company may offer an attractive combination of price, quality, and convenience to its customers in return for loyalty, a profitable business relationship, and cooperation in providing critical feedback. It offers a blend of benefits to its employees in return for their productivity and partnership, and it offers owners financial benefits or the achievement of some worthy social service in return for resources invested and risks undertaken. Thoughtfully managing this exchange is the single most strategic activity affecting long-term success. Few give it the attention it deserves.

Effective measurement systems enable organizations to concretely assess and improve the exchange of value with their stakeholders. Yet corporate measurement is typically unbalanced, failing to pay enough attention to one or more key stakeholder groups such as the corporation's customers or its employees. Even core owner measures are commonly lopsided, focusing on financial factors while leaving critical operating indicators unaddressed. Such weaknesses have been duly noted in recent years by authors advocating various remedies, including "balanced scorecards," "performance prisms," and "success trees." Their common priority in measurement is to monitor progress in delivering value to a broader range of stakeholders. Although still not widely practiced, the approach is compelling, especially in a competitive environment in which stakeholders have choices.

Failure to achieve stakeholder balance in work teams is even more common. The consequences are severe because it is the front line that produces the bottom line. Although defined at the top, corporate strategy is implemented through work teams. Premium-service strategies require knowledgeable, friendly, efficient, and responsive service providers. Premium-quality strategies require motivated and competent production workers. Despite their strategic impact, work teams rarely understand either the overarching corporate goals or their part in achieving them. It is rarer still that they are guided by effective measurement. This inside-out, bottom-up perspective is easily overlooked and underappreciated in executive discussions of strategy and measurement. Yet most of the heavy lifting is done here in these work groups of a dozen or fewer, in which people labor shoulder to shoulder, sharing a common mission, common leadership, common resources, and common stakeholders. It is here that measurement is most intuitive and actionable, and it is here that measurement is weakest. A work team guided by balanced feedback from its customers, employees, and owners will be far better positioned to navigate whatever turbulent changes lie ahead.

In a world in which discovery is aided by smart machines and the whole of human knowledge doubles every five years, in which DNA has been mapped and cars are navigated by satellites, who would deny that change has never been more pervasive and certain? The underlying forces are unstoppable. Technological breakthroughs abound. A worldwide market economy fosters ever more intense competition, causing customers to expect more, product life cycles to shorten, and processes to become more complicated. Add to this myriad powerful demographic, political, and economic forces. Collectively, they create pressing consequences for organizations and their work teams if they fail to change fast enough.

And yet these daunting challenges also bring extraordinary opportunities. Many products and services can now be "mass customized." Today, "have it your way" applies not only to hamburgers but also to cars, clothing, computers, and college educations. Entire supply channels have been integrated to provide faster, better, cheaper delivery to customers. Even relationships often can be managed with one-to-one precision. Twenty-first-century innovators are reinventing themselves, rewriting their missions, and reengineering their processes to make themselves more holistic, more personal, and more proactive. There are unprecedented opportunities to build dynamic "learning organizations," in which anyone with competence to contribute can do so, and better decisions can be made nearly in real time. These opportunities apply directly to work teams, inviting development of new skills and advancement to more fulfilling roles with greater involvement. Like it or not, all of these changes increase both the risks and the rewards in the workplace by multiplying the number of choices available to customers, employees, and owners. *Measuring and managing the corporate exchange of value with core stakeholders has never been more important, and it is becoming more important.*

However, the robust and tightly structured change-management systems, such as "continuous improvement," "benchmarking," and Process Reengineering, which have been featured prominently in the business literature for the past two decades, have not met expectations. A postmortem points to at least three reasons for widespread underperformance. Foremost among them is that too many of the people affected simply did not want to change. Fear, complacency, and a failure to crisply define and communicate vision added to a host of other essentially cultural dysfunctions. A second reason is that people did not know what to do. The process itself was often poorly defined and planned; resources were frequently inadequate. The words often sounded right enough: "Quality comes first" and "Excellence matters most." But such initiatives were more slogan than substance. A third reason for failure is that people did not know how to do it. They simply lacked the critical skills. Training and support were inadequate or poorly invested, and all too often the processes themselves were unnecessarily complicated and unwieldy. In the end, behavior at work is not unlike behavior elsewhere. It is substantially defined by habits, and habits do not change without compelling motivation, clear definition, and effective skills.

For most workers, daily routines still remain remarkably constant for lengthy periods. But when the storms come, often in the form of strategic realignments leading to structural reorganization, they can bring a tidal wave of change. One colleague rightly observed, "It sometimes takes a long time for things to happen quickly." How, then, can work teams better anticipate and navigate these turbulent times? An essential part of the answer is that they must become more closely connected to their core stakeholders. Meeting, and preferably exceeding, their legitimate expectations is essential to the deployment of any balanced corporate strategy, and that requires defining and measuring value delivered and value received.

What would it mean to measure what matters? Such an undertaking is in part conveyed in this amusing story: Deep in the Black Hills of South Dakota, a ferocious blizzard was raging. The new minister of the country church waited anxiously at the door to see if any parishioners would brave the elements that first Sunday morning. At last, one old farmer rode up, dismounted his horse, and approached the door. "Sir," said the minister, "the weather is so severe that it appears that you'll be the only one able to get here, and, frankly, I'm not real sure what to do." The sage old fellow looked him straight in the eye and said, "Reverend, when I haul a load of hay out into the field to feed to my cattle and only one cow shows up, I still feed it." Warmed by these words of encouragement, the minister mounted the pulpit and began his oration. More than two hours passed as he shared with power and passion all that was on his heart. After the closing benediction, the minister hurried over to his solitary parishioner. "Sir," he said anxiously, "please tell me what you think." The old fellow looked up somewhat dazed and weary and replied, "Reverend, when I haul a load of hay out into the field and only one cow shows up, I don't give her the whole load."

This book is not intended to serve up the "whole load" on measurement. We leave that to others, with the caution that the impact may not be unlike the effect on that old farmer. We write instead to professionals in organizational effectiveness seeking to counsel work teams from a more holistic and balanced perspective. We write to workflow professionals seeking a simpler and conceptually sound approach. Most of all, we write to leaders in work teams throughout the company who seek to cut to the chase and to measure what matters. *It is this exchange of value between work teams and their core stakeholders that matters most.* There are always at least three such stakeholders:

- **Customers:** the recipients of goods or services produced by the team

- **Employees:** individuals working together under a common supervisor, sharing common resources, and pursuing a common purpose

- **Owners:** founders, investors, and their representatives, including the corporate chain of command

For each stakeholder, we propose a simple process to define and measure the value exchange with the company, both value received and value delivered. By beginning with stakeholder value in mind and taking priority steps to clearly define and measure effectiveness in delivering it, one brings new perspective to measurement;

XIV   MEASURING WHAT MATTERS

it is the perspective of the team's core customers, employees, and owners. It is a perspective that informs assessment and empowers the collective effort toward continuous improvement. Best of all, *it can be acted upon immediately, by any motivated leader at any level.*

In Chapter 1 we discuss this conceptual framework more fully. Chapters 2, 3, and 4 explain how to apply this commonsense process to a team's owners, customers, and employees. These chapters include exercises that encourage immediate application of the model and a case study that progressively unfolds each stakeholder's perspective. Chapter 5 brings the insights and findings together into one mosaic, demonstrating stakeholder interdependencies and the importance of crafting a comprehensive purpose that captures their common interests.

In Part 2 (Chapters 6 through 10), we provide several powerful tools, using case studies, that target some of the most pervasive and expensive problems facing work teams, beginning with a chapter on trust. Trust is the lubricant reducing human frictions among stakeholders and fostering corporate purpose. No perspective is more effective in the long term to engender trust than the common concerted effort to understand and improve the delivery of value to *all* stakeholders. Chapters 7 through 9 focus on leadership, teamwork, and performance assessment. Chapter 10 closes our study with a case demonstrating the power and potential for using targeted measures to better understand both people and process. Throughout, we provide a way of thinking about data and how to use it. The philosophy and the applications all reflect the underlying human issues that anyone who wants to make a difference needs to consider.

Acknowledgments

Most important to the quality and tenor of this book has been the help and bold support of Connie Kallback, our editor. She has made the entire effort a very human and collaborative process—a truly memorable partnership.

Without the help of Patrick Sanaghan and Julie Roberts, our chapter on the utilization of numbers in support of team development would not have been possible. Without something of value to measure, there would have been no chapter.

Finally, I would like to acknowledge the many clients and students with whom I have engaged over the years and from whom I have gotten the encouragement to attempt new designs, new strategies, and new approaches. Experimentation can occur only if there is a laboratory for testing new ideas. Receiving their enthusiastic support in the real world laboratories of business and education has been a huge gift.

—Rod Napier

This project was more than a book; it was a catharsis. In many ways it afforded an opportunity to synthesize a lifetime of learning into a handful of insights. I am deeply indebted to my many teachers—authors, colleagues, and mentors alike.

To the hundreds of authors whose ideas introduced new perspectives, I am truly grateful. None have affected my thinking more than Dr. Stephen Covey, whose books on principle-centered leadership and personal effectiveness are among the best ever written.

A handful of professional colleagues have shared in much experiential learning. These include Gary Shapiro, Pam Mills, Bill Simpson, Roger Reynolds, John Turk, and Roxi Hewertson. To the reader these are just names. To me, these people have shared in a lifetime of learning.

And, of course, there are a very few, very special mentors. Thanks to Ken Blanchard, who taught me that a few actionable, powerful, and simple insights can change the world; Jay Morley, who taught me the importance of rigorous process; and my coauthor and partner, Rod Napier, who taught me that process is more than work flow; it is as much or more about how people work together.

And, most of all, I will forever be indebted to Hal Craft, one of the most principle-centered leaders I have ever known, a man of enormous integrity.

Lastly, I thank my wife, Gretchen, and son, Jason, whose insights, edits, and encouragement added much to the pages that follow.

—Rich McDaniel

About the Authors

Rod Napier was a professor in the areas of group and organizational dynamics at Temple University for a decade during the early years of the group dynamics movement. Currently he teaches in the Center of Organizational Dynamics at the University of Pennsylvania and is a Teaching Fellow at the Wharton School. He is an applied theorist who uses his experiences consulting with a wide range of institutions to shape the strategies he then translates into books (a dozen to this point) for leaders and managers. He co-authored *Groups: Theory and Experience,* which is in its seventh edition and remains one of the leading texts in the field of group dynamics. Other books include *The Courage to Act, Tools and Activities for Strategic Planning,* and *Intentional Design and the Process of Change.* He is working on a book exploring the impact leadership seduction has on every aspect of organizational life.

His clients have included Bechtel, Exxon, the United Nations, CBS, the University of Pennsylvania, Wellesley College, the University of Virginia, Solaris Health System, the United States War College, Outward Bound USA, the cabinet of the Nicaraguan govenment, Merck, and the Pennsylvania Power and Light Company. He has done groundbreaking work in Ghana, West Africa, South Africa, Chile, Mexico, Russia, and Finland.

He is the father of three wonderful daughters who have taught him about the woman's movement and are adult best friends. He is married to Julie Roberts, his partner of eighteen years.

Rich McDaniel is Associate Vice President of Campus and Business Services at Cornell University, where he has been a committed student and practitioner of organizational change management for more than three decades. This has included a leadership role in an ambitious service excellence campaign, the implementation of

Total Quality Management, a major investment in Process Reengineering, a decade-long values-based leadership initiative, and more conventional approaches to achieve and document high levels of stewardship.

He has also pioneered award-winning process innovations, including Web-based course management systems, print on demand of customized acadmemic materials, and supply channel integration. While president of the National Association of College Stores, he published *Connections,* a book on strategic planning to guide industry-wide change, and later cofounded the Retail Alliance Inc., a consortium of large, independent collegiate retailers sharing a common vision to define and disseminate best practices. His current activities include efforts to achieve measured "best in class" support services.

He and his wife, Gretchen, live in upstate New York.

A Framework for Measurement

1

Measuring What Matters

Exchanging Value with Stakeholders

Efforts to find the right way to keep score have been management's version of the search for the Holy Grail.
—JOAN MAGRETTA

Telling a manager to measure what matters is akin to advising dieters to watch their weight. It's almost too obvious to mention. Yet competing approaches proliferate much like diet plans. While desired results such as service excellence, effective teamwork, or productivity come only to those willing to step on the scales, finding the right way to keep score in organizations has proven elusive. Despite an abundance of advice, confusion persists and performance suffers. The dilemma is illustrated by the story of a man in a hot air balloon who, upon realizing that he was lost, reduced altitude and spotted a woman below. He descended a bit more and shouted, "Excuse me, can you help me? I promised a friend I would meet him an hour ago, but I don't know where I am."

The woman called up, "You are in a hot air balloon hovering approximately thirty feet above the ground. You are between 40 and 41 degrees north latitude and between 82 and 83 degrees west longitude."

"You must be an engineer," responded the balloonist.

"I am," replied the woman, "how did you know?"

"Well," answered the balloonist, "everything you told me is technically correct, but I have no idea what to make of your information, and the fact is I am still lost. Frankly, you've not been much help so far."

The woman below retorted, "You must be in management."

"I am," replied the balloonist, "but how did you know?"

"Well," said the woman, "you don't know where you are or where you are going. You have risen to where you are due to a large volume of hot air. You made a promise that you have no idea how to keep, and you expect people beneath you to solve your problems. The fact is, you are in exactly the same position you were before we met, but now, somehow, it's my fault."

Defining What Matters

Measurement in most organizations is a mess. We err in every conceivable way. We measure too much or too little. We make measures incomprehensibly complex or overly simplistic. Our measures are too often lopsided and unbalanced. There is a pressing need for a commonsense framework for measurement, a way to measure what matters. Ironically, the things that matter most are readily apparent.

Purpose Matters

Whether public or private, organizations are created and sustained to accomplish something. Without shared purpose organizations are lost, adrift like the hot air balloon of the story. Ideally, that "purpose" is defined in statements of vision, mission, and strategy, statements that give meaning and direction to all effort. Purpose can be translated into measures, and measures into action. What can matter more than a measurement that conveys in accurate and understandable terms where you are in relation to where you aspire to be? Why, then, do so few organizations clearly define, fully communicate, and conscientiously align the efforts of all units with their purpose? Why isn't corporate purpose the very standard to which every major activity is held? Why do so few, especially those who labor in work teams, understand the corporate purpose and priorities, and how their activities contribute to them? These are challenging questions.

Process Matters

Purpose is accomplished through process. Process defines the blend and timing of human and material resources used to get things done, and it determines productivity. Where there is competition, it is process that distinguishes winners from losers.

Yesterday's Industrial Revolution was a process revolution. The use of machines to leverage manual work combined with process refinement to enable breakthroughs in performance. Manufacturing was transformed through the mechanization of routine activity, the use of interchangeable parts, and specialization of individual efforts. The slow and expensive production of a few highly skilled artisans gave way to mass production by many less-trained but better-coordinated specialists. Costs and prices plummeted, while at the same time quality often improved.

Today's Information Revolution is also a process revolution. The use of smart machines connected by worldwide networks is being combined with process refinement to leverage our abilities to understand, customize, and streamline underlying processes. Empowered by timely, accurate, and strategic information, entire supply channels can be integrated, fostering dramatic productivity gains as partners collaborate to orchestrate just-in-time exchanges from business to business. Occasionally, all this even begins with an initial interaction with the consumer defining the very product or service to be produced. Harnessing the power of information to refine process has been one of the key competencies enabling both Wal-Mart and Dell to grow from obscurity to dominance in a single generation. Some, like Microsoft's Bill Gates, go so far as to predict an eventual transition to a seamless economy and a new era of productivity enabled largely by better process. While much of the glamour and visibility of these high-tech visions have faded in the market adjustments of the new millennium, the changes predicted are moving forward, in fits and starts but with undeniable surety.

Yet poor process is so commonplace that most of us have come to accept it almost without question. Take, for example, getting your morning cup of coffee. Coffee drinkers can procure their fix from hundreds of self-service purveyors, ranging from gas station convenience stores to conference buffet tables. Few processes are simpler than the preparation of a cup of coffee. One must obtain an empty cup, pour coffee into it, add the cream and sugar, and dispose of the trash. Why, then, is it so rare to find the necessary materials to support this simplest of workflows laid out in the order needed from left to right on a single counter? Coffee drinkers often find themselves bouncing and bumping about among the caffeine-deprived, desperately searching for the next link in the supply chain.

Too often workflow processes evolve without design. That's one reason why robust process improvement methodologies have occupied center stage in the business literature for decades. In the 1980s, Total Quality Management (TQM) penetrated the service sector, extending its elaborate methods to foster "continuous process improvement." In the 1990s Process Reengineering went a step further, seeking to entirely reinvent targeted processes using newly available technologies. The expanded use of "benchmarking" sought to compare process outcomes in a standard way in order to spot best practices with intent to incorporate the processes that made them great.

This fact that poor process is commonplace means that it won't be necessary to master Six Sigma statistical techniques, popularized by General Electric, or other complex methods to find opportunity to improve. Pick any discrete function in your own company with which you are familiar. Perhaps it is a workflow in accounts payable, receiving, or some task assigned to an administrative office. Now mentally reenact the routine processes practiced in that unit in the same commonsense way that you might review the process flow to obtain a cup of coffee. It may help to imagine that you are embarking on a brief process journey and that you are a box or an invoice or a piece of mail. Are the steps in the process documented anywhere? Have they changed materially in the last five years? Has anyone reviewed them seeking a better approach? Is it likely that someone else doing similar work might be doing it faster, better, or cheaper? Is the process measured? For most of us, the answers are humbling. Much of what we do is done in the way it is because of inertia, not design.

People Matter

Founders create organizations because their purposes require the contributions of many people. These people bring together diverse competencies and collective wisdom to a common enterprise. While every complex purpose requires a mix of resources—such as machinery, money, and materials—no resource is more vital to success than the people. People are so important because they are more than resources: people think, and thought defines and refines both purpose and process. However, people also have feelings. When they feel disaffected, alienated, offended, apathetic, angry, uninformed, or fearful, their contribution and productivity will decline. When they feel motivated, involved, informed, loyal, and empowered, their contribution and productivity will increase. This "law of the heart" is as predictable and measurable as gravity.

In a sense, organizations are living organisms. They are created by people (owners) to serve people (customers) through the efforts of people (employees). The corporate purpose is much more likely to be achieved when leaders systematically align the legitimate interests of their human stakeholders, an alignment that must encompass both the head and the heart. In a world full of choices, corporate purpose is best achieved through a thoughtfully designed exchange of value, one that both balances and leverages the common interests of customers, employees, and owners. A successful organization seeks to provide ALL of its core stakeholders more of what they value in exchange for more of what the company values, the greater fulfillment of its purpose.

Engaging these messy human interests requires more than rational review and improvement to work flows. Even though inadequate attention to human factors is by far the biggest reason for failure, somehow human factors get lost in most of the literature on process management. Indeed, a closer look at the scholarship exposes two very different perspectives on process. The industrial engineer considers process primarily as workflow, that is, the orchestration of activities to accomplish tasks effectively and efficiently. In contrast, the human resources professional views process as the orchestration of interactions among people to get things done. Both perspectives are essential. Bringing them together into a broader view, one designed to consciously pursue common interests creates a context for synergy.

Paying Attention to What Matters

Much of the power of leadership is bound up in what leaders pay attention to and what they ask for. Some of the time the attention is informal; other times, it is conscious and measured.

Informal Attention

Even the most subtle frown, gesture, or preoccupation of a leader may carry severe unintended negative consequences. However, strategically directed attention can bring unprecedented rewards when it is focused on the things that matter most: purpose, process, and people. Decades ago, Ken Blanchard made this point powerfully in one of the most insightful business books of the time, *The One Minute Manager*. The book's theme was that even the briefest anecdotal exchange between managers and employees pertaining to things that matter—such as sharing goals, praise, or a respectful reprimand to help realign someone's efforts—can have a dramatic and positive impact. In the early 1980s author Tom Peters popularized a related notion that he termed "management by walking around." Peters claimed that leaders in excellent organizations make it a priority to get out where their people work, where they can pay attention to things that matter.[1] A cursory glance at most executive calendars reveals that these well-established insights of long ago remain largely neglected. Although some managers exercise this power of attention like a child with a loaded gun, most dispense it sparingly and with at least a modicum of intuition. However, few seize the opportunity in a thoughtful and systematic way, leaving the potential benefits untapped.

Measured Attention

To measure what matters is to pay attention to the things that will have the greatest impact in achieving purpose, improving process, and serving people. When we take the time to thoughtfully define and measure the things that matter most, we define expectations concretely and harness the collective energy of the many to the common corporate enterprise. In doing so, leaders convey "This is what counts!" It is hard to overemphasize how powerful measured attention can be when it is well conceived and deployed, or how destructive it can be when done poorly.

Wise measures are few

Albert Einstein once said, "Not everything that can be counted counts, and not everything that counts can be counted." Determining what counts and how to count it requires wisdom—the wisdom to define and measure what matters, whether that is related to purpose, process, or people. Quality guru Joseph Juran once observed, "Performance will depend disproportionately on a few things done really well." His insight, now popularized as the Pareto Principle or the 80/20 rule, was that for many phenomena, 80 percent of consequences stem from 20 percent of the factors that cause them. In other words, there are usually just a few things that are very important. Successful organizations take the time to define and measure and steadfastly pay attention to these "vital few" things in order to give them a sustainable focus. Stephen Covey put it this way: "The main thing is to keep the main thing the main thing."[2]

Wise measures are simple

American physician and poet Oliver Wendell Holmes stated, "I wouldn't give you a fig for simplicity on this side of complexity; but

I would give my life for simplicity on the far side of complexity." In other words, simple insights that accurately convey underlying complex truths are to be sought after. In part, that is because they are easier to understand, to share, and to act upon. Einstein took it further by observing that if you can't explain something simply, you don't know enough about it.

Wise measurements offer insight

The power of measurement is bound up in comparisons. Imagine receiving a weekly report from a warehousing and distribution center that says that the average number of units received per person per hour the previous week was 50. Is that good or bad? You can understand or interpret the measure through comparison. You might make internal comparisons, to the manager's intuition, to prior years' results, to other parts of the business cycle, to differing rates among individuals, or to established targets and standards. You might extend the frame of reference by adding external factors like industry benchmarks or even a functional "best practice" gleaned from an entirely different type of business. In our example, if you learned that the rate of 50 units per person per hour represents a peak productivity month compared to an average of 35 in all others, you would immediately turn your attention toward understanding why. What is it that enables higher productivity in one month or causes lower productivity in another? Or what if an external comparison established that the best practice in receiving efficiency is actually 150 units per person per hour? If the comparison is valid, you would experience an immediate paradigm shift as you apply this new frame of reference, one that originates outside the company.

Some cynically suggest that good politicians routinely make bad performance look good by comparing it to even worse alternatives. Because anyone can manipulate a comparison, whether he or she is in the public or private sector, managers need to be on the alert and to behave rightly. Good managers know that honest comparison is the seedbed of insight. They are attentive to measures even when they highlight internal weaknesses, because performance gaps can provide pointers to opportunities for rapid and dramatic improvement.

Creating Stakeholder Value Matters

In the end what matters most is the creation of value. All organizations have that as their common calling. And they have a commitment to all corporate stakeholders, including their customers, employees, and owners.

Values as input

When principle-centered leaders consciously embrace and hold the organization accountable to a short list of good values, over time they create cultural norms that determine how people treat others, both inside and outside the organization. Well-crafted corporate values such as truth, respect, teamwork, integrity, and excellence provide a plumb line against which every individual action or decision can be tested. Collectively, they establish a kind of corporate constitution and bill of rights rolled into one and supersede even the authority of rank. Good values not only allow firms to attract and retain the best people, they also nurture trust—and trust binds people together in ways that encourage risk taking, innovation, productivity, and service excellence. Perceived behavior in demonstrating these values can also be reliably measured.

Value as output

Peter Drucker once observed that "value creation is the animating principle of management and its chief responsibility."[3] If measured stakeholder value is not the holy grail of management, it is at least hallowed ground. Directing attention to the people on whom an enterprise depends and to the value exchanged with them creates a powerful force in advancing stakeholders' collective interests.

Value creation and stakeholder choice

In the end, organizations must please their stakeholders because the stakeholders have choices. Without choices, stakeholders must accept whatever value proposition is offered them. Customers are often restricted in their choices when they deal with unregulated monopolies, government services, organizations insulated from market forces, or insides of companies, where one service team supports another. Such customers simply cannot readily go elsewhere. Similarly, employees are restricted in their choices by job markets, access to training, and regional limitations affecting an individual's ability to move. Even owners are encumbered by labor unions, by market factors limiting ability to sell, and by structural factors limiting their ability to easily change purpose. Wherever choice is restricted, the potential exists for one stakeholder to take advantage of another. In the short term at least, such circumstances seem to validate the contention of the ancient Greek historian Thucydides, who said, "The strong do what they can and the weak suffer what they must."

However, long-term organizational success requires mutually advantageous results. And stakeholder choice is on the rise! Customers have never had so many options, and in the future they will have still more. As the job market transitions to a service-knowledge economy and a generation of baby boomers heads into retirement, we can predict a future where employee strategy will move to center stage. It is increasingly clear that corporate purpose is best served by a conscientious effort to create value for ALL stakeholders. It is that effort to which we now turn our attention.

Aligning the Company's Core Stakeholders

An organization and its stakeholders are to varying degrees interdependent. On the one hand, the company needs all stakeholders' support and constructive involvement to succeed. On the other hand, stakeholders too have a personal stake or vested interest in the success of the company. Some—such as corporate suppliers, government regulators, and communities where business is conducted—may operate on the periphery. However, at least three closely interconnected stakeholders always have a disproportionate interest, involvement, and impact on the company: customers, employees, and owners. Defining and aligning their overlapping in-

FIGURE 1
Aligning Core Stakeholders

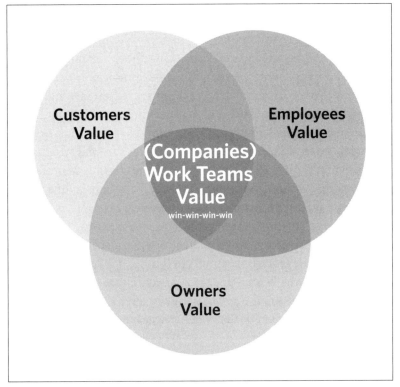

Customers
Value

Employees
Value

(Companies)
Work Teams
Value

win-win-win-win

Owners
Value

terests (as illustrated in Figure 1) positions the firm to target win-ning strategies whereby each group of people gets enough of what they value to remain loyal. Customers want products and services that deliver timeliness, quality, and value. Employees want a fulfilling work experience where they are not only fairly paid but are also appreciated, involved, and productive. Owners want the efforts and resources of the firm to be tightly focused and efficiently invested in pursuit of their clearly defined purposes. Mutually advantageous outcomes don't come about by accident; they require design—the conscious effort to define, measure, and deliver both stakeholder satisfaction and contribution.

Applying Stakeholder Value to Work Teams

Like the speed of the pit crews at an auto race, productivity in organizations is substantially determined by the way people work together in teams. Work teams are clusters of employees laboring side by side, week after week. They work under a common leader, share common resources, seek to fulfill a common and specific purpose, and serve a common set of customers (often internal to the company). This is where life in organizations is lived out. Some teams are project or special purpose teams. However, most are natural work groups defined by the organization's formal structure of functions: accounting, receiving, finance, purchasing, manufacturing, or various service functions. They typically consist of a supervisor and a dozen or fewer team members. Their activities form vital links in a chain of value connecting internal processes to external outcomes. Most of the organization's resources are expended here. Most of the work is accomplished here. It is here that corporate strategy is largely implemented. It is here that stakeholders are most easily defined and the value they receive measured. Yet it is here that measurement of that value is weakest.

Stakeholder Value Exchange Model

Managing the exchange of value between a work team and its stakeholders requires measuring both stakeholder satisfaction (with value delivered) and stakeholder contribution (i.e., corporate satisfaction with value received). This feedback informs an ongoing adjustment process to refine and improve the value package. Figure 2 illustrates this exchange of value.

Defining and measuring the satisfaction and contribution of a work team's core stakeholder raises five commonsense questions, which are presented in Table 1. For each stakeholder the work team must answer the following questions: (1) Who are they? (2) What do they value and expect from the team? (3) How well is the team doing at meeting or exceeding those expectations? (4) What does the team (as a representative of the organization) value and expect

FIGURE 2
Aligning Core Stakeholders

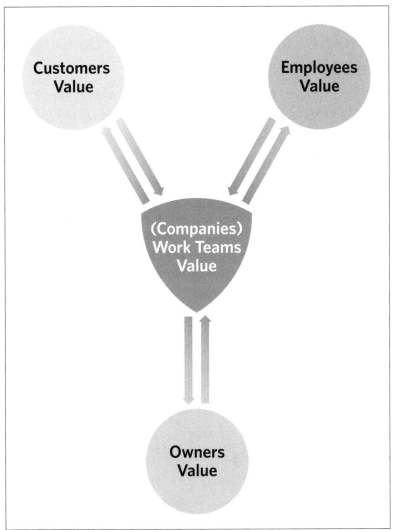

from the stakeholder? (5) How well is the stakeholder doing at meeting or exceeding those expectations?

Empowered with measured feedback, the organization can define a strategy for winning change, change that is designed to

TABLE 1
Stakeholder Value Exchange in Work Teams

	Customers	Employees	Owners
Who are the stakeholders?			
Value delivered: stakeholder satisfaction What does the stakeholder value and expect from the work team? How well is the work team doing?			
Value received: stakeholder contribution What does the work team value and expect from the stakeholder? How well is the stakeholder doing?			

achieve ongoing realignment by targeting value creation for ALL core stakeholders. Let's examine each of these questions in further depth.

Who Are the Stakeholders?

Understanding what stakeholders value begins with defining who they are. Customers are the intended recipients of the products or services created by the work team. In the case of internal work teams, that is typically the next link in the value chain as work-in-process moves from one department or unit to another. Employees include the team supervisor or leader and all team members—full-time, part-time, and temporary staff. Owners are the founders, investors, risk takers, and their designated representatives, including governing boards and those to whom they delegate authority within the organizational structure. Owners define, refine, and validate the organization's purpose and assess its process.

These definitions can enable any team to quickly identify individual stakeholders at a superficial level. However, understanding people requires more. For example, in the 1950s, V. Raymond Edmond was president of Wheaton College, a prestigious Christian liberal arts school in the Midwest. To this day, stories abound of his exceptional care for students. It seems that Edmond made a deliberate effort to know the students, seeking to learn names, majors, interests, and personal needs. His care even extended to praying for them. Upon seeing each familiar face as he would cross the campus, it was not uncommon for him to break into a broad smile, calling the person by name and then conversing on personal matters that few college presidents would take the time to learn. The students loved him! His legacy has left an imprint on the culture of the campus, which remains vibrant generations after his passing.

The value of personal relationships has also long been understood by successful salespeople. Well-known author Harvey Mackay outlined how, in his envelope business, he would routinely track scores of customer attributes, many—such as hobbies, political affiliation, and birthdays of family members—having no direct linkage to the business requirements.[4] Mackay understood the value of knowing customers as people and building relationships that went beyond business basics. Today's Customer Relationship Management tools greatly expand the breadth and depth of information tracked to include demographic, psychographic, and even transactional information, all as part of a large-scale effort both to customize the value package and to nurture more personal relationships. The same approaches apply with equal justification to managing relationships with ALL stakeholders, including those with employees and owners.

Understanding one's customers, employees, and owners is a powerful starting point to inform and direct strategic thinking and decision making about how best to meet their needs. Applying this frame of reference within the work team is both practical and compelling; the scope is narrow and achievable, the interactions among stakeholders tend to be frequent, and a common purpose can be clearly defined.

Value Delivered: Stakeholder Satisfaction

Organizations both deliver and receive value from their stakeholders. Understanding what they value and expect, and measuring success in delivering it, is essential to inform efforts to improve.

What do stakeholders value and expect from the work team?

Within the boundaries of corporate purpose, work teams need to thoughtfully assess what each of their stakeholders values and expects from their services. The fastest and simplest approach to finding out is simply to ask the team members what they think stakeholders want. After clearly identifying the team's specific customers or owner representatives as described above, ask the simple question, "What is it that we do for them that they value and expect?" Be patient. Because most work teams have never been asked, it may take a few minutes after the initial shock to get a discussion under way. However, team members have clear ideas based both upon both their general experiences and their work experiences. These ideas often result in a good initial list, and the creation of such a list reinforces both the common sense of the overall process and the reasonableness of the stakeholders' expectations. This approach also cultivates support and buy-in.

Another approach is to ask the experts. Entire libraries have been dedicated to the topics of defining customer expectations in particular product and service categories and determining what employees value from their workplace experience. While the specific expectations of owners will vary by industry and function, the task of thinking through their interests in the work team and searching out key performance factors is always fruitful. You will want to gather these insights early on.

Ultimately, to both validate and expand your findings, you will need to ask the stakeholders. Talk to them one-on-one or in informal discussion groups. Design these interactions in ways that enable you to test ideas from earlier inquiries and that allow stakeholders to suggest new ones. This somewhat open-ended and anecdotal approach is all part of a learning process that will lead naturally to, and inform, more systematic feedback from surveys and other instruments. Collectively, these methods allow stakeholders to speak for themselves. Right or wrong, their perception matters.

Customers generally value such things as fair prices (if they pay); knowledgeable, friendly, responsive, and efficient service providers; and timely and convenient transactions. Employees value such factors as a positive and supportive work environment, recognition for good performance, involvement in decisions that affect them, and, of course, fair pay. As suggested earlier, owners value achievement of the purposes for which they invested resources and undertook risks, that is, making sure that what each work group is doing contributes as effectively as possible to the core mission of the firm, and that their processes to do this work are as efficient as possible.

Interestingly, stakeholders often do not value benefits in the same way. One time-tested distinction notes what might best be thought of as maintenance factors. For example, few employees will be impressed to receive an accurate and timely paycheck, and few customers will search out the leadership of an organization to praise them for providing a product or service when needed. However, if these basic expectations are not met, stakeholders often become quite dissatisfied. Other factors, however, can be deeply motivational. When a supervisor takes the time to appreciate someone on her team for a job well done or a customer or colleague recognizes exemplary service, it is not uncommon for the story to be repeated both in the workplace and at home. There is synergy in aiming high. In effect, a team's commitment to excellence or exceeding stakeholder expectations in strategically important categories will be both materially and emotionally rewarding, creating a multiplier effect as high performance standards feed more intrinsic motivators. Yet stakeholder expectations are typically not well defined, measured, or recognized in work teams.

How well is the team doing?

Only after the team understands who its stakeholders are and what they value can it begin to measure how well it is doing in delivering those benefits. One way that the team can accomplish this for customers and employees is through commonsense surveys designed both to identify those things stakeholders consider most important and to rate the team's performance by indexing the extent to which it meets or exceeds expectations. Results enable the team to define and focus on strategic successes, factors that are important and rated well, and strategic weaknesses, factors that are important but done poorly. This process can be effective in focusing attention on the work team's most strategic outcome, meeting or exceeding their stakeholders' expectations. With experience, the process as it is refined over time invariably leads in the right direction.

Where stakeholder perceptions fall below expectations, two possibilities exist: either expectations are unreasonable and must be lowered or performance is below standard and must be raised. To determine which is the case, you can introduce other ways to set standards and measure performance. Instead of asking customers if they perceive that the service was friendly, you might instead send in paid shoppers to determine if the service providers were demonstrating friendly behaviors such as smiling or greeting customers within a specified period and in a particular way. Instead of asking if the product or service was reliably delivered when the customer needed it, you might measure the number of times "out of stock" was the response to customer requests. Instead of asking if employees perceive that wages are fair, you might compare compensation to the rest of the industry or to similar businesses in the community. Both perception and specification measures are important and build directly from the core purpose of reliably delivering what stakeholders value.

For owners, different measurements are needed. While owners universally value "purpose alignment" (accomplishing the goals of the company) and "process performance" (doing it faster, better, or cheaper) from their work teams, they frequently employ anecdotal or perception-based methods to assess whether they are getting the desired results. Supervisors also exercise this kind of judgment in varying degrees with each performance review, and managers often base business decisions on gut feel. Moving on to more robust measures requires thoughtful definition of the work team's purpose and critical review of its processes. Although the need is compelling, ideal owner measures for work teams are rarely readily available. They require careful thinking and serious effort. When guided solely by seat-of-the-pants assessments applied in an ad hoc fashion, work teams are left adrift.

Value Received: Stakeholder Contribution

At the same time that work teams must deliver value to their stakeholders, stakeholders have duties to the team and the organization. Assessment must cut both ways, measuring both value delivered and value received. Customers can be expected to be profitable and are often expected to share essential feedback or collaborate on efforts to improve services. Employees can be expected to demonstrate character in their behavior and competence in their work. Owners can be expected to provide sufficient resources, establish clearly defined purpose, and support a just or fair work culture. Explicitly defining what work teams value from their stakeholders and measuring how well reasonable expectations are being met is essential to continuous improvement in this bilateral exchange of value. Where expectations are not being met, the organization suffers and remedial action is required.

The Winning Exchange of Value

By measuring the overall effectiveness of value creation and exchange, attention is focused where it can foster continuous improvement. Performance gaps are to be expected and can lead to further inquiry. If customers indicate that the service quality is unfriendly and unresponsive, attention is directed in a timely way to understanding why. Ways of finding out might include informal meetings, simple follow-up surveys, or just targeted questions asked routinely by team members. The answers obtained foster a growing understanding of what to change. Desired changes can then be implemented, and the measurement continues into new cycles, with performance being improved or refined with each effort.

Metrics may identify multiple problem areas in serving stakeholders. Not surprisingly, these different problems are likely interrelated. Poorly treated employees often provide poor customer service, and both results will show up in the measurement. Similarly, changes should generally be designed for mutual advantage. Why would employees help to identify inefficient process when the time saved may cost them their jobs? Winning change seeks the common good first; it includes a commitment to work team excellence in customer service, a commitment to high performance teamwork that yields a fulfilling work experience for employees, and a commitment to best practices achieved through best processes.

At first blush, this outcome may seem somewhat Pollyannaish. Rest assured that it is not. Measurement of effectiveness will unearth problems, put undiscussables on the table, and require tough decisions. It will reveal unproductive employees who need some combination of training, discipline, motivation, transfer, or dismissal. It will bring to light customers who are not within the range targeted for service or are undesirable for other reasons. The process may also uncover unreasonable owner expectations that must be confronted and corrected. Measuring each work team's effectiveness in satisfying its stakeholders will bring these tough decisions directly into your path. It will also bring to the surface performance that deserves recognition and celebration. Both results are essential.

The strategic significance of bringing stakeholder balance to measurement has already been discovered at the level of the enterprise; it is used today in more progressive organizations to direct overall strategy. In this book, however, we unapologetically focus on interconnected and interdependent work teams, the very engine of value creation. We argue that organizations must do more to embrace three-dimensional value creation in work teams. Most of the measurement done in work teams has been insufficient and decidedly unbalanced. Like rowing a boat with one oar, unbalanced measurement only leads in circles. We are excited to bring balanced stakeholder assessment to work teams, where we find common leadership, focused mission, shared work duties, and common stakeholders. This is where measurement is weakest and opportunity is greatest. This is where change can be defined and implemented one bite at a time, where any team leader or supervisor can choose to move forward with commonsense processes starting today.

Summary

Despite widespread efforts to find the right way to keep score in organizations, most organizations are poorly measured. There is a need for a simple conceptual framework to measure what matters. We have seen that purpose matters; virtually all organizations are created and sustained to pursue a specific purpose. Process matters; all work is accomplished through process, yet poor process is commonplace. People matter; organizations are founded by people (owners), to serve people (customers), through the efforts of people (employees). The likelihood of successfully achieving a corporate purpose goes up precipitously when the legitimate interests of these human stakeholders are consciously aligned. Such an alignment must encompass both the head and the heart.

Much of the power of leadership is bound up in what leaders pay attention to. Measurement is focused attention. To measure what matters is to pay attention to the things that will have the greatest impact in achieving a purpose and refining a process. As a general rule, it is wise to identify a few simple measures that make insightful comparisons and allow one to assess the exchange of value between the company and its core stakeholders.

Values are sometimes described as standards of behavior. Shared organizational values can create a productive cultural context. Values are also good for business because they nurture trust and direct attention toward common and mutually advantageous ends. Organizations governed by principle-centered values are predisposed to meeting the expectations of all stakeholders.

All organizations have at least three core stakeholders on whom they depend for success. Customers are the recipients of value created. Employees are workers enlisted by the firm to act as stewards in pursuit of the corporate purpose. Owners are the founders, the investors, and their representatives. Where customers, employees, and owners exercise discretion, long-term organizational success requires conscious effort to target and achieve winning results.

Work teams are broadly responsible to implement strategy, yet their perspective is rarely considered and their energies are not systematically aligned. Stakeholder value can be most easily defined, measured, and improved in work teams. That is because these teams generally share a focused mission, common leadership, common resources, and common stakeholders

An organization's success is determined by its exchange of value with stakeholders. Organizations create and deliver value to their core stakeholders, and they receive value from them. Measuring the stakeholders' satisfaction with value delivered and the organization's satisfaction with the value it receives in return (or stakeholder contribution), informs efforts to continuously improve. An index of this value-for-value exchange is arguably the holy grail of measurement because it is the outcome that matters most. In assessing value given and value received it is necessary to ask these simple questions: (1) Who are the stakeholders? (2) What do they value from the work team? (3) How well is the team doing at delivering what its stakeholders value? (4) What does the work team value from them? (5) How well is the stakeholder doing at delivering what the team (on behalf of the organization) values?

Measuring the value exchange encourages synergy, the process by which two parties win more by working together than they could individually. They win not only by sharing a fixed benefit but also by creating new benefits—in effect, by growing the pie.

2

Owners Come First

Exchanging Value with Owners

You read a book from beginning to end. You run a business the opposite way. You must start with the end, and then do everything you must to reach it. —HAROLD GENEEN

In the mid-nineteenth century Ezra Cornell founded the university that today bears his name. He did so with the aid of a friend and colleague, Andrew Dickson White, whom he engaged to become the university's first president. These men shared a passionate conviction that the time was right to pioneer a new kind of educational institution, one "where *any person* can find instruction in *any study.*"

Cornell and White's idea was to open access to higher education to men and women of all races and socioeconomic backgrounds. It was to expand and liberate scholarship to foster the unfettered study of philosophy, literature, government, history, and science. And it was to afford students unprecedented choice in defining a personal course of study. These were revolutionary ideas in that day, ideas for which the founders willingly made great sacrifices.

When organizations are newly founded, passion and excitement run high. Purpose is clear to all, regardless of rank or function. Dreams of new products or services to be delivered in new ways to new customers are widely shared. Risks are great, but there is also the compensating promise of great reward, whether in the form of personal fortune or some worthy social good. In this way, at minimum, owners come first.

Who Are the Owners?

An organization's founders are first among its population of owners. They are the initial architects of purpose, defining mission and vision and the strategy by which their goals are to be pursued. Typically, owners are also investors or donors and entrepreneurs who place at risk their money, their reputations, their time, and other precious resources that equip the firm to achieve its calling. Over time, most will delegate high-level decisions to representative governing boards and recruit senior executives to serve their interests in operational matters. These leaders then recruit others who recruit others who recruit still others, until work teams are in place either to produce the goods and services integral to the corporate purpose or to support those who do. In this way everyone is bound by a common stewardship to owners to represent their interests within the scope of responsibility and authority entrusted to them. Those closest to owners, serving on boards and in the executive ranks, will find these words obvious and barely worth mentioning. But far below, deep down in the organizational structure, in the work teams, these are foreign words. There, owners are strangers. The descriptive word most commonly used is "they" and to many, "they" are to be suspected, feared, and resisted. The need for understanding is great.

Exercise 1 begins the process to understand a work team's owners and to manage the team's relationship with them. (A completed sample of this exercise, Sample of Exercise 1, appears on page 57; the sample relates to the First Bookstore team used for illustration throughout Part 1.)

EXERCISE 1

Who Are Our Owners?

Directions: Complete the required information below.

Definition: Owners are founders, investors, and risk takers. They are the architects and guardians of the organization's purpose. They commission others at various levels—from governing boards to work teams—to accomplish that purpose, entrusting to them the necessary resources and authority to act, and rightfully holding them accountable for those actions.

Founders

Describe your organization's founders.

_____

_____

_____

_____

_____

Board of Directors

Name   Title   Comments

_____

_____

_____

_____

_____

_____

_____

_____

_____

EXERCISE 1 cont'd

Chain of Delegation

Describe the direct line of authority linking the board of directors/ trustees to your work team.

Name	Title	Comments

Work Team

List members of the work team.

Name	Title	Comments

Understanding owners as people and managing relationships with them will help equip your team to better meet their expectations. However, doing this will require more than simply listing names and titles. What can you do to better understand them?

FIGURE 3
Owner Value Exchange

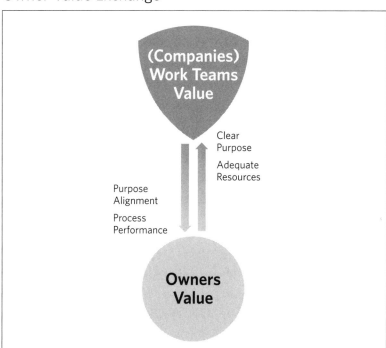

Value Delivered: Owner Satisfaction

As illustrated in Figure 3, work teams routinely exchange value with the owners of their organizations. Clearly defining what it is that each party expects and assessing how effective their respective efforts are at delivering it creates a baseline for continuous improvement.

What Do Owners Value and Expect of Work Teams?

Owners value purpose alignment from their work teams
Several hours into a transpacific flight, the pilot announced on the intercom that he had both good news and bad news. "The bad

news," he said with regret, "is that we're lost. But the good news," he was quick to add, "is that we're making really good time."

This story and others like it remind us that purpose comes first in all human endeavors, both personal and corporate. The purpose might be to grow produce, to manufacture a product, or to provide a service. It may be motivated by the intent of generating profits or serving society. *Purpose establishes a foundational reason for being, the achievement of which is of overriding value both to owners and to the organizations they create.* As Harold Geneen, former CEO of ITT aptly put it, in business you always "start with the end and then do everything you must to reach it."[1]

To accomplish the owners' purpose, employees are recruited, organized, and deployed into complementary and interdependent work teams. In successful organizations, carefully crafted processes link these teams together, with each unit supporting the whole by adding value as work in process moves forward in a carefully orchestrated, purpose-driven symphony.

However, as organizations grow, work efforts often become compartmentalized. The unifying theme infused by the founders' purpose can be forgotten or even become irrelevant. Ongoing refinement and redirection of purpose is easily neglected in the pursuit of daily routines. Poor communication by the leadership and among interdependent work teams adds to the cacophony and leads to widespread misalignment. Even though it may appear for a season as though they are making good progress, without midcourse correction to redefine purpose and realign scarce resources to it, companies gradually lose their bearings.

Owners value process performance from their work teams

Midway into another transpacific flight, the plane shook forcefully. Moments later the pilot reassuringly announced, "Ladies and gentlemen, no doubt you felt the vibration as one of our four engines dislodged and fell into the ocean. Please do not be alarmed. Our plane has been designed to fly with the remaining three engines; however, the trip will take approximately one hour longer." The plane shook again forty-five minutes later, and the pilot returned to announce that another engine had been lost. He finished by saying, "Unfortunately, our trip will take about an hour longer." Ninety minutes passed uneventfully before a third massive vibration occurred and the pilot announced the loss of yet another engine. "Regrettably," he concluded, "our trip will be approximately an hour longer." Visibly annoyed, one of the passengers nudged his neighbor. "Can you believe this?" he complained, "If this keeps up, we will be up here forever."

All work in all organizations is powered by process. For that reason no subject has received more attention in the business literature. Techniques that have been advocated include incremental but "continuous process improvement," rapid and complete Process Reengineering and the use of targeted benchmarks comparing process outputs to identify and copy best practices. All are intended to empower organizations to pursue their purposes more fully. Disciples of such techniques have often sought lofty transformational goals for their organizations, spending huge sums while often reaping disappointing returns. Reasons for these results vary, but they include overly broad scope, overly complex methods, and employee resistance. Poor process makes work take longer and cost more. As with the plane losing its engines, the loss of process power will initially slow things down and will eventually bring down an organization.

How Well Is the Work Team Doing?

Given that purpose alignment and process performance are so highly prized by owners, how might they best be assessed in a given team? How can team members know that they are doing the right things, those things that directly support the collective purpose? And how can they know that they are doing them effectively? *By comparison. By explicitly defining and comparing the team's purpose and assessing the fit to the broader corporate purpose, team priorities can be continuously realigned. By defining and comparing the team's processes to internal and external standards, team activities can be continually improved.*

Purpose alignment
As with making good time in a lost plane, working efficiently without clear purpose simply makes no sense. Purpose obviously comes first and matters most, both to the owners as individuals and to the organizations they create. And it falls primarily to the owners and their senior representatives to spell out the purpose in clear and compelling terms. This corporate charter is embodied in the organization's directional statements, including mission and vision statements, describing what to do, and strategy and values statements, describing how these ends are to be accomplished. Collectively, they create a kind of corporate compass with which to inform midcourse corrections.

- **Directive Mission:** A mission statement describes a present purpose. It is a carefully crafted statement answering several essential questions: (1) Who are we? (2) What do we do here? What is the targeted value package that we are here to create? (3) For whom? Who are the targeted stakeholders to be served by this value package? (4) Why? What is the reciprocal benefit sought for our organization? At a high level, the mission statement defines the value exchange envisioned by the owners. Well-crafted statements of mission are directive in that they inform decision making.

- **Prescriptive Vision:** A vision statement describes a future purpose by defining what the organization aspires to become if successful; it presents a picture of how it wishes to be perceived, positioned, and described in three to five years. Powerful visions pursue excellence and require a stretch to accomplish. Yet they are specific, targeted, and achievable. Effective leaders regularly communicate these aspirations to their core stakeholders such that, as they become widely understood and supported, they also become integral to the organization's very identity and sense of destiny. As such, they also inform decision making.

- **Connecting Strategy:** Strategy describes how purpose is to be accomplished. It is made operational through thoughtfully prioritized goals and objectives clarifying what needs to be done, by whom, when, and with what resources. Maintaining a line of sight linking individuals at all levels to a short list of overarching strategic corporate priorities is a powerful way to align internal efforts.

- **Shared Values:** Values describe common standards of behavior that govern how people treat one another as they work together toward a common purpose. They provide a kind of moral compass. Of course, a company culture can be driven by poor values or Machiavellian behavior that is brazenly selfish, disrespectful, uncaring, or manipulative. Such an approach can succeed for a time to the degree that stakeholders are either uninformed or their choices are limited. However, market forces are empowering stakeholders today with both information and alternatives. Clearly defined values inform decisions and can be measured.

To be successful, companies must do more than define purpose; they must align collective efforts to fulfill it, both among core stakeholders and structurally among internal work teams.

Stakeholder alignment

Where stakeholders have choices, organizations must consciously target a mutually advantageous purpose to deliver value to the targeted population of customers, employees, and owners on whom they depend. These value propositions have to be aligned. For each stakeholder, who is to be served and with what combination of value elements, and how are these value elements to be created and deployed? For example, Wal-Mart targets price-conscious customers. But to deliver that value proposition of "always" delivering low prices, Wal-Mart must have a complementary employee strategy of achieving high levels of productivity around a narrowly focused set of services. This kind of productivity requires state-of-the-art systems and logistics. The overall approach must also add up in a way that appeals to a targeted investor profile. *Purpose alignment requires complementary and coordinated stakeholder plans.*

FIGURE 4
Structural Alignment

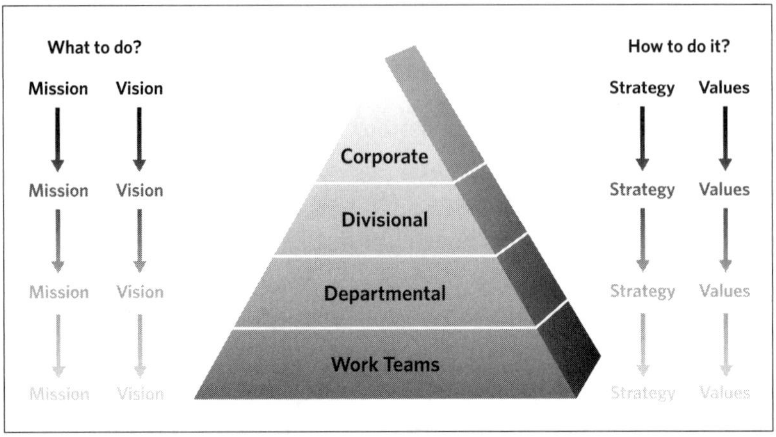

Structural alignment

As illustrated in Figure 4, *corporate mission, vision, strategy, and values must cascade downward throughout the organization, layer by layer and function by function.* This information is essential to inform and direct the efforts of work teams. Only through careful and conscientious comparison of one with the other can the activities of work teams be aligned. Any serious effort to do so will unearth pockets of misalignment. Some of the things being done may not contribute substantially to the greater purpose while additional things may need to be done to achieve that purpose.

At the lower levels of the pyramid, where most work teams operate and most strategy is deployed, two observations are striking. First, the corporate purpose and priorities are not well understood. Few can articulate the mission or vision; fewer still know enough about the intended strategy to identify priority goals. *Second, the work team's purpose and fit is not well defined.* In one recent survey, only 37 percent of the workers indicated that they clearly understood what their organization was trying to achieve and why. Only 20 percent claimed that there was a clear line of sight between their team's tasks and the organization's goals.[2] Few readers will need outside research to validate this. Those in organizations know from firsthand observation. Unit-specific mission, strategy, and priority goals are often missing altogether. And it is here, among the least powerful, that gaps in living up to the standards of behavior described by corporate values tend to be greatest. Workers are left to operate in the dark. Life in the accounting department, on the manufacturing floor, among the IT staff, in customer service units, and so forth is left to play out in a surprisingly ad hoc fashion. Structural alignment requires that work teams both define and align their priorities with the company's priorities, and it requires that they affirm and hold themselves accountable to the company's values.

Exercise 2 is intended to help a work team apply these principles. (A completed sample for the DC team, Sample of Exercise 2, is on page 64.) It calls for gathering and reviewing all of the organization's purpose documents, including mission, vision, and strategy statements for the company, the division, and the department, and whatever may already exist for the work team. You will find that each describes what is to be done and for whom. The result will be a core statement of purpose. Then assess how well the activities and priorities of your work team fit within this corporate purpose. Consider areas of activity that may not be needed at all. Perhaps they can be done better elsewhere in the company, or perhaps they can be outsourced or even discontinued. Consider, as well, other duties that do appear mission-critical and at present are not adequately addressed. This process will inform your efforts to assess how well you are doing at meeting owner expectations for purpose alignment.

Process performance

Although purpose must precede process, process is the only way that anything gets done. Owners therefore prize efficient process in work teams. By that they mean process (1) that is timely, (2) that creates quality goods and services, and (3) that requires no more resources than necessary to get the job done. Yet poor process abounds. It shows up in badly designed work flows requiring unnecessary steps or complexity, in failure to use appropriate tools or technologies, and in high error rates resulting in waste and costly

EXERCISE 2

Owners Value Purpose Alignment: How Are We Doing?

> **Directions:** Gather and attach documents describing your organization's corporate purpose for the company, for organizational units in your chain of command, and for your work team. Use them to inform your team's effort to describe the intended value proposition for each targeted stakeholder category. Then assess how well the activities of your team fit that purpose.

Corporate Purpose			
	Customers	Employees	Owners
Describe the target population to be served.			
Directive mission What is our present value proposition/ package to serve them?			
Prescriptive vision What is our future value proposition/ package to serve them?			
Connecting strategy What are the company's most important priorities?			

EXERCISE 2 cont'd

Divisional/Departmental Purpose

	Customers	Employees	Owners
Describe the target population to be served.			
Directive mission What is our present value proposition/ package to serve them?			
Prescriptive vision What is our present value proposition/ package to serve them?			
Connecting strategy What are the divison/ department's most important priorities?			

EXERCISE 2 cont'd

Work Team Purpose

	Customers	Employees	Owners
Describe the target population to be served.			
Directive mission What is our present value proposition/ package to serve them?			
Prescriptive vision What is our present value proposition/ package to serve them?			
Connecting strategy What are our work team's most important priorities?			

Within the framework of the organization's purpose:

What services or activities should we consider discontinuing?

What services or activities should we consider adding?

rework. *Poor process is so common because unless the work team is vigilant in reviewing their processes on an ongoing basis, inefficiencies remain unseen, slowing down the work and adding expense.*

For most people in work teams, abstract discussions about purpose alignment or process performance are about as appealing as having a root canal. But life at work is anything but abstract. Workers spend most of their waking hours there. What the industrial engineer calls process may sound like jargon to them, but it describes well-worn routines that are as familiar as the faces of fellow workers with whom they share the routines. This is the very world they know best. Even a commonsense assessment can unearth significant opportunities to improve. Such improvements do not require massive culture changes, the uncompromising support of the senior executive staff, or organization-wide commitments to transformational methods like Total Quality Management or Process Reengineering. Those tools and allegiances sometimes help, but *in most cases, a single team can act immediately within the scope of its existing authority and resources.*

Many overlapping methods and tools are available with which to evaluate process. They fill the pages of countless books that describe techniques to stratify and catalog them, comprehensive procedures to map and measure them, and insightful ways to analyze and improve them. But along the way they often leave behind the very people responsible for understanding and implementing them. Department managers, unit supervisors, project leaders, and workers are left in a cloud of unnecessary complexity and stupefying jargon. At the level of the work team, where the scope of activity is narrowly focused on a handful of familiar and tightly connected functions, a different path, a simpler one, can be taken, on the thesis that even a commonsense review can yield great reward. In effect, the Pareto Principle is validated once again, this time by applying it to the very methods we prize, selecting from the many the vital few that are most intuitive and powerful.

Process can be defined as "one or more tasks that add value by transforming a set of inputs into a specified set of outputs (goods or services) for another person (customer) by a combination

FIGURE 5
Process: Steps to Take to Create Value

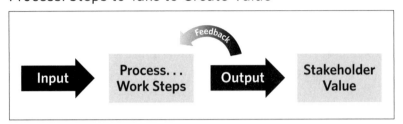

of people, methods, and tools."[3] These elements are illustrated in Figure 5. Work teams might understand it simply to be those steps routinely taken to create something of value. Team members always share at least a gut-level appreciation that their customers and owners would value getting more accomplished and getting it done faster, better, or cheaper. When challenged to rethink and improve familiar processes, motivated and involved work teams will find ways to do just that. This baseline review requires four simple steps: identify, document, evaluate, and improve the team's key processes. Let's take a closer look.

Identify key processes

Unless the work team is already aware of major process defects, a good place to begin a review is to take an inventory, listing all processes through which their work is accomplished. The responsibilities of an accounting work team, for example, might include accounts payable, reconciliation of receipts, accounts receivable, the generation of income statements, and a host of lesser functions. The accounts payable function alone may encompass several dozen subprocesses, ranging from setting up a new vendor for payment to reconciling vendor statements. However, *these processes are not all of equal significance. A handful will consume most of the time and resources or have a markedly greater strategic impact or risk.* In accounts payable, for example, that short list of critical processes might include invoice entry, check writing, and reconciliation of vendor statements, because those subprocesses collectively consume the majority of the staff time and other resources. Improving these vital few activities will have a disproportionate impact on the team's overall efficiency, so they deserve priority.

Document key processes
Understanding these priority processes requires that they be documented by developing an explanation of the present flow of work and a picture of how the steps fit together. Many techniques have been developed over the years to do this, some of them requiring specialized training such as flowcharting, data flow diagramming, and functional mapping. These techniques have their place, and clearly better methods create the potential for better results. But many operating managers and supervisors open up one of these toolboxes only to find such a bewildering array of options that the review is brought to a grinding halt. This is unfortunate, because much value can be gained even by writing down each step. As the team does this, it can also include copies of related documents, computer screens, and other supporting materials. One useful interactive technique to develop this big picture of the work flow is to write these steps on sticky notes and place them on a blank wall to represent the place of each in the work sequence and its relationship with other steps. *Remember that the underlying purpose here is to make the present work flow more understandable to the reviewers and to be as clear as possible about what each process is intended to deliver.* Examples of deliverables might include tickets booked, invoices authorized, deposits made, parts assembled, merchandise checked out, and meals served. *Begin the review with the deliverable for each process clearly in mind.*

Evaluate key processes
Evaluation raises the obvious question, how well is our process doing at delivering these intended results? It requires a few good measures. A good measure of a key process would provide insight into (1) *speed* (i.e., timeliness or cycle time), (2) *quality* (i.e., variability or error rate) and (3) *cost* (i.e., resources consumed per unit of input). Consider a commonplace process such as account clerks

entering invoices into a computer in order to validate the completeness of an order and authorize payment. In this process, the number of invoices accurately entered per person per hour might be economically tracked. A measure like this directly connects the primary input, staff time, to the primary output, correctly entered invoices. While few process measures are as easy as this, *putting a meter on the primary work flows of a work team informs the team how to score. This measures what really matters.*

Discussions of this sort can get lost in a quagmire of confusing concepts and buzzwords, made all the more challenging by the fact that every process measure must be customized to the inputs and outputs of the process being measured (as illustrated in Table 2). However, if these key processes are to be completed faster, better, and cheaper, work teams must find ways to define and measure their speed, quality, and cost.

Measuring the performance of key processes is an essential beginning, but it is only through comparison that evaluation can occur. Internal comparisons are easier and less expensive than external ones. An internal comparison might be as simple as comparing a result to the supervisor's intuition or gut feel. Or it might be the more robust evaluation that comes from comparing performance over time, comparing the production of individual producers, or comparing with units performing similar duties elsewhere in the company. Such comparisons can be surprisingly easy and insightful. In our example of invoice entry, we might find that the average number of invoices entered per person per hour increased 50 percent during the peak season, or that some workers could produce twice as much as others, or even that the performance of another office in the same company was markedly better. A short list of thoughtful internal comparisons like these can powerfully redirect attention to key problems and opportunities.

External comparisons can extend the reviewers' understanding and insight. A frame of reference that reaches outside the company to a targeted group of peers or that cites industry norms and best practices can uncover even more dramatic opportunities for improvement. For example, you might find that the performance of a comparable operation in another company far exceeded your inter-

TABLE 2

Process Measures

Sample Processes	Speed	Quality	Cost
Travel agency ticketing	Ticket cycle time	Ticket error rate	Cost per ticket issued
Phone services	Number or percentage of calls answered in 3 rings or less	Number or percentage of calls fully resolving the customer problem	Cost per call handled
Shelving	Number or percentage of items shelved within standard time	Shelving error rate	Cost per item stocked
Custodial services	Percentage cleaned versus standards defined	Number of defects per week cited in facilities inspection reports	Cost per gross square foot cleaned
Insurance claims	Resolution time	Number or percentage of claims satisfactorily resolved	Cost per claim resolved

nal best practice. Such a comparison would immediately shift expectations.

Table 3 illustrates internal and external comparisons for the invoice entry example. Feedback like this raises obvious why questions. Why does average productivity vary from a low of 70 invoices per person per hour in the off-season to 100 in the peak season? Why does individual employee productivity vary from a low of 50 to a high of 110? Why is it that peers outside the firm can generate average performance of 100 per hour (and as high as 130) while this

TABLE 3

Invoice Entry

Process Measure	Internal Comparison			External Comparison		
Invoices Entered per Hour	Work Team Average by Season		Range of Individual Averages	Work Team Average	Peer Average	Best Practice
	Low	High	Low High			
	70	100	50 110	85	100	130

team averages only 85? *Only when the team reviewers understand why these results occurred do they become equipped to take the final step, making improvement.*

Improve key processes

At last we come to the payoff, process improvement. By identifying, documenting, and evaluating priority processes, a team can direct its attention to opportunities to improve. Understanding why process performance varies can enable a team to compile a short list of improvements. Perhaps entire steps can be eliminated, new equipment can be used, the flow of work can be altered or automated, a policy can be changed, people can be retrained, or a host of other shifts can be made. A well-conducted review will almost always discover significantly better ways to work. In the case of the invoice entry example, the team might have found the following:

- Elements on invoices to be entered could be highlighted to make key information more easily spotted by account clerks, thereby improving the speed and accuracy of data entry.

- The computer application could be upgraded to reduce the number of fields entered on each invoice by looking up and populating default information already available, such as vendor address or terms.

- A direct system link could be built with major suppliers, allowing the automatic transfer of invoice data and thereby eliminating the function entirely.

- Purchasers could be asked to consolidate billings to reduce the number of invoices.

Despite the obvious potential of process reviews in work teams, they are routinely overlooked. The very routine of day-to-day work contributes most to this oversight. The press of daily duties, unexamined assumptions that current methods are acceptable or perhaps unchangeable, deeply ingrained work habits, and even the notion that it is someone else's job to do the thinking create a tangle of self-imposed constraints that can shut down all but the most dedicated and persistent efforts to improve.

Exercise 3 provides an overview of a simple approach your work team can use to assess the performance of its processes. You can adapt it for use as an exercise for members, collectively or individually, to complete or simply as an overview for listing, documenting, evaluating, and improving your key processes. The exercise is designed to lead you toward your vital few processes, measures, and opportunities to improve.

Value Received: Owner Contribution

Now that we've looked at owner satisfaction, we turn our attention to owner contribution. Two important questions demand an answer: *What does the work team value from its owners? How well are the owners doing at meeting the work team's legitimate expectations?*

Owners and the organizations they create expect their work teams to do only those things that contribute to the corporate purpose and to do those things well. In other words, they value both *purpose alignment* and *process performance.* But work teams also have legitimate expectations of their owners that need to be made explicit and consciously evaluated. Two are universal: clearly defined purpose and adequate resources.

EXERCISE 3

Owners Value "Process Performance": How Are We Doing?

Directions: Answer the process review questions below.

Identify Key Processes

Processes are steps taken to create value for your team's stakeholders. They are not all of equal significance. Generally a handful will represent most of the time and resources consumed or have a markedly greater strategic impact or risk. Unless the team is already aware of a process problem or opportunity, pick processes for review that are the most resource intensive.

% of Team
Resources
Consumed

Process 1 _____ _____%___

Process 2 _____ _____%___

Process 3 _____ _____%___

Process 4 _____ _____%___

Document Key Processes

Process chosen for review: _____

Clearly define what this process is intended to deliver:

_____

_____

Describe each step followed to achieve that result. You will find it helpful to include copies of related documents, computer screens, and other supporting materials.

Step 1 _____

Step 2 _____

Step 3 _____

Step 4 _____

EXERCISE 3 cont'd

Evaluate Key Processes

The purpose of evaluation is to assess how well the process is delivering the result described on page 48. The key to successful evaluation of the process is comparison that will help your team determine if the desired results can be achieved faster, better, or cheaper.

- Internal comparisons capture differences in productivity by season, by worker, and by department within the firm.

- External comparisons are more difficult and expensive, but they have the potential to spot better processes outside the firm.

Choose a mix of internal and external comparisons. Based on this feedback, identify and investigate the greatest gaps to define a short list of "opportunities to improve."

_____

_____

_____

_____

_____

Improve Key Processes

Select priorities from the list of opportunities.

What will you do to improve this process?

_____

_____

_____

_____

_____

- **Clearly defined purpose**. It is ultimately the owners' responsibility to ensure that the corporate purpose is clearly defined, understood, and supported throughout the company. Defining the corporate purpose requires a directive mission, a prescriptive vision, a connecting strategy, and shared values. To be actionable, the corporation must also have a short list of overarching corporate priorities and goals that work teams can easily understand and apply in assessing their internal efforts. Teams cannot align their activities effectively without clear direction and priorities from the top. One way to assess whether owners are succeeding is simply to ask the team members: What are the company mission, vision, and strategy? What are the present overarching corporate priorities and how do they impact our priorities? If team members don't know or care, it is left to the owners and their representatives to take the initiative.

- **Adequate resources.** Owners must also assume responsibility to provide sufficient resources to equip corporate work teams. If becoming competitive requires new systems, training, or investment in better facilities or equipment, owners and their representatives must be accountable to make these resources available. A simple way to ascertain whether that is a problem in a particular team is to ask members what additional resources are necessary to achieve their clearly defined purpose and what the return on investing in them is. Then evaluate each suggestion on its own merits using criteria (financial and otherwise) that are clearly understood by all.

It may seem presumptuous to suggest that companies and their work teams should hold owners accountable. Yet it is essential to the long-term collective interests of all, including owners, that they do just that. A graceful way to provide feedback on legitimate needs is to make it clear that the intent is to improve return to the owner when identifying a deficiency. The message is essentially, "We will better achieve the purpose you have charged us with if these changes are made."

First Bookstore Case Study: Owners

Regardless of the size of an organization, work teams are small. The most common type, the natural work team, operates within the conventional organizational structure. It typically employs fewer than two dozen individuals, who share a common purpose, common resources, and common leadership. We have chosen a receiving department supporting a retail business to illustrate the case for owners, customers, and employees over the next three chapters. However, we might just as easily have selected an accounting office, a maintenance crew on the second shift in a manufacturing firm, or the servers on the dinner crew in a cafeteria-style restaurant. All insights and methods will broadly apply.

We do not intend the case study to be the final word on measurement. Instead, we seek to illustrate a simple, commonsense approach to measure and evaluate the value exchanged between a team and its core stakeholders by posing five questions for the team to ask about their stakeholders:

1. Who are they?

2. What do they value and expect from the team?

3. How well is the team doing at meeting or exceeding those expectations?

4. What does the team value and expect from the stakeholders in return?

5. How well are these stakeholders doing at meeting or exceeding those expectations?

Because changes often impact all three core stakeholders and in varying degrees require their support, gathering feedback from all of them can powerfully inform efforts to prescribe and implement winning change. We therefore take up this subject in Chapter 5.

Background for the Case Study

First Bookstore is a fictional private retailer serving a large state university campus by selling primarily textbooks and related academic support materials and college memorabilia from two off-campus but prime locations. Founded in the mid-1970s, the store has flourished for nearly three decades by pursuing a premium service strategy. Its core customer category is a population of roughly 40,000 students. Two-thirds of them are traditional students, 18–22 years of age and in residence there to pursue their studies full-time. The remaining third are nontraditional students; these are mainly middle-income older commuters who are attending school part-time, often while working full-time. Other important campus constituencies include the teaching faculty of nearly 2,500, approximately 5,000 support staff, an alumni population of nearly 350,000, and a large number of campus visitors. To provide its services, First Bookstore employs 90 full-time staff members, a part-time work force of up to four dozen students, and on occasion up to 50 full-time, short-term temporary staff.

At the time of this study, the business had recently fallen on hard times. After three years of modest decline, annual sales had temporarily stabilized at approximately $30 million, but the bottom line had suffered and the future looked even more challenging.

Lupe supervised the distribution center (DC), a small cadre of people charged with receiving and distributing the store's resale merchandise. The work there was routine. Apart from seasonal shifts in product mix and volume, every day seemed pretty much like the day before. There was comfort in this routine, the comfort of familiarity, habit, and sameness. These routines generally kept everyone busy, at least busy enough that none of them were even aware of the assumptions being reaffirmed day by day, assumptions that they were doing the right things in the right way. It was as though a fog had slowly drifted in, bringing with it profound stupor.

In the short space of a year, not one but two new competitors had opened, and they were hungry and fierce. Combined with all the other business woes, it seemed that the distribution center's comfortable world had undergone economic shock therapy. It had become clear that these comfortable routines, long taken for granted, must now be questioned. The owners would expect it; in fact, they would soon require it. With the need to act becoming urgent, Lupe understood that any changes must be thoughtful and well targeted. They must be informed by a clear understanding of the owners' interests. Who are they? What do they value and expect from her team? And most important of all, how well is the team doing at meeting or exceeding these expectations? It was obvious that only after answering those questions could she target the right changes.

Who Are Our Owners?

As Lupe pondered these questions, she soon remembered Jon. Jon Levine had built First Bookstore's two retail outlets almost thirty years before. Although he had died, the present board of directors consisted of twelve family members, to whom the president and general manager, Jim Malone, now reported. Jim had worked for the family since the company began and had become the boss. Lupe decided to begin her quest to better understand her firm's owners that very morning, by meeting with Jim.

After exchanging pleasantries, Lupe jumped right in. "Can you help us understand our owners, Jim? With all the changes going on, we feel we need to know a lot more about them and what they expect from the company and the DC. Jon passed away shortly after I was hired about a decade ago, and I'm afraid I don't know much about the current owners. Take me back to the beginning."

"Sure, Lupe, I guess I know the history as well as anyone. Originally, Jon founded the business because the faculty on campus was dissatisfied with the two existing bookstores. At that time even their most basic services were deficient; for instance, no one even bothered to follow up on open textbook orders to make sure that the books would be on hand when classes began. But even then Jon envisioned something far more. He saw the opportunity to build a business on relationships and to really understand his customers.

That was long before the idea caught on. He liked to say, 'The faculty is the very heart and soul of this business, and they deserve to be treated that way.' But, at the same time, he understood that the students weren't happy either.

"Service excellence was Jon's mantra. His vision was to offer 'legendary service' to students and faculty, service so good that people all over campus would be telling stories about the store. He set out to do this by hiring remarkable people. He called them 'people people.' You know what I mean, the kind of folks who just love the service business. It was obvious to Jon that success in business depended on matching people to purpose, and he invested what most people would consider extreme efforts to find the right fits. That's why the second part of his vision was to create a fulfilling work experience for those special people—a place to work that was productive, fulfilling, and fun. Jon knew that a service business stands or falls on the strength of the employees who provide the service.

"Of course, I wouldn't suggest for a minute that profit didn't matter. Believe me, it mattered then just like it does now. The family depends on those quarterly dividends. That's why the third aspect of his vision was that we would become the 'home of best practice.' That meant doing the right things right. Jon had a deep-down conviction that profits result from a winning strategy designed to ensure that all the core stakeholders get what they value most. Believe it or not, that's even why he named the business First Bookstore. He thought of it as a place where people would come first, whether they were customers, employees, or owners, and he flatly refused to compromise by suggesting that one was above another. Delivering value to all of them was a hot button for him until the day he died. It worked, too. In the first five years he managed to win more than 60 percent of the market share away from well-established competitors."

Lupe was thoughtful. "Some aspects of that legacy remain to this day, although a lot has changed, too. I'm wondering, since the owners no longer work in the company, how do you interact with them now? Do they meddle or pretty much stay out of the way?"

Jim grinned, "I guess the real answer is 'none of the above.' They don't have the time, interest, or competence to run the business and, thankfully, they know it. But they do weigh in on the things that matter to them. I guess they have been mostly concerned about meeting the financial goals, especially in the past few years. They do have a lot at stake. But if Jon were alive today, he'd surely be concerned about other things, like making sure that everyone knew why we are here, where we are going, and how each individual fits into the bigger picture. He was pretty careful to spell out the store's mission and vision describing what we were about, as well as the strategy and values spelling out how we would go about accomplishing our goals."

"I barely remember Mr. Levine, Jim. But he sounds like a guy who really seemed to know what mattered. I remember him saying that 'you can get almost anything you want in life if you just help enough other people to get what they want.' It sure sounds as though that's the way he led the company. What made those early years such a big win?" Lupe reached for a pen and prepared to take notes.

"Well, Lupe, I guess you'd have to say that the early years were more than a win, they were a win-win-win-win. The store won, the customers won, the employees won, and, of course, Jon won. And the beginning of all of this winning was that early commitment to shared values. We don't talk about them as much as we should anymore, but you still see them on our walls, on our letterhead, and just about everywhere else. Actually, I think Jon would have had them tattooed on our foreheads if he thought he could get away with it. They are truth, respect, teamwork, excellence, and integrity—those are values that we all developed together. In a sense those values drove everything else. Let me explain.

"The first value is truth. We have a responsibility to weigh in where it matters most, even when what we have to say is not easy to hear. The commitment to respect relates to the first; it's so important to treat everyone with respect even when you don't agree and regardless of whether they are customers, co-workers, colleagues, business partners, or the guys who empty the trash. Our rule of thumb was simply to treat people the way they would want to be treated. Pretty original, eh?

"Next is to be a team player. Teamwork matters a lot to us because most of our work is done in teams. Teams create the potential to tap complementary skills and to incorporate new insights. We depend on teams to deliver high performance standards.

"Then there is excellence—the only result worth striving for. Well, I guess you can't be excellent at everything, but Jon knew that setting high standards in strategically targeted outcomes for all core stakeholders would feed on itself. It powerfully molds our self-identity. Jon made the whole thing personal by constantly challenging us to 'take excellence to heart.'

"After setting such high standards of behavior, integrity is essential. It means walking the talk. Without it, this values stuff is just a bunch of lofty platitudes. A real commitment requires accountability, and accountability requires measurement. The right values tend to point you in the right direction, especially when you are competing in a service business like ours."

Lupe had been scribbling furiously (see Sample of Exercise 1) but put her pen down. "I honestly don't recall a time when those values were not plastered all over the place, but I'm wondering if our vision has changed. Are we still trying to achieve legendary customer service, a fulfilling and productive employee work experience, and the home of best practice for our owners, and if we are, how would we know when we've accomplished it?"

Jim was nodding as he continued. "You make a good point. Jon challenged us to be the best, to be people committed to excellence. His early vision statement sought to capture what that meant. To his credit, it provided a clear, specific, and compelling destination. I mean you could feel the heartbeat in it. To a considerable degree a vision like that could provide a useful guide to decision making. But it lacked measurement, some way to determine where we were on the journey. To that degree it wasn't prescriptive enough. I'm certain that we could do better now. We might even define and measure 'legendary customer service' and a 'fulfilling and productive work experience' based upon a satisfaction survey of some sort and

SAMPLE OF EXERCISE 1
Who Are Our Owners?

Directions: Complete the required information below.

Definition: Owners are founders, investors, and risk takers. They are the architects and guardians of the organization's purpose. They commission others at various levels—from governing boards to work teams—to accomplish that purpose, entrusting to them the necessary resources and authority to act, and rightfully holding them accountable for those actions.

Founders

Describe your organization's founders.

First Bookstore was founded by Jon Levine to provide better course materials services to faculty and students. However, Jon saw a much bigger opportunity. He would treat ALL of his core stakeholders as though they came first by giving them more of what they valued than they expected. This meant that the company would succeed by delivering a thoughtfully defined value package to each of its core stakeholders. It worked . . . the company took root and grew rapidly. Jon was passionate. Those early days must have been exciting.

Board of Directors

Name	Title	Comments
Jon Levine Jr.	Chairman	Older son 15%
Mary Levine		Jon's spouse 15%
Jon Levine III		Grandchild 5%
Robert Levine		Grandchild 5%
Joan Alcott	Vice chair	Daughter 10%
Jim Alcott		Joan's spouse 10%
Sarah Alcott		Grandchild 5%
Kevin Alcott		Grandchild 5%
Jim Alcott Jr.		Grandchild 5%
Marty Levine	Treasurer	Younger son 10%
Wendy Levine		Marty's spouse 10%
Sam Levine		Grandchild 5%

The stockholders are all Jon's heirs and no longer take an active interest in the business. They depend on the company's quarterly dividends. It would seem helpful to get better acquainted with them.

Chain of Delegation

Describe the direct line of authority linking the board of directors/trustees to your work team.

Name	Title	Comments

Jim Malone—CEO & General Manager and immediate supervisor. Jim remembers the founding purpose and was coached by Jon. However, the founding purpose is clearly not his. Whatever he may say, his immediate concern is to deliver the financial numbers. Jon's commitment to the stakeholders as a means to that end has waned and perhaps even disappeared. It would be good to get closer to Jim and to make sure he will support our efforts to rekindle the founder's balanced approach to winning.

Distribution Center Work Team

List members of the work team.

Name	Title	Comments
Lupe Rodriguez	*Team supervisor*	
Rena Casden	*Lead person*	
Joe Switzer	*Material Handler 1*	
Pat Callahan	*Material Handler 1*	
Harvey Watson	*Material Handler 1*	
Pete Doran	*Material Handler 2*	
Ed McGiff	*Material Handler 2*	
Jason Ditzell	*Material Handler 2*	
Merritt McMurty	*Material Handler 2*	
Dave Weidman	*Driver*	

Understanding owners as people and managing relationships with them will help equip your team to better meet their expectations. However, doing this will require more than simply listing names and titles. What can you do to better understand them?

'home of best practice' as being in the top quartile within our key industry statistics."

Lupe reflected quietly for a full minute before responding. "Measured excellence in serving our customers, employees, and owners is certainly enough to spark that fire in the belly. It's a worthy enough destination if you can get your hands around it. There's something in it for everybody. But we still have to live in the present, don't we?"

"You're right about that. That's why good companies invest the time to capture today's purpose in a descriptive mission statement, one that answers the big questions," said Jim.

"You must be kidding, Jim." Lupe replied. "Most managers would find it more interesting to watch grass grow than to read, much less write, a mission statement. The statements are worse than boring; they're downright irrelevant. I always thought companies use them more as PR or as something to fill up the annual report."

"You couldn't be more wrong, Lupe. A directive mission statement describes the organization's very reason for being. If done well, it answers four practical questions that should direct day-to-day activities: Who are we? What do we do? For whom do we do it? Why do we do it?

"We are First Bookstore, a business dedicated to putting the interests of all our stakeholders in equal and high regard. We are here primarily to provide academic support materials for faculty and students, although staff, alumni, and campus visitors also use our services. But we know excellence in service requires dedicated employees, and one doesn't get dedicated employees without meeting their needs. That's why we include serving our employees as well as our owners in our mission. The 'why' is fairly simple: we are here to support the university's greater purposes, especially teaching, while earning an excellent return on investment."

"Point taken," said Lupe. "A directive mission spells out today's purpose in ways that help keep the company targeted, and a prescriptive vision lays out a future destination that is clear and compelling. To be useful, both have to provide a meaningful guide to decision making. Ours seems to do that. But obviously that's still not enough. Movement forward doesn't happen by accident, or because you write it out on a piece of paper. What am I missing?"

"You're missing strategy. That's the map to get us from here to there. In fact, we spend most of our effort reviewing and reframing the strategy through which we hope to fulfill that purpose. New competitors, new technologies, shifts in our customer demographics, and so forth require ongoing reassessment and adjustment. For example, even today, key faculty members remain at the epicenter of our customer strategy. Their support and recommendations greatly impact student perception and behavior. Of course, with 2,500 faculty members, we have to target the most important opinion leaders. Did you know that fewer than 100 faculty members teach the large-enrollment classes that represent 50 percent of our textbook business? It's amazing to me that our competitors can't seem to figure that out, and I sure hope they never do! Part of our customer strategy is to give teachers of these classes the VIP treatment they deserve.

"First Bookstore has always sought what Jon called a 'winning strategy.' He believed that long-term profitability in this business could best be achieved the old-fashioned way, by earning it. Earning it meant a fair exchange of value between the company and its three core stakeholders. In the early days, he would even have a written customer strategy, an employee strategy, and of course the internal operating and financial strategies to serve the owners' interests. I must confess that in the turmoil of recent stressful business conditions we have lost that balance. I guess we have become much more focused on purely operational and financial issues. Your visit reminds me of better times. Now, I know I have some of those old documents here somewhere." Jim rummaged about in his desk, finally laying his hands on the information shown in Figure 6, the company's statements of mission and vision, and handed them to Lupe.

"How, then, do you go about implementing so ambitious a strategy? What's the role of the board, and everyone else for that matter? How do you ensure that the right things get done by work teams like ours?"

FIGURE 6
First Bookstore: Mission and Vision

Our Vision: To Be the Best . . .

- Giving the best value to our customers. Our service to core customers will become legendary, so good that it will foster unsolicited stories across campus.

- Providing the best value for our employees. We will create a fulfilling and productive workplace for our employees.

- Being the home of best practice for our owners. Our operational and financial performance will consistently exceed comparable industry norms. We will become the undisputed leader in our industry, the home of best practices.

Our Mission . . .

To serve faculty, students, staff, alumni, and campus visitors by providing a specialized selection of reasonably priced products and services, including course materials, general books, technology products, campus memorabilia, and various convenience items. We will consistently exceed the expectations of our customers, employees, and owners by delivering more of what they value than they expect.

"The board annually approves our proposed business plan, Lupe. Then it's my job to implement it. I delegate parts of that effort to you and the other department heads, and I'm sure you do the same. The strategy defines clear targets, but to act on them, the targets must be converted into priority goals and objectives, which cascade throughout this whole business. I know it sounds a bit corny, but Jon always taught us that in the final analysis we're all managers around here, even the sales associates on the front lines and the clerical staff in the business office. We have entrusted virtually everyone with varying levels of stewardship in pursuing the interests of our owners."

It seemed a stretch at first to suggest that even entry-level employees represent the owners, but on reflection Lupe thought the logic was solid enough, and Jim obviously believed it. She still couldn't help musing to herself how odd that notion might seem to those who served on the front lines. She also realized how much of the company's founding passion had died with Jon, leaving only ghostly vestiges behind. The company had grown and changed. More than half the staff had turned over. Jim was a great guy, but he was no Jon Levine. He was more hands-on, more detail oriented, and he was certainly no visionary. While he was savvy operationally, the big-picture stuff was not his forte, and one was unlikely to hear him praising the thousand and one little things that encourage the kind of excellence the mission called for. Whatever the intent, work life for most employees at First Bookstore had degenerated into just plain work—what you do when you show up each day, and what you do to pay the bills each month.

Lupe had a much better sense now of who the owners were and what they expected on the whole. "They want us to live the values. They want us to contribute to accomplishing the overall mission in such a fashion that we also pursue the bigger vision. They expect that we will do this by meeting or exceeding stakeholder expectations, by pursing a winning strategy." But something critical was still missing, and it troubled her. What did vision, mission, strategy, and values mean for her work team in the distribution center? She knew that Jim was her best hope for getting help to figure that out.

What Do They Value and Expect?

"Jim, I really appreciate your time," said Lupe. "My people might consider this sort of talk a bit lofty, but I'm pretty sure most of that's just a smokescreen. They want to know what the company stands for, where it is going, and why. *But most of all, they want to know how we fit in to all this.* What does this mean to us, especially now? How do the mission, vision, strategy, and values of the whole company impact our distribution center? What specifically do the owners expect of us, and how do we stack up against those expectations?"

Jim looked Lupe straight in the eye as he replied. "Let me put it as plainly as I know how. More than anything, our owners want two things from you and your team. They want purpose and process. Our purpose is pretty clearly defined by our mission, vision, strategy, and values. *Do only those things necessary to support our corporate purpose.* Every bit of resource that you consume doing anything else is no longer available to help us do what we were created to do. *And do what you do well.* Every bit of resource frittered away through poor processes is no longer available to help us do what we were created to do."

How Are We Doing at Purpose Alignment?

Jim's words reverberated in Lupe's mind, *"Do only those things necessary to support our corporate purpose. And do them well."* As she returned to her office, she realized that her next steps would require no more thought than putting one foot in front of the other. Until now she had considered talk about mission, vision, strategy, and values to be abstract and irrelevant to the successful operation of a real work team like hers. But in a little more than an hour, Jim had profoundly changed her thinking. How could she possibly hope to align her team's purpose with the company's without first clearly defining both and making careful comparisons between the two? Only then would she be able to assess the effectiveness of the efforts and resources they consumed in supporting the broader priorities of the firm. The insight struck as a blinding flash of the obvious. Lupe immediately set out to prepare the information shown in Sample of Exercise 2.

As she reviewed her hastily prepared chart, Lupe saw gaps in every major category. How could it be otherwise? Only an hour ago, the mission, vision, and strategy of the firm were largely unknown. This effort to define them raised two alarming observations. The primary statements of corporate purpose had not been consciously revised or reevaluated since the days of Jon Levine and they no longer reflected corporate practice. The second observation was even more problematic. The activities of her own work team had gone largely unexamined for as long as Lupe had been there.

She recalled a new freight tracking system implemented a few years back. It had enabled the team to consolidate several freight carriers into one, saving at least a couple of hours each day. Later, she had checked in with the team, hoping to redirect their time and

Owners Value Purpose Alignment: How Are We Doing?

Directions: Gather and attach documents describing your organization's corporate purpose for the company, for organizational units in your chain of command, and for your work team. Use them to inform your team's effort to describe the intended value proposition for each targeted stakeholder category. Then assess how well the activities of your team fit that purpose.

First Bookstore

	Customers	Employees	Owners
Describe the target population to be served.	- 2,500 faculty (especially 100 large-enrollment classes) - 40,000 students -350,000 alumni/campus visitors	- 90 full-time professionals - 4 dozen part-time students - Up to 50 temporary staff	- Jon Levine, original owner and founder - 12 member-owners of the board, all family - Jim Malone CEO and supervisor
Directive mission What is our present value proposition/package to serve them?	**Core value:** *To provide reasonably priced course materials, books, technology products, campus memorabilia, and convenience items.* **Jon's mission:** *exceed expectations by delivering more than expected.*	**Jon's mission:** *exceed expectations by delivering more than expected.*	*The owners expect a good return on investment. Some depend on the dividend income.* **Jon's mission:** *exceed expectations by delivering more than expected.*
Prescriptive vision What is our future value proposition/package to serve them?	**To be the best . . .** *By providing "legendary service" to our customers*	**To be the best . . .** *By providing a "fulfilling and productive work experience" for our employees*	**To be the best . . .** *By becoming the undisputed "home of best practice" for our owners*
Connecting strategy What are the company's most important priorities?	- Service excellence - Competitive prices - VIP services to key faculty - One-stop shopping	- Recruit and promote "people people" well-matched to work purpose	- Consistently exceed stakeholder expectations - "Do only those things that contribute to the company's purpose" - "Do them well"

SAMPLE OF EXERCISE 2 cont'd

The Distribution Center at First Bookstore

	Customers	Employees	Owners
Describe the target population to be served.	-Merchandise buyers -Accounting staff -Retail operations staff	- 10 full-time staff - Up to 10 temp-orary staff	- Our primary owner contact is Jim Malone
Directive mission What is our present value proposition/ package to serve them?	- To receive - To store - To distribute the store's products	Exceed expecta-tions by delivering more than ex-pected.	Exceed expecta-tions by delivering more than ex-pected.
Prescriptive vision What is our future value proposition/ package to serve them?	**To be the best . . .** By providing "leg-endary service" to our customers—service so good that our cus-tomers will tell stories about us	**To be the best . . .** By providing a " fulfilling and pro-ductive work expe-rience for our employees"	**To be the best . . .** By becoming the undisputed "home of best practice" for our owners
Connecting strategy What are our team's most important priorities?	What is the com-pany strategy?	What is the com-pany strategy?	What is the com-pany strategy?

Within the framework of the organization's purpose:

What services or activities should the team consider discontinuing?

Mail handling
Campus deliveries

What services or activities should the team consider adding?

Expanded campus mail out services

capture those savings. Only then did she discover that they had taken on new mail-sorting responsibilities from the business office upstairs while two key people were temporarily out on leave. By the time the office personnel returned, the new routines had been firmly entrenched. This was a sobering reminder that much of what gets done at work is not carefully planned and sometimes doesn't even make sense.

She also faced the nagging question of whether her team should continue to be involved in campus deliveries. The five thousand packages that they distributed each year had to be worked in to their core services as time permitted. It had become a nuisance job, requiring between two and six hours each day. They just couldn't cost-justify the equipment, vehicles, systems, and other resources to become really good at it, and they knew it. Besides, two local package delivery firms already provided better services, and at very low costs. Perhaps the DC should be outsourcing this function. The idea was both intriguing and a little disconcerting. Lupe now pondered these matters from a different perspective. Her team was a part of something bigger, and a realignment would be needed if they were to follow Jim's instruction to do "only those things necessary to support the company purpose."

How Are We Doing at Process Performance?

But Jim had asked for more than just doing the right things. He had asked that whatever activities their team genuinely needed to do also be done well. It was common sense that any serious effort to understand and improve the team's work would require the involvement and commitment of the members. Yet it was equally apparent that this would involve more than just bringing everyone into a room and asking for opinions. First, each of the team's key processes would need to be identified and documented; then the team could come together for further documentation and evaluation, and, where appropriate, to determine improvements. Lupe set about the task of preparing by gathering the information that they would need.

Identify key processes

The DC carried out three key processes: receiving, storage, and distribution. Together, these processes consumed nearly all of their resources. Receiving consisted of unloading trucks, checking in merchandise, and then routing the merchandise either into temporary storage or to the sales floor. Once stored, products remained until requisitioned for picking and transfer to the sales floor. Distribution entailed making bulk deliveries and pickups as well as deliveries on and off campus. When Jim asked them to "do what you do well," he was referring to these very functions. Could these functions be done faster, perhaps by decreasing the cycle time from the loading dock to the sales floor? Might they be accomplished better, with fewer errors, or changed in other ways that add value? Could they be provided cheaper, reducing costs by improving processes? Even though repeated untold thousands of times, these processes had never before been systematically reviewed.

Lupe began by listing these processes in priority order (see Table 4), along with an estimate of the percentage of their unit's time committed to doing the work. Then, starting with the most resource-intensive process, receiving, she repeated the effort for the key subprocesses as shown in Table 5.

Document key processes

Because textbook receiving was the largest and most resource-intensive subprocess, Lupe went on to document this key process by describing each step, inserting graphs, charts, forms, and computer screen prints that she knew her whole team would easily understand. As she prepared into the late hours, she couldn't escape the thought that this was a strange twist of fate. For many years she had intended to write out these very steps in order to preserve them in the event key people were to leave unexpectedly. Now that she finally was getting around to it, her purpose was to do the exact opposite: to change the steps.

Evaluate key processes

Having chosen textbook receiving as a priority process for review and having documented the work flow, she was now ready to

TABLE 4
DC Processes

1. **Receiving**	**50%**
2. Storage (picking-transfer)	30%
3. Distribution	
Campus	10%
Off-campus mail out	5%
4. Other processes	5%

TABLE 5
Receiving Subprocesses

1. **Receiving textbooks**	**50%**
2. Returning (textbooks)	20%
3. Receiving (other product categories)	20%
4. Returning (other product categories)	5%
5. Other receiving processes	5%

evaluate the process. She knew instinctively that talking through each step with her staff and others affected by the process would be helpful. However, that discussion would be much improved if it could be informed by thoughtful measurement. The simplest measurement would be tracking the outputs for each major activity. For receiving, each order generated a log entry. Orders were then received line by line, with each line representing varying quantities of items received. The number of logs, lines, and items received could easily be measured and monitored.

Although the DC had not previously tracked these activities, Lupe immediately recognized the value in doing so. Their team was there to receive, store, and distribute merchandise. A routine measurement would, at minimum, keep everyone focused on these mission-critical outputs. Besides, even a cursory analysis had exposed the obvious seasonality to the workload driven by the academic cycles. Products were ordered, received, shelved, sold, and re-turned in a predictable cycle, and careful attention would surely help the team improve their efficiency over time. While this came as no surprise, the numbers developed in Figure 7 (page 70) made these extremes more apparent.

Yet as insightful as these activity indicators were, Lupe realized that they were inadequate. It would be far better to link these out-puts to inputs, to link production levels to the primary resources used to accomplish them. In effect, Lupe needed a different kind of measure, one that could capture the productivity or efficiency of the process. Because people are the primary resource (or input) used to receive, Lupe prepared the chart shown in Figure 8, show-ing the average number of items received per period per person. She noted that even there, performance varied markedly with the business cycle.

The process walk-through

After assembling the needed background information, it was at last time to meet with the team, and Lupe was ready. Excitement was in the air as the DC team entered the room that Monday morning. There was anxiety to be sure. Everyone knew that the firm had posted another operating loss the past quarter, and they knew that the future would become a whole lot more challenging as new competitors were gearing up for a life-and-death struggle. Even so, Lupe's enthusiasm was unwavering. The team trusted her, and she was confident that they could both define and implement the nec-essary changes on their own. Today's meeting would be the first of several intended to review the team's major processes step by step, beginning with the most resource intensive, the textbook receiving process.

Lupe had firmly declined Jim Malone's offer to bring in a con-sultant. "No one knows more about how things work around here and where the process potholes are than we do. Besides, any con-sultant worth his salt will start out asking us what needs to change. We can do that much on our own." There was, however, one big concern. Years of routines and deeply embedded habits create

FIGURE 7

Activity: Items Received

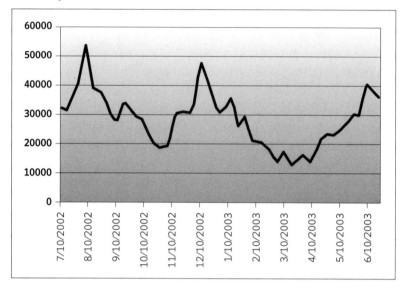

FIGURE 8

Productivity: Items Received per Employee per Hour

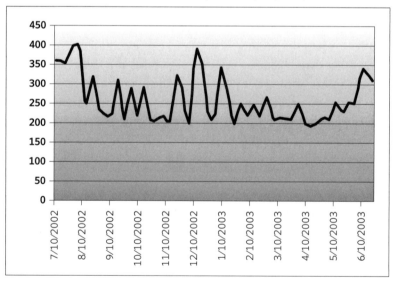

blind spots, sometimes preventing people from seeing even obvious problems and opportunities. That's why Lupe came armed with data strong enough to direct attention to problem points and clear enough to force the team to reckon with the biggest question: why?

Lupe looked at the people sitting around the table and began. "We've worked together a long time. We're good people. We're a good team. We work for a good company. But our market has changed, and we're going to need to change with it. The boss has asked this of us: '*Do only those things necessary to support our corporate purpose. And do what we do well.*' If we have made one mistake around here, perhaps it is that we've taken too much for granted. We have assumed that everything we do deserves our efforts and that our best efforts are good enough simply because we try hard. When you have as much to do as we do, it's understandable that reviewing how our work gets done is likely to get shuffled to the back burner. But a review is just what's needed now, and no one knows more and is better qualified to do it than we are. So today we're going on a process walk together. It will be familiar territory because we have all walked along this same path many times before. We know these processes, in some sense better than we know our best friends. On the one hand that's a good thing. We have lots of experience. But on the other, that very experience can blind us, making us incapable of reinventing the way we work. So, let's try to open our eyes to the process glitches, the dumb policies, and the human frictions that mess things up. Let's sort out the opportunities to streamline our own work, perhaps by redesigning our space or redefining the flow of work, by upgrading the tools we use, or even by reassigning parts of it."

"But, Lupe," Pete interrupted, "what happens if we do everything you say? Won't some of us end up losing our jobs? That sounds to me like a death wish."

Lupe sighed. "It may appear that way at first, but consider this, Pete. The company expectations are fair. The process is fair. Clinging to wasteful practices would be wrong. We're here at the table today, entrusted with an initial self-assessment. Even if we find ways to work smarter and cut staffing levels here, attrition and transfer alone might provide less painful ways to do what we need to do. It seems to me that we have to be more concerned about the death spiral that occurs when everyone digs in and resists essential changes until we all go down."

Some intense conversation followed. But in the end, everyone knew that Lupe was right. Changing these processes was essential; it was just that the prospect of changing familiar routines was daunting. At the same time, everyone knew the problems that were a part of every workday. The opportunity to get them into the light of day and to finally be heard was strangely encouraging. No one, including Pete, who had been there the longest, could recall any time when a systematic effort like this had ever taken place.

Lupe passed around some of the background information on the team's processes (see Tables 4 and 5, page 68) as she described the need to stay focused on the major processes without getting distracted by the petty stuff. She then concluded, "It's about textbooks. They represent 65 percent of our corporate sales. They are the very core of our collective mission. They consume 70 percent of the time and resources we invest in receiving, and receiving is the most important service we provide. Let's begin there."

Lupe used sticky notes to describe each discrete step, placing them on the wall to make it easy for people to understand the flow and the relationship of tasks to one another. When a form or report was mentioned, she even passed copies around and taped one to the wall next to the step it referred to. As she did, the ideas began to flow as though the cork had been popped on a bottle of champagne. As they reviewed each step, even the most reserved members of the team got into the discussion.

Pat cautiously began, "During our peak periods the trucks get lined up, overloading the processing area. Maybe we could use the online freight company systems to coordinate truck arrivals."

"Speaking of trucks, why not bring more products in on pallets so that we can use the forklifts to unload trucks and clear the staging area more quickly?" inquired Ed.

Rena was next. "Maybe some of the products could be held at the freight company's regional centers to smooth out the workload here on site. Once we go into overload there are lots of things that have to be reworked."

Joe was nodding in agreement as Rena spoke and then added, "Could the textbook buyers help us by ordering some of the products a little sooner so that the books arrive when we have the manpower to deal with them better?"

Pete spoke up, "Back to the unloading process for a minute. I think the staging area should be closer to the loading dock. It sure would speed things up. It's not that an extra thirty feet makes that much difference, but it does if you multiply it by five thousand trips a year."

"I am pretty concerned with the overcrowding in our staging area," said Jason. "Can't we figure out a way to use the overhead space so we can at least turn around in there? It seems like we should be able to figure out a better racking system."

"I'll second that one," Merritt echoed. "I'm the one who has to do most of the shelving. Not enough room is a big problem, but if you could at least have the quantity of books on each tag I wouldn't have to be constantly rearranging shelf space. Also, the tags are barely big enough to read."

In just under two hours more than two dozen ideas on how to streamline the flow of work had surfaced, and there was little question that most could be done with little or no help from the outside. Of course, there was more to do. There would be other processes to review, and even these changes would have to be evaluated further, resourced, assigned, and completed. But the team's interaction had resulted in thoughtful evaluation and, perhaps as important, the commitment of the very people whose support would be essential in moving forward.

Lupe declared a well-deserved break. When they returned, she passed around the activity indicators shown in Figure 7 (page 70) and asked, "What do these measurements tell us?

"That the business is incredibly cyclical for one thing, Lupe." exclaimed Pete, "That really isn't a surprise to us, but it goes from under 20,000 to more than 55,000 units per week to be received and shelved. That's quite a shift."

"Are we doing a good job when we're in these peaks, guys? Are we productive? Would Jim Malone be happy with us?" Lupe wanted to know.

"I think we are," said Rena. "Just look at the numbers. Besides, you know how hectic it is. I don't see how we could work any harder."

"I know what you are saying, Rena, but we just completed the walk-through of our receiving processes and noticed all sorts of things that we are doing that slow things down, and we saw other things that we could do to speed things up. Are we doing as good a job as we might? I don't really see how numbers like items received per day can ever answer that question, since we don't know how much it costs us to do this work. I've got another chart for that," as she handed out Figure 8 (page 70). "It shows the average number of items received per person per week. Because we log on the computer every time we receive—and because the temporary staff stays pretty much in textbooks—I was able to get a reasonably close number without much effort. What do you think now? Are we doing our work well, as Jim requested?"

"Yikes!" exclaimed Joe. "Our receiving rate even during our peak cycle when we should be at our best is all over the ballpark. It goes from a high of almost four hundred per hour to a low of under two hundred. And some of those lower points are during times when we should have lots of work. I can only conclude that we are bringing in too many temporary workers, and it sure looks as though we could schedule them a lot better."

"That's got to be a part of it, Joe, but I imagine there's more to the story. Lots of times the books aren't here to receive when we're ramping into the cycle. Perhaps we can work with the buyers and the major publishers to bring them in on more of a planned schedule. Maybe we could even pay our temporary staff more with the idea that if we didn't have work on a given day they might only work a half day," said Rena.

"Yeah, but that would be kind of tough on them, wouldn't it? said Dave. How would you like it if the company did that to us?

Maybe we could put together a short list of projects that could be done with the extra time. No matter how good we get at the schedule, there will always be pockets of dead time."

Harvey waved the latest graph. "Man, I never would have figured this stuff out without looking at these numbers. We're all busting our humps to get the job done; I never would have figured it out just based on how I feel at the end of a day."

"That's the basic idea of these measurements, guys," confirmed Lupe. "It's sort of like this: if you're not keeping score, it's all just practice. Without measuring our success in delivering what our owners value, how can we expect to know how well we're doing? How can we expect them to know?"

Lupe resumed after a thoughtful pause, "Even these numbers don't tell the whole story, do they? We see we can learn a lot from internal comparisons. This variation in our productivity raises some pretty tough questions. My guess is that if we broadened the comparison to include our peers, or even distribution companies that are much bigger than we are, the gaps would be even bigger. I'm going to take a look at these external markers. The next time we talk let's see if there are some easy ways we can learn from those outside our team" (see Table 6).

Lupe's assessment found what most honest work teams would find: significant opportunities to improve. The *purpose review* suggested that there were gaps in applying mission, vision, and strategy, resulting in misalignment; the team was doing some things that were not mission-critical or was not doing others that were. For example, the team had good reason to consider outsourcing campus delivery services, returning mail services to the office, and eliminating some other functions. The *process* review also uncovered significant opportunities to improve the efficiency of the team's core textbook processes. Using simple measures and comparisons such as these to direct the team's attention to what their owners value is a powerful way to realign activities to purpose and to improve productivity.

TABLE 6
Sources for External Comparisons

Benchmarks
Where processes are measured in a standard way, benchmarks can extend the process comparison outside the firm. Trade and professional associations often advocate and sponsor benchmarking activities.

Site visits
Visiting businesses that have developed superior processes creates an opportunity for experiential learning and is often effective. Site visits can also foster buy-in from key staff charged with implementation.

Peer or consultant reviews
Often outside experts can be commissioned to review a firm's processes and render findings that reflect both anecdotal and quantifiable outside comparisons.

Process certifications
Comprehensive national or professional process standards are available for some processes. Examples include ISO certifications, Baldridge service standards, and standards defined within professional associations.

Outsourcing
Sometimes functions are not mission critical and can be outsourced. When this is the case, firms can often compare the costs and service quality offered by such a firm with those provided internally.

Summary

Owners operate outside the organization and exchange value with it. There must therefore be a mutually advantageous exchange of value between the company and its owners. Managing that exchange requires careful delineation of who the owners are, what their contribution is, and what their expectation is for value returned.

Who are the owners?

The owners are the founders, investors, and risk takers. They are the architects and guardians of the organization's purpose. They employ a chain of delegation to commission others at all levels, from governing boards to work teams, to accomplish that purpose, entrusting to them the necessary resources and authority to act, and rightfully holding them accountable for those actions. While the roles and responsibilities of owners are generally well known to those at the top, to most workers, the owners are strangers. They are often misunderstood, suspected, resisted, and feared.

What do owners value and expect of work teams?

To improve owner satisfaction, work teams need to understand what owners expect and assess how well they are meeting those expectations. Owners value and expect their work teams to be aligned with the overall corporate purpose such that the resources invested there are either committed directly to the functions that the firm was created to accomplish or provide essential support to others who are. Owners also value process performance, meaning that the resources they invest in the firm are used to best advantage in pursuing the purposes of the firm.

How is the team doing at meeting expectations?

Organizational purpose can be defined by shared values, a directive mission, a prescriptive vision, and a connecting strategy. These directional indicators should cascade throughout the organization and be further defined by congruent goals and objectives that ultimately inform and direct the efforts of work teams. Only through careful and conscientious comparison of goals and objectives with corporate directional indicators can the activities of work teams be fully aligned. *Yet at the lower levels of the pyramid, the corporate purpose is generally not well understood. And the work team's purpose and fit are not well defined or coordinated.*

Even though purpose is accomplished through process, inefficient process is commonplace. Advanced methods to evaluate process have their place. However, even the most elementary review of process, if well intended, typically unearths significant opportunity to improve, because work teams easily overlook poor process due in part to deeply embedded work routines or habits and a natural apprehension of change. Commonsense process review consists of (1) identify, (2) document, (3) evaluate, and (4) improve key processes. *Even though process reviews have obvious potential to dramatically improve the operations in work teams, they are routinely overlooked.*

Owner contribution

Work teams also have legitimate expectations of owners. Teams must define what those expectations are and assess how well the owners are doing at delivering them. For example, work teams value and expect owners to clearly define purpose throughout the organization and to provide clear expectations for each unit to use in assessing how well its efforts align. They also expect owners to provide adequate resources to do work entrusted to them.

By clearly defining and measuring the exchange of value between work teams and owners, organizations can foster ongoing improvement in value delivered and value received.

3

Customers Come First

Exchanging Value with Customers

> *The only thing that matters in business is developing customer value.* —KARL ALBRECHT

The president of Doggie Vittles Dog Food Company summoned his managers to an emergency meeting in his office. Pacing the room, he barked out a series of questions.

"Men and women! Tell me! What dog food company has the most nutritious dog food in all of America?"

"Doggie Vittles, sir!" the managers shouted back.

"And what dog food company has the most attractive packaging of any dog food company in America?"

"Doggie Vittles, sir!" they replied in unison.

"And what dog food company has spent more on advertising than any other dog food company in America?"

"Doggie Vittles, sir!" they yelled back.

The president then paused before shouting out a last question. "Then why aren't we selling more dog food than any other dog food company in America?"

The room became very quiet. Finally, someone in the back of the room spoke up.

"Well, sir, it's because dogs just don't like it."[1]

Whether selling dog food, educating adult learners, or providing health services, successfully delivering what customers value is critical to the mission of any organization. Long before facilities are constructed or equipment is requisitioned, before employees are hired or capital is invested, organizations begin with customers in mind. Even profit comes as a by-product of providing the things and experiences that customers value. This insight has prompted many, like customer service guru Karl Albrecht, to suggest that it is customers who matter most and must therefore come first.[2]

The primacy of customers in market economies can be seen in the vast array of consumer choices, as competitors rush to provide nearly every imaginable product and service. Despite almost universal awareness that this exchange lies at the center of corporate purpose, most organizations lack effective feedback systems. To be effective, feedback must adequately measure both customer satisfaction with the value delivered and company satisfaction with value received. Without feedback, companies waste precious time and resources, often learning too late that the dogs just don't like it.

Consider for a moment the many organizations with which you have interacted during the past week. Your list may include grocery stores, restaurants, snack shops, department stores, the auto repair garage, gas stations, hotels, banks, and Internet services. Now add work-related customer interactions with suppliers and commercial service providers. Even this list is incomplete. How about interactions with schools, houses of worship, civic groups, charities, government agencies, and the plethora of other nonprofits that provide important services and depend on your support? Of these several dozen organizations with whom you have had transactions, how many regularly ask for your feedback? How many use it to consciously assess and improve their customer value package? If loyalty is the gold standard for customer relationships, how many have earned yours? We can safely predict that the answer is very few.

This casual approach to managing customer relationships is particularly alarming in the light of well-known customer service economics. For example, most managers understand that customer retention is good strategy. It costs four to six times more to win a new customer than to retain an existing one. But retention requires making few mistakes. A whopping 80 percent of customer satisfaction depends on doing things right the first time. Yet 95 percent of the corporate resources committed to customer relations are consumed with fixing reported problems. Retention also depends on managing mistakes well. This includes both warmly encouraging critical feedback and acting immediately to fix reported problems. But dissatisfied customers rarely tell the offenders of problems. As many as 96 percent of them never complain; they just leave. However, they do tell just about everyone else—on average between eight and ten others. When problems are promptly resolved to the customer's satisfaction, up to 95 percent will do business again with the firm. Even then it will take roughly twelve positive encounters to make up for one negative one.[3]

Service matters to customers. Poor service is the number one reason customers defect to other businesses. In exit interviews, 68 percent cite an attitude of indifference. Businesses with poor service quality are also less profitable, averaging only 1 percent return on sales while businesses with high service quality average 12 percent and charge significantly higher prices.

Perhaps the most alarming observation is that even satisfied customers are defecting in record numbers. Customers who classify themselves as "very satisfied" are four to seven times more likely to come back to purchase again within eighteen months.[4] In most markets the bar has been raised to a new height. Customer satisfaction is no longer sufficient. The simple truth is that delivering enough value to customers to earn their long-term loyalty requires a level of attention that few companies have been willing to invest.

It has never been more important for an organization to explicitly define, monitor, and improve the value exchange with its customers. To do that, it needs to answer a couple of obvious questions: Who are the targeted customers? Among those things that the customers value and expect, what is the intended value package and how well is the company doing at meeting or exceeding customers' expectations in providing it? Answers to these questions can inform an honest assessment of customer satisfaction with value delivered. However, organizations also need to assess the corporate satisfaction with value received, the customer's contribution to the company. More specifically, what is it the company values from these customers and how well are customers doing at meeting or exceeding reasonable expectations? This process at the corporate level can inform and advance a customer strategy intended to improve the value-for-value exchange over time.

As patchy and ineffective as corporate feedback systems can often be, customer feedback within work teams is far worse. Although work teams serve a much more targeted population of customers and provide a narrower and more homogeneous range of services, few systematically evaluate the exchange of value with customers. It is that opportunity to which we now turn our attention.

Who Are the Customers?

Try asking any dozen employees at random who their customers are. Their responses will almost certainly reveal alarming naïveté. One staff member in an accounting office said, "We don't really have customers." Another, in security, commented, "I suppose everyone is our customer." Between "no one" and "everyone" lies a wasteland of confusion yielding widespread mediocrity in delivering value. At a time when many suggest that the key to competitive advantage lies in nurturing intimate lifelong relationships with core customers, a time when some even go so far as to predict a customer revolution as we transition into a customer economy, the very work teams charged with implementation are both unable to identify their customers and fail to understand how serving them contributes to a broader corporate strategy.

Everyone Has Customers

Customers are the people served by work teams. They are the next link in the value chain, the recipients of value created. One team serves another that in turn serves still others in the process of eventually crafting a value package for delivery to the final customer.

For example, in an accounting office, the work team processes transactions such as paying invoices or collecting and depositing receipts. They may then summarize the transactions into meaningful financial information, thoughtfully formatted to support decision making. Those services are rendered to a targeted population, such as department managers or administrators, people with legitimate expectations. The managers or administrators expect, among other things, that these transactions will be handled in a timely and accurate manner and will yield reliable and relevant financial information. They also expect to be treated professionally, to be able to access office staff when needed, and to get reliable answers to questions. *Defining this finite set of customers for whom the team's efforts are expended is a foundation for customer measurement.*

Internal and External Customers

Historically, attention has focused on external customers. Their satisfaction and loyalty is a mission-critical outcome, crucial to the corporate purpose. However, *most work teams serve internal customers*—others inside the same company. Teams in HR, IT, accounting, administrative support, receiving, procurement, and manufacturing are responsible for work in process that they pass on to other work teams. As such, they share in a common corporate purpose, and at some point in the corporate hierarchy they are accountable to a common authority. Money rarely changes hands among these internal work groups. However, when the service is mediocre internal customers cannot easily leave for a better provider.

External customers are the recipients of the products or services that are provided by the organization and envisioned in the corporate mission. In the private sector, these customers typically pay for value received and can choose among competing providers. However, a large proportion of the goods and services produced, even in Western market economies, is delivered through government or other nonprofit channels, often without direct payment or competitive alternatives. From the perspective of work teams, then, both the payment for services and the choice of service provider is the exception and not the rule. *Whenever customers cannot elect to go elsewhere, measurement is essential.*

Important Customers Come First

Because their mission is narrowly focused, work teams typically have a few customers or customer categories that have a disproportionate impact on successfully achieving it. Those customers are quite simply more important than others, and they deserve priority. Others may be less important because they are small, strategically irrelevant, or unprofitable. Teams must identify important customers and give them special attention. They must manage relationships with these customers closely in order to better understand their needs and customize services to meet them. They will need to make sure that feedback from these customers is not indiscriminately commingled with that of others. Exercise 4 will help your team identify these special people. Its purpose is both to define the connection between serving internal and external customers and to help build a foundation for managing relationships.

Value Delivered: Customer Satisfaction

Work teams routinely exchange value with their customers (see Figure 9, page 89). By clearly defining what each party values and assessing how effective its respective efforts are at delivering it, a team can create a baseline for continuous improvement. The baseline can also inform efforts to better match the mix of customers served to the corporate purpose over time.

What Do Customers Value and Expect of Work Teams?

One way to find out is by *asking the team.* Team members collectively bring to the table many years of firsthand contacts with customers and an intimate familiarity with the processes in place to serve them. Asking them to put themselves into their customer's position by defining what they would value is an effective way to gain considerable insight. For example, a team of travel agents

EXERCISE 4
Who Are Our Customers?

Directions: List your company's and work team's customers in the left column, and record descriptions of each in the right column.

Definition: Customers are the people served by work teams. They are the next link in the value chain, the recipients of value created. One team serves another that in turn serves still others in a chain that eventually crafts a value package for delivery to final customers. A few important customers or customer categories typically have a disproportionate impact on the team's success.

Company's most important customers/customer categories	Customer description

EXERCISE 4 cont'd

Company's most important customers/customer categories	Customer description

Briefly describe how the team's efforts to serve internal customers contribute to the company's efforts to serve external customers.

_____

_____

_____

_____

_____

What can we do to better understand our customers?

_____

_____

_____

_____

_____

FIGURE 9
Customer Value Exchange

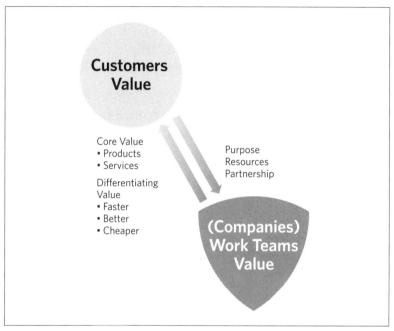

might know from firsthand experience that their customers value disclosure of the cheapest ticketing options, easy connections between flights, a 24-7 hotline to call if something goes wrong en route, specific amenities on the aircraft, and travel perks such as upgrades. A repair team installing and maintaining appliances in homes might observe that their customers value punctuality for the service appointment, reliable work with no follow-up necessary, and questions answered in layman's language. *Involving the team not only taps members' experience, it focuses attention on their collective purpose to serve, nurtures a deeper understanding of needs, and fosters commitment to improve.* However, team members' input alone is insufficient. It can have blind spots created by routines, bias, and an understandable discomfort with change. Therefore, the starter list must be enhanced with further inquiry and validation.

A second approach might be termed *ask the experts*. For obvious reasons, few topics have been more extensively researched than inquiry into what customers value. Some scholars have sought to define models applicable across broad classes of activities. For example, Zeithaml, Parasuraman, and Berry did groundbreaking work over a decade ago in which they proposed the following five key dimensions of service quality:[5]

- **Reliability:** the ability to perform the promised service dependably and accurately

- **Responsiveness:** the willingness to help

- **Assurance:** the knowledge and courtesy of employees and their ability to convey trust and confidence. Assurance encompasses employees' competence, courtesy, credibility, and security.

- **Empathy:** the provision of caring and individualized attention.

- **Tangibles:** the appearance of the physical facilities, equipment, personnel, and communications materials

We can easily apply these core value elements to the activities of a work team. What are the team's core functions, and how reliable are they? In what respects and to what degree do the team's customers value assurance, empathy, and responsiveness? What tangibles, such as physical facilities and equipment, are employed, and how might they be changed to enhance perceived value? In this way, the team's developing list can now be challenged and supplemented from these broader perspectives.

Another way to glean expertise is from industry- or activity-specific publications, Web searches, and professional or trade associations. These models of what customers value will, at minimum, orient work teams to the kinds of things their customers might appreciate.

With rare exception, the final judge of customer value is the customer. It therefore behooves the team to *ask the customers* and consider that input as definitive. It is generally best to begin this process in open-ended and loosely formatted conversational forums intended to simply gain understanding. One-to-one and one-to-many meetings can be used to review the team's developing list and to explore related discussions. This will extend the insight of the team representative(s) and help prepare for more formal assessments to come. Exercise 5 provides some structure for this process of gathering input as to what customers value and expect from your team.

How Well Is the Work Team Doing?

Because even satisfied customers often defect to the competition when a better offer comes along, long-term success in markets where customers have choices requires more than satisfaction or meeting customer requirements. Organizations must set the bar considerably higher by aiming instead for "customer delight," "legendary service," or even "raving fans." *The target is to exceed expectations often enough and by a margin sufficient to build loyalty.* This kind of corporate vision for excellence requires the direct and indirect contributions of every member of every work team, even those serving backstage and out of view.

Customers expect what might be termed *core values.* When they go to a grocery store core values might include a reasonable selection of foods, a clean and orderly design, carts next to the door, and people readily available to provide checkout services. However, when the selection includes a breadth of specialty foods, pastries, and hot entrées; when the facilities are beautifully presented; when assistance is given in carrying purchases to the car; when the prices are low or the checkout service is unusually friendly, customers are pleasantly surprised, as expectations are exceeded. This is *differentiating value.* Core value delivers the basics. Differentiating value does it faster, better, cheaper, or easier. Customer-driven organizations conscientiously match a targeted package of value elements to a targeted population of customers with the intent to exceed expectations. Work teams can do the same.

After categories of value are clearly defined, each element must be assessed to determine both its relative importance and the performance of the work team in delivering it. Importance can be

EXERCISE 5
What Do Our Customers Value and Expect?

Directions: Use the following methods to determine what customers value and expect from your team:

Ask the employees. Begin the process by asking members of the work team to define what they think their customers—employees—value.

Ask the experts. Review information available from books, professional associations, Web sites, and other resources to gain insight regarding what customers value most.

Ask the customers. Validate and edit this list through direct feedback from the team's customers.

Record your findings below, describing each element as clearly and succinctly as possible. Adapt the length of the list to your needs.

What products and services do we provide that our customers value and expect?

calibrated by using a 1 to 5 scale, from Not at all important to Extremely important (see Figure 10).

A team's discovery of what its customers consider important will prompt two classes of response. If team members agree (because the category is both mission-critical and highly valued), they will act to continuously monitor and improve performance in providing it. However, if they disagree (either because their customers value elements not considered mission-critical or they do not value others that are) it is the responsibility of the team to make changes or manage customer perception. For example, for nutritious dog food to be an important differentiator, the responsibility falls to the company to convince its customers that the element is important; if it can't do that, it will need to change the strategy.

After the team determines what the customer considers important, it can then seek to determine the customer's rating of the team's effectiveness or performance in delivering this value. One common approach is to survey customer satisfaction. This is certainly acceptable. However, where an organization sets a standard "to consistently exceed expectation on strategically targeted categories of perceived value," it will prove especially powerful to rate performance against that expectation on a scale ranging from 1 = Far below expectation to 5 = Far exceeds expectation.

For example, Figure 10 summarizes feedback in which 20 recent customers were surveyed on the reliability category for an appliance repair service team. Of the 20 respondents, 15 rated reliability as "extremely important" while 5 rated it as "very important," for an average rating of 4.75. The high priority given to this category is not surprising, but what may be surprising is that customers often consider outcomes like this a basic competency, thus raising expectation to high levels. Anything less than a near-perfect record is likely to generate criticism, discontent, and defection. As illustrated in the example, asking for comments on high or low ratings makes it possible to better understand the responses.

For most work teams, identifying their core customers, defining what the customers value, and monitoring success in meeting the customers' expectations is achievable without outside assistance

FIGURE 10
Summary of Findings for Assessing Value Delivered

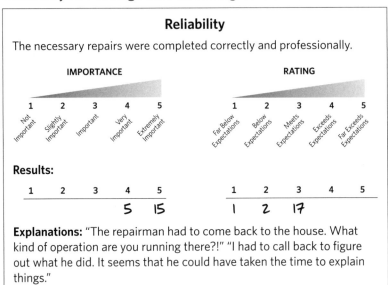

Reliability

The necessary repairs were completed correctly and professionally.

IMPORTANCE	RATING

1   2   3   4   5   1   2   3   4   5

Not Important / Slightly Important / Important / Very Important / Extremely Important   Far Below Expectations / Below Expectations / Meets Expectations / Exceeds Expectations / Far Exceeds Expectations

Results:

1	2	3	4	5		1	2	3	4	5
			5	15		1	2	17		

Explanations: "The repairman had to come back to the house. What kind of operation are you running there?!" "I had to call back to figure out what he did. It seems that he could have taken the time to explain things."

from consultants or specialists. And measuring their performance in this way will powerfully inform the teams' efforts to improve customer satisfaction.

The cycle of service—mapping moments of truth

Years ago, Jan Carlzon, former CEO of Scandinavian Airlines, popularized the idea that every occasion in which a company engages a customer is a *moment of truth*.[6] There can be thousands of these moments in a single week for a single team. They occur with every face-to-face exchange, every phone call, every e-mail, every voice mail or piece of correspondence. In these moments expectations are missed, met, or exceeded. Collectively, the moments determine perception. *Customer perception must be managed moment by moment.*

A *cycle of service* is a collection of these customer connections involved in a single service event, whether it be a trip to the emergency room or ordering takeout at the local Chinese restaurant. Reviewing and assessing these moments of truth fosters deep insight into the building blocks that determine perception and illuminates practical places to improve. Consider, for example, the customer's perspective on the cycle of service involved in returning a new car to the dealership for a service warranty checkup:

- **Moment:** At the time the customer buys his car the salesperson was knowledgeable, friendly, efficient, and responsive. Enrolling in the service checkup program was fast, easy, and free.

- **Moment:** After three months, the first routine service is due. The customer receives a friendly and professional card in the mail personally signed by the salesperson. The salesperson introduces a dedicated service manager who is being assigned to his account.

- **Moment:** Five days later the customer is called at work as a follow-up reminder. The call is friendly, polite, and professional. The customer schedules an appointment.

- **Moment:** On the day of the appointment the customer brings the car to the shop. This face-to-face encounter is positive. The facilities are clean and orderly. The personnel are knowledgeable and friendly. In fact, the customer was expected by his personal service agent and warmly greeted. The drop-off takes less than five minutes, and the shop then shuttles him directly to the office.

- **Moment:** Later in the day, the customer receives a phone call informing him of the status of the work. He is notified that two other minor problems were found and fixed at no charge. He is told when the work is to be completed.

- **Moment:** The customer is picked up at the end of the day at the designated location and comfortably shuttled back to the facilities. The driver is courteous and helpful.

- **Moment:** Back at the dealership checkout is even faster than the drop-off. His representative comes to the counter to explain the work done and to answer questions.

- **Moment:** Two days later, the customer is contacted again to verify that the repair was successful and that he was satisfied. The service agent also conducts a short questionnaire; the customer's perception of value delivered in most categories exceeds expectations.

Every point of customer contact was a moment of truth, which contributed to the customer's perception of value delivered. Collectively, this cluster of contacts results in the perception rating measured in the questionnaire. Linking the two can be an effective way to involve the work team in a systematic, data-driven review of their work. When a given cycle of service involves two or more work teams, they might come together for the review or, at minimum, clearly identify the customer contacts for which they are responsible and work to improve any low ratings.

Measuring value specifications

Questionnaires measuring perception are subjective. They reflect an unconscious comparison of value received to customers' internal notions about what they should have received. Even so, perceptions cannot be safely ignored. Improving ratings with important customers in strategically sensitive categories can be accomplished in only two ways: either by lowering customers' expectations to more reasonable levels or by improving services in ways that they will recognize and value. Both are supported by efforts to specify and measure underlying factors that drive these perceptions. For example, in the case of reliable equipment repair services, the firm might measure the number of times that repairs needed to be reworked. In the case of a retailer who wishes to measure friendly service, it might specify the criteria—such as smiling, greeting, and offering assistance—that it expects its sales associates to meet. It could then enlist paid shoppers to measure the degree to which these friendly behaviors were exhibited. This additional information could then be used to bring perceptions into alignment over time.

Using the short list of important customers identified in Exercise 4 (page 85) and the concisely defined list of what your team's customers value as prepared in Exercise 5 (page 90), you can now gather feedback using a format like the one provided in Exercise 6. The exercise contains three main parts. The first is intended to help you sort customers into meaningful categories to better evaluate responses. Supplying checkboxes for the categories simplifies the process. The second, in chart format, gathers feedback on both importance and performance in delivering each value element. Adapt the chart to your own specifications. The third, the open-ended questions following the chart, allows customers to alert the team to issues and concerns that are important to them but were overlooked. (See the completed Sample A of Exercise 6 on page 106.)

Value Received: Customer Contribution

We now change our focus to what the team values from its customers and how to define and measure its customers' perceptions of how it is actually doing.

What Does the Team Value from Its Customers?

When organizations serve customers they expect something in return. This value received typically includes customer contributions to (1) fulfill and refine the corporate purpose (as defined by its mission and strategy), (2) directly or indirectly provide resources, and (3) partner with the organization for mutual advantage.

Purpose

Corporations typically pursue their purpose with respect to their customers through a strategy that describes both the target population of people to be served and the value proposition with which to serve them. Nordstrom provides a value package of premium service at a premium price to a targeted population of more affluent customers. Wal-Mart positions itself on the other end of the

How Are We Doing at Meeting or Exceeding Customers' Expectations?

Work Team Customer Questionnaire

Help us serve you better. Complete the survey by filling in the circle below that best describes where you work and then follow the directions below.

○ _____   ○ _____

○ _____   ○ _____

○ _____   ○ _____

Directions: Please circle the number to score each service, focusing on the *importance* to you and your *rating* of how we're doing. Please explain high or low ratings.

Core Products and Services

Using the list of valued products and services (Exercise 6), clearly define each core service. Then, frame up the customer feedback on each element of perceived value.

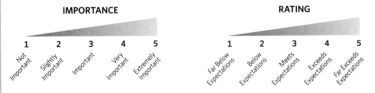

Explanation: Strongly solicit explanations for all responses that are rated above or below expectations.

continuum, offering an equally compelling low-priced value proposition but to a very different population of customers. Ivy League universities target and serve a different population than do community colleges. Even government agencies such as welfare services are created to serve narrowly defined needs for targeted groups of beneficiaries. Organizations need to regularly reassess

EXERCISE 6 cont'd

Other Value-Added Enhancements

Using the list of valued products and services, clearly define value-added enhancements to core services that differentiate your team in the eyes of its customers.

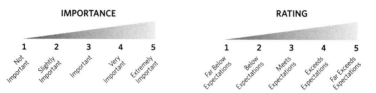

IMPORTANCE					RATING				
1	2	3	4	5	1	2	3	4	5
Not Important	Slightly Important	Important	Very Important	Extremely Important	Far Below Expectations	Below Expectations	Meets Expectations	Exceeds Expectations	Far Exceeds Expectations

Explanation: Strongly solicit explanations for all responses that are rated above or below expectations.

Open-ended questions: Add open-ended questions that give customers the opportunity to share strongly held views or other advice pertaining to the perceived value of products and services provided.

and refine this match to ensure that their limited resources are effectively deployed. It is also important for them to use customer feedback to refine that purpose over time.

Resources

Customers also directly and indirectly provide resources to organizations. In the private sector, the profit motive is apparent. However, even among nonprofits, funding is often linked to some index of people served such that success leads to additional public or private funding. Successful work teams may also lay legitimate claim to more of the corporate resources.

Partnership

Work teams also value their customers' willingness to partner with them by providing essential feedback, collaborating on strategic initiatives like new products or services, or providing references to new prospects.

How Well Are the Customers Doing?

For each work team, expectations like these can be clearly defined and measured using the process illustrated earlier in Exercises 4, 5, and 6. This process might include explicit assessment of customer contribution in fulfilling or refining the corporate purpose, in returning resources, or in partnering initiatives as noted above. Questionnaires can pinpoint problems and opportunities in managing the perceived contributions of the team's customers. Whatever the methods used, a deliberate effort to review customer performance is both strategic and straightforward.

The First Bookstore Case Study: Customers

Lupe's team was a hard-working group of ten individuals whose primary duties centered on the receipt, storage, and distribution of First Bookstore's resale products. They rarely saw paying customers. Apart from an occasional phone call, e-mail, or piece of correspondence, most of their effort supported other work teams. This distance made it harder for them to appreciate the founder's conviction that service excellence would distinguish First Bookstore in powerful ways.

Of course, they understood what it meant to be a customer. Like everyone else, they were active consumers who could recognize a good value when they saw one. But that just didn't seem to apply in a distribution center. Deep in the bowels of the business, they were just workers alongside other workers. The notion that some of them were customers seemed foreign.

Who Are Our Customers?

Of the ninety full-time staff, there were only eighteen with whom the DC interacted almost daily and for whom most of their labors were expended. Six were buyers, responsible to procure resale products. The DC received the merchandise, stored it, distributed it, and occasionally even returned it to suppliers. The team also served another half dozen people in the accounting office, for whom they validated the accurate receipt and return of products and created an audit trail to support the payments and credits routinely processed there. Their final group of customers worked in retail operations. The operations team consisted of six key people charged with management of the store's selling activities. The DC served them by getting products shelf-ready, occasionally pricing them or adding security devices, and moving merchandise to and from the sales floor as needed. Efforts on behalf of these three groups consumed nearly all of the team's time and resources.

Had anyone asked members of Lupe's team whether they were committed to excellence, most would have taken offense, presuming that their dedication and diligence should have been obvious from their deeds. However, in a context where the c-word was rarely used, where neither the company's nor the team's customers had even been identified, much less understood, the isolation of the DC should have come as no surprise. One indicator was the increasing use of terms like *we* and *they;* it was obvious that sooner or later these criticisms would find more open expression. The need was becoming urgent that the DC better understand not only their customers but the company's customers as well, and how serving one group contributed to serving the other. With that modest goal in mind, Lupe completed Exercise 4 introduced earlier in this chapter (p. 85) and shown here in Sample of Exercise 4. She realized that it fell far short of customer intimacy, but even this foundational effort would not come easily.

What Do They Value and Expect?

Lupe believed that business was essentially common sense, and it seemed pretty obvious that if they were going to improve their service for their customers they would have to begin by determining what it was that the customers valued. She introduced the topic at their weekly team meeting. After explaining and thoroughly discussing her chart (Sample of Exercise 4), she asked the team this question: "Based on your experience, what do our core customers

SAMPLE OF EXERCISE 4

Who Are Our Customers?

Directions: List your company's and work team's customers in the left column, and record descriptions of each in the right column.

Definition: Customers are the people served by work teams. They are the next link in the value chain, the recipients of value created. One team serves another that in turn serves still others in a chain that eventually crafts a value package for delivery to final customers. A few important customers or customer categories typically have a disproportionate impact on the team's success.

Company's most important customers/customer categories	Customer description
Faculty	As a category, our faculty drives decisions and sales in the store's primary product line, academic materials. There are 2,500 teaching faculty. Of them, 100 teach large-enrollment classes that represent more than half of the store's sales.
Students	We serve more than 40,000 FTE students. Two-thirds might be classified as traditional students. They are 18–22 and live on campus. The remaining nontraditional students are adult learners, who are generally holding down jobs and commuting part-time to classes on campus.
Staff	There is a campus-wide staff of nearly 5,000. These are people working to maintain buildings, run the administration, support research, and provide student services.
Others	There are others who visit campus or have ongoing relations with it (e.g., alumni, conference attendees, and research collaborators).

SAMPLE OF EXERCISE 4 cont'd

Company's most important customers/customer categories	Customer description
Buyers	We hardly know these people. They appear
Gary: Team supervisor	overworked and stressed most of the time,
Chuck: Technology products buyer	especially Gary and the book people.
Debbie: Book division buyer	
George: General merchandise buyer	
Nora: Book buyer	
Mike: Insignia products buyer	
Office staff	Perhaps because we work in the same build-
Susan: Team supervisor	ing, and interact often, our people know
Bob: Asst. supervisor	each other.
Bill: Accounts clerk	
Kim: Accounts clerk	
Diane: Accounts clerk	
Darlene: Accounts clerk	
Retail operations	This team seems disorganized and
Shelly: Team supervisor	stressed, especially during biannual peaks
Chris: Store 1 lead	in the business cycle when new terms begin.
Kathy: Assistant, store 1	
Guy: Store 2 lead	
Linda: Assistant, store 2	
Ken: Merchandising and display	

Briefly describe how the team's efforts to serve internal customers contribute to the company's efforts to serve external customers.

There is a clear line of sight between the receiving, storage, and distribution of resale products that we do for our internal customers and ensuring that the external customers get what they need.

What can we do to better understand our customers?

Relationships with the buyers and the operations team are strained. A top priority for us is to consider going to their staff meeting.

value and expect from us? If you had one of their jobs, as buyer or office staff, or in sales floor operations, what would you want the DC to do for you?" Before long ideas were flowing freely.

"I guess I would expect the staff to be knowledgeable about the systems, procedures, and especially the status of things. They'd need to be able to answer my questions," said Dave.

Joe chimed in, "Yeah, and of course that means being able to get to people when needed by one means or another—e-mail, phone, and sometimes in person when things are urgent."

As the discussion continued, the team observed that, in the end, their primary duties were to receive, store, and distribute things. Surely it was to be expected that they would be able to provide these core services well. At a minimum, that meant doing their work quickly and accurately. After all, "that's what we're here for," observed Pat wryly.

"Still, I think they really want something more than these basics," said Merritt thoughtfully. "Remember last month when Mike's merchandise came in the day before he needed it for an advertised promotion? A group of us worked late that night to get it all out for him. We kind of knocked his socks off, if you know what I mean. He went around telling everyone for the next three days."

"The opposite is just as true, too," said Dave. "When we blow it, we sure hear about it. Only yesterday Gary was whining that it is taking way too long to get his merchandise to the sales floor."

"Well, accuracy is critical as well," added Joe. "The accounting office gets pretty persnickety because a mistake in receiving takes a long time to correct with the vendors, and it could even cause the buyers to screw up their next round of orders." Several other admissions of less than stellar service led to some embarrassed snickers along with a pretty good starter list within just a few minutes.

Lupe ended her morning meeting with a question. *"Who should we ask to determine what our customers really value and how we're doing at delivering it?"* Following a brief pause, Jason grinned and offered, "Well, duh, I guess we'd have to ask them, wouldn't we?"

In the span of barely an hour, their work team had identified many of the things they were pretty sure their customers would value and expect from them. They even agreed that their customers deserved the final say. Lupe ended the meeting by agreeing to ask for customer feedback. It was a first.

Before going to the customers, however, Lupe wanted to get more background information. She compared her work team's list to information posted on the Internet by their professional association and even by a few other firms outside her industry doing distribution activities. She also called colleagues and accessed some materials gathering dust in the company library to get a more informed and comprehensive view of what customers tend to value from similar operations. With this additional input, she prepared an unabridged list of what she believed her customers would value most.

During the next few days Lupe took advantage of opportunities to meet with representatives from the buyers, office staff, and retail operations, her three major customer groups. Her goal was simple: to test and expand their list. These conversations were open-ended and free flowing. She asked each customer whether these were the most important items and how her team might better assess their success in delivering them. She also asked questions like the following: "What could we do that would most improve the value of our services to you? What should we stop doing that you find unproductive? What other ideas, recommendations, and comments do you want to bring to our attention?" After listening carefully to what they had to say, she shared the evolving list (Sample of Exercise 5) adapted from Exercise 5 (page 90) in an effort to validate its findings and to ask if this is really what customers valued from the DC.

Lupe realized that even if her list was incomplete, she still had to be substantially on the right track; besides, she could refine the list over time. Of course her customers would value these things. Her co-workers had thought so, her colleagues had thought so, and now her customers, the final authorities, had agreed.

What Do Our Customers Value and Expect?

Our customers value our core services. By that they mean . . .
- Receiving services. *Our receiving services are timely, accurate, and efficient.*
- Storage services. *Our storage and transfer services are timely, accurate, and efficient.*
- Shipping services. *Our off-campus outgoing mail services are timely, accurate, and efficient.*
- Campus delivery services. *Our campus delivery services are timely, accurate, and efficient.*

Our customers value professional staff. By that they mean . . .
- Accessible. *They can get help when needed.*
- Friendly. *They are treated in a friendly and courteous manner.*
- Responsive. *Their requests are addressed in a timely and professional manner.*
- Knowledgeable. *Staff members understand how to meet their needs and get things done right.*

Our customers also value . . .
- Effective communication. *Our communication is clear, timely, and complete.*
- Orderly facilities. *The distribution center facilities are clean, orderly, and professional looking.*
- Easy-to-use systems and procedures. *The systems and procedures are easy to use and efficient.*
- Convenience. *The location, hours of service, and overall accessibility of service meet their needs.*

How Are We Doing?

The next logical step would be to assess how effectively her work team was providing the things on her list. To do this, she would need to ask her customers for their feedback in a more systematic fashion. She envisioned a simple questionnaire, one that would be easy to understand and administer. Knowing that some elements would be more important than others, she wanted her questionnaire to gather feedback on the relative importance of each factor. Realizing that customers rate services by comparing them against what they expect, Lupe also wanted to structure the questionnaire to directly compare their perceived rating with expectations. After all, exceeding customer expectations in delivering value was the very definition of Jon's founding vision for legendary service. She knew that high or low ratings would direct her attention to problems and opportunities. While that would be helpful, it fell short of explaining why the customer gave that response. For that reason, she incorporated the opportunity for clarification of each rating in the questionnaire and intended to strongly encourage her customers to explain any high or low ratings. The survey instrument concluded with some open-ended questions intended to draw out further insights and assessment.

Lupe presented her evolving draft for validation and follow-up discussions with selected customers. "Is this right?" Lupe asked. "If we scored well here, would we really be meeting your requirements?" She intended to ask for feedback on a routine basis in order to track progress over time, and she was sure that it would be relatively easy to put on the Web, making ongoing collection and tabulation easy.

To increase the survey's response rate and reliability, Lupe requested and received thirty minutes at the biweekly staff meetings of each of her three major customer groups. During that time she explained her goals to improve service by defining and delivering more of what they valued. She also explained the questionnaire presented in Sample A of Exercise 6, taking questions and clarifying where needed. Finally, she administered the survey instrument and collected the attendees' completed responses on the spot. As she left the room, she thought to herself how fortunate she was to be serving internal customers who were so easily accessible and who were both interested and motivated to support her efforts to improve the quality of service.

The ease with which the data were tabulated surprised Lupe. She began the process by sorting the questionnaires into three piles, one for each of her team's three core customer groups, the buyers, office staff, and retail operations staff. She then summarized the results for each group on a separate form as shown in Sample B of Exercise 6 by placing a mark to represent each response in the importance and performance ratings boxes and adding them when completed. Whenever a customer provided an explanation, Lupe carefully transcribed it onto the master form to preserve that insight for future reference.

SAMPLE A OF EXERCISE 6
How Are We Doing at Meeting or Exceeding Customers' Expectations?

Distribution Center Customer Questionnaire

Help us serve you better. Complete the survey by filling in the circle below that best describes where you work and then follow the directions below.

○ Office   ○ Buyers   ○ Sales Floor Operations

Directions: Please circle the number to score each service, focusing on the *importance* to you and your *rating* of how we're doing. Please explain high or low ratings.

Receiving

Receiving services are timely, accurate, and efficient.

IMPORTANCE

1	2	3	4	5
Not Important	Slightly Important	Important	Very Important	Extremely Important

RATING

1	2	3	4	5
Far Below Expectations	Below Expectations	Meets Expectations	Exceeds Expectations	Far Exceeds Expectations

Explanation:

Storage

Storage and transfer services are timely, accurate, and efficient.

IMPORTANCE

1	2	3	4	5
Not Important	Slightly Important	Important	Very Important	Extremely Important

RATING

1	2	3	4	5
Far Below Expectations	Below Expectations	Meets Expectations	Exceeds Expectations	Far Exceeds Expectations

Explanation:

SAMPLE A OF EXERCISE 6 cont'd

Distribution Center Customer Questionnaire

Shipping

Shipping/outgoing mail services are timely, accurate, and efficient.

Explanation:

Campus Delivery

Delivery services are timely, accurate, and efficient.

Explanation:

Accessible Staff

Staff are accessible when needed (by phone, e-mail, or in person).

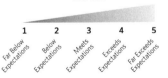

Explanation:

SAMPLE A OF EXERCISE 6 cont'd

Distribution Center Customer Questionnaire

Friendly Staff
The staff treats me in a friendly and courteous manner.

IMPORTANCE   RATING

Explanation:

Responsive Staff
My requests are addressed in a timely and professional manner.

IMPORTANCE   RATING

Explanation:

Knowledgeable Staff
The staff understands how to get things done right.

IMPORTANCE   RATING

Explanation:

SAMPLE A OF EXERCISE 6 cont'd

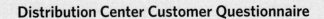

Distribution Center Customer Questionnaire

Facilities

Facilities are clean, orderly, and professional.

Explanation:

Systems and Procedures

Systems and procedures are easy to use and efficient.

Explanation:

Convenience

The location, hours of operation, and overall accessibility of service meet my needs.

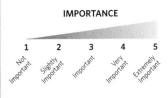

Explanation:

Distribution Center Customer Questionnaire

Communication

Communication is clear, timely, and complete.

IMPORTANCE

1   2   3   4   5

Not Important   Slightly Important   Important   Very Important   Extremely Important

RATING

1   2   3   4   5

Far Below Expectations   Below Expectations   Meets Expectations   Exceeds Expectations   Far Exceeds Expectations

Explanation:

Overall Assessment

How well does the distribution center serve your needs?

IMPORTANCE

1   2   3   4   5

Not Important   Slightly Important   Important   Very Important   Extremely Important

RATING

1   2   3   4   5

Far Below Expectations   Below Expectations   Meets Expectations   Exceeds Expectations   Far Exceeds Expectations

Explanation:

What can we do better to serve you?

_____

_____

_____

What should we know that our customers might not otherwise be inclined to tell us?

_____

_____

_____

SAMPLE B OF EXERCISE 6
Tabulated Customer Results from Buyers

Receiving

Receiving services are timely, accurate, and efficient.

IMPORTANCE   RATING

Results:

1	2	3	4	5
	2		4	

1	2	3	4	5
	2	3	1	

Explanation: "It takes too long . . . sometimes over a week. What are you guys doing over there?"
"You make far too many mistakes."

Storage

Storage and transfer are timely, accurate, and efficient.

IMPORTANCE   RATING

Results:

1	2	3	4	5
1	2	3		

1	2	3	4	5
2	1	3		

Explanation:

SAMPLE B OF EXERCISE 6 cont'd

Shipping

Shipping/outgoing mail services are timely, accurate, and efficient.

Results:

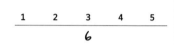

Explanation:

Campus Delivery

Delivery services are timely, accurate, and efficient.

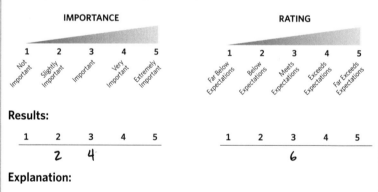

Results:

Explanation:

Someone long ago told Lupe that feedback is a gift. If so, this was one present that she would have happily returned. She immediately saw that serious problems were showing up in the responses of both the buyers and the retail operations team. However, to gain greater insight, Lupe entered the three summary forms into a simple spreadsheet prepared to compute and plot average performance rating and average importance data on the X and Y axes respectively. The results, illustrated in Figure 11, clearly cordoned off a *danger zone,* where her team's performance fell well below customer expectation in areas considered important to its customers, and a *success zone,* where it performed well. The approach seemed particularly well suited to measuring the corporate vision for legendary service. The graph also helped direct Lupe's attention right where it needed to be, on problems and opportunities requiring immediate action. The only problem was that there were precious few categories where they were exceeding customer expectations.

Before she could review the data with her team, Lupe would first need to digest it and then design that team interaction. She set about to review each of the three major customer groups. As she considered the buyers' group's data, she targeted the obvious problems in the danger zone:

- **Receiving:** As might be expected, the buyers considered receiving the most important service provided in the DC. However, five of the six buyers rated it below expectation. Their ire was especially apparent in the explanations provided:
  - "It takes too long . . . sometimes over a week. What are you guys doing over there?"
  - "Why can't I get my merchandise sooner?"
  - "Promotional merchandise often reaches us too late, causing stress."

While the other core services seemed to meet minimum standards, they certainly fell short of excellence. Besides, those services were less essential to the buyers.

FIGURE 11
Buyers' Customer Service Assessment

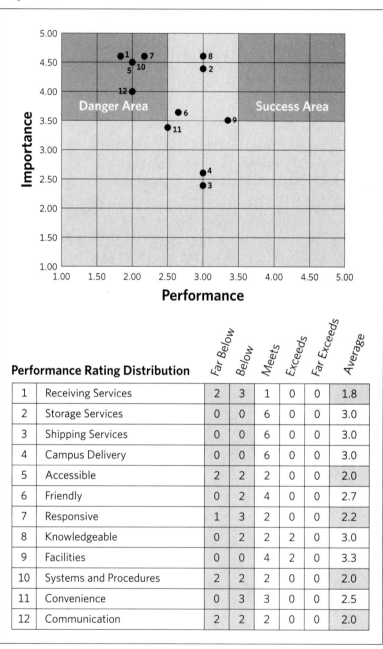

Performance Rating Distribution

		Far Below	Below	Meets	Exceeds	Far Exceeds	Average
1	Receiving Services	2	3	1	0	0	1.8
2	Storage Services	0	0	6	0	0	3.0
3	Shipping Services	0	0	6	0	0	3.0
4	Campus Delivery	0	0	6	0	0	3.0
5	Accessible	2	2	2	0	0	2.0
6	Friendly	0	2	4	0	0	2.7
7	Responsive	1	3	2	0	0	2.2
8	Knowledgeable	0	2	2	2	0	3.0
9	Facilities	0	0	4	2	0	3.3
10	Systems and Procedures	2	2	2	0	0	2.0
11	Convenience	0	3	3	0	0	2.5
12	Communication	2	2	2	0	0	2.0

- **Responsive and accessible staff:** Four of the six individuals surveyed rated the DC's performance below expectation. Again, the explanations exposed obvious frustrations.
  - "Answer the phone!"
  - "Respond to my e-mail in a timely manner; I have to plan promotions."
  - "Why don't you stay open the same hours as the store so we can get to you?"
  - "Joe is mean spirited . . . fix him or fire him!"
  - "People seem stressed out every time I ask for something. What's going on over there?"

- **Communication:** Four of the six buyers also rated communication below what they expected. Their explanations seemed to highlight a common problem:
  - "I have to call to find out anything. Isn't there a better way to know the status of my orders?"
  - "Talking to you is like talking to myself . . . only I learn less."
  - "The DC is like a black hole."

- **Systems and procedures:** The DC's systems and procedures were also poorly rated with four buyers rating it below expectation. Explanations included the following:
  - "I can't believe all the manual logs and ledgers you guys keep. The only thing missing is an abacus."
  - "Things don't seem well organized."

Relations between the DC staff and the buyers' group had been strained for some time. However, no one predicted the scope and intensity of that dissatisfaction. The picture painted by the data was one where a major customer group, arguably their most important one, considered the DC to be missing the boat on their most critical performance measures. Improving their ratings in these areas would have to be their highest priority.

Customer Contribution

Lupe felt queasy as she reviewed the data again and again. She was surprised, embarrassed, and, frankly, more than a little irritated. She knew that there had been occasional day-to-day conflicts and complaints, but how could her team have gotten so far out of touch with its most important customers? How could she put these data in front of the people on her team who thought they were working hard and doing a good job? Surely they would be demoralized and defensive. These very people prided themselves on excellence, even naively claiming to be best practice. Such words seemed empty when confronted by overwhelming evidence to the contrary. It was then that Lupe remembered a proverb that her father had often quoted: "The matter appears clear until the second man speaks." Customers may come first, but they aren't always right. No one is. She needed to hear the rest of the story, to understand the perception of her own people with respect to their customers' contribution. After all, there are legitimate things that service providers value from their customers. These reasonable expectations must also be carefully defined, measured, and addressed.

When Lupe called the staff meeting early that Monday morning, she was anxious to dig into the data with her people. But she knew better. She therefore began the meeting by asking, "What do you value from your customers in the buyers' group, the office staff, and the sales floor operations team?" Team members seemed almost flattered that anyone would want to know their point of view, and a spirited dialogue started up almost immediately. It came as no surprise that many of the same attributes as in the survey data percolated up again. "These people need to provide their core functions professionally just as we do," said Pat, "and that includes planning ahead." Others suggested that the buyers, too, needed to be knowledgeable, friendly, and responsive, and more than anything *they should work with us* as part of the same organization.

Of all the team's ideas, the one most highly prized was the notion of partnership. Rena said it best: "We just need to be working together as partners if we're going to really serve the store's customers the way they want us to."

"How are they doing as partners and collaborators?" Lupe asked. "How well are we working together?"

"Atrocious is too mild a word!" exclaimed Merritt. "They make our life unbearable, especially the buyers." There was quick agreement and the discussion seemed to go downhill from there.

- "We can't get our work done. They call and e-mail constantly, and most of the time, the call is about something anyone with half a brain could have figured out. Their interruptions cause delays, and then they have the gall to criticize us."

- "They buy late for promotions, and that causes last-minute pressures to receive things and get them to the store."

- "Many times, they place their orders on the phone and forget to enter them into the computer. Products arrive at the loading dock, and we don't have a clue as to why they are there. We have to set the order aside, figure out who might have placed the order, and then try to track them down."

- "Why can't the buyers work together so that all their merchandise doesn't arrive on the docks during the same cyclical peak periods when we are already swamped?"

The team went on with some energy for the full hour. *Lupe realized that the same survey instrument used to measure how well her team served her customers could easily be adapted to measure how well their customers met her team's legitimate needs and expectations.* In the week that followed, Lupe prepared and administered this questionnaire within her staff. It was similarly formatted and intended to measure the perceived collaboration with each customer group. This time however, the results, tabulated in Sample B of Exercise 6 and displayed graphically in Figure 12, were entirely expected. They were the mirror image of the customers' perception. In effect, the members of the DC group were as frustrated with their customers as their customers were with them. It was only then that something quite profound came into view. The DC and its customers had fallen into a lose-lose spiral: poor

FIGURE 12

The DC's Customer Collaboration Assessment

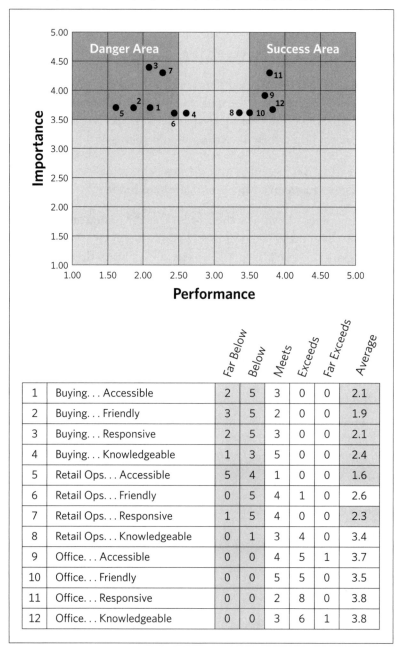

		Far Below	Below	Meets	Exceeds	Far Exceeds	Average
1	Buying. . . Accessible	2	5	3	0	0	2.1
2	Buying. . . Friendly	3	5	2	0	0	1.9
3	Buying. . . Responsive	2	5	3	0	0	2.1
4	Buying. . . Knowledgeable	1	3	5	0	0	2.4
5	Retail Ops. . . Accessible	5	4	1	0	0	1.6
6	Retail Ops. . . Friendly	0	5	4	1	0	2.6
7	Retail Ops. . . Responsive	1	5	4	0	0	2.3
8	Retail Ops. . . Knowledgeable	0	1	3	4	0	3.4
9	Office. . . Accessible	0	0	4	5	1	3.7
10	Office. . . Friendly	0	0	5	5	0	3.5
11	Office. . . Responsive	0	0	2	8	0	3.8
12	Office. . . Knowledgeable	0	0	3	6	1	3.8

collaboration begat poor service, which in turn further eroded collaboration and service. There was an urgent need to address the situation. Further interactions within the DC team and with their customers would be needed to better understand problems and to find ways to solve them. Wisely, Lupe decided to focus first on the buyers, the team's most strategic customer group and the one that perceived the team's performance as weakest. She called a joint meeting with the buyers and a half dozen of her team members who were most directly involved in providing services for them. As the day approached for the meeting, tensions mounted.

The Meeting

Lupe entered the room last with a bundle of papers tucked under her arm. Everyone was already seated around the rectangular table. The corporate buyers—George, Chuck, Mike, Debbie, and Nora—sat on one side, with Gary, the unit manager, uncomfortably perched on the edge of his chair at the far end. Rena, Ed, Pat, Dave, and Joe had taken seats on the opposite side. Only one seat remained. But before taking her place, Lupe stood for a moment, studying everyone's faces. Judging from the general lack of eye contact and the uneasy silence, she knew that no one would be falling asleep in this meeting. And yet, this was a first. Nothing quite like it had occurred before. One way or another, this was bound to be a momentous day.

As she surveyed the room she called each of the buyers by name. "George, Chuck, Mike, Debbie, Nora, Gary, we want to thank you for giving us this time. As you know, our company is navigating through some rough waters right now, and those of us in the DC have been taking a really hard look at ourselves, hoping to find ways to make our services faster, better, easier, and, of course, cheaper. That's a pretty tall order because we always thought of ourselves as being hard workers, committed to good service. That's why we were shocked by some of the customer data we have been getting back. You guys are our customers and the primary reason we have jobs at all. Frankly, we have to do a better job. We have some pretty tough feedback to review with you today, and the only ground rules for this meeting are defined by our company values. We must be *truthful*. There is going to be a temptation to skirt the really hard stuff, and we simply can't do that. At the same time we must be respectful when we share. Anything less just causes everybody to shut down, and nothing good comes from that. Of course, we also know the company believes in the kind of *teamwork* that gets things done. That's going to be hard to deliver, but if we do we have a shot at *excellence,* and that is our ultimate goal. Judging from this feedback, though, it's pretty clear we're not there right now. Are we ready for this?"

The strained expressions faded noticeably. Nora and Debbie even managed faint smiles. Fortunately, Gary jumped in with a consoling message in kind. "Lupe, we want to share with you and your whole team how much we respect what you're doing here. I know it has to be tough to get this feedback. It's like putting a sign on your derriere saying "kick me." Whatever the problems may be, there can be little doubt that we share a part of it. Let's go for it."

"You asked for it, Gary, and 'it' is data—data about your perceptions of us and our perceptions of you. Obviously, perceptions aren't everything. But let's start there." Lupe handed out Figure 11 (page 114) , which summarized the buyers' group's feedback to the team, and Figure 12 (page 118), which summarized the DC team's assessment of their customers. "Judging from this information, we are both missing the boat. We want to do better. There is only one road to improvement, and it can't be traveled alone. Next year at this time, we want to score at least 4 on everything. That means we're going to commit to exceeding your expectations. If we're going to do that, we need to agree on some fair standards and then perform up to them. I was hoping that we might get that process going this afternoon by starting with receiving. It's the biggest part of what we do for you and what you value most. You guys know better than anyone that our business is intensely seasonal, so there will be times when we get behind. Still, there can't be room for excuses. Five of the six of you indicated that we fail to meet your expectations for receiving. To help us understand what we need to do, we thought we might look at the way we work together in getting your merchandise received to sort out what's working and what's not. Would that be OK?"

"Sounds great," said Gary. "Since books are our biggest purchase, Debbie, why don't you walk us through your interactions with the DC, starting with purchase orders. I guess Lupe is asking that we especially tune in to those points in the process where the activities of one team affect those of the other and therefore affect our perceptions of each other." It was as though the starter's flag had just been waved at an auto race. The group took off blazing through a cycle of service, knowing that victory meant finding ways to ratchet up service quality.

"The buying decision comes first," said Debbie. "Most of the time we decide what to order based on what we know of the market or our own sales data. However, in the case of textbooks, we buy whatever the professor tells us he needs for the course. There's an unwritten rule about teaching faculty; even though it is the students who buy these books, their instructors decide what they buy, so we take very good care of the instructors. Frankly, we do whatever it takes to make sure they are pleased. That's why we need fast turnaround from you guys, even when their requests come late, which I admit often happens.

"Once we define how many to buy, we source the books. Generally you can get them new or used, and for many of the new titles, you can get them either from a wholesaler or the publisher. We typically choose the publisher to get better terms."

"But wait just a minute, Debbie," interrupted Rena. "There are hundreds of publishers, and when you use them for small purchases, we end up with scores of small orders to receive, arriving at all hours of the work day from dozens of freight companies. Many of those books don't sell and eventually get returned, leaving the business office with hundreds of small vendor credits that are difficult to use. I know you get an extra 3–4 percent, but much more than that gets lost overall. Would you be willing to reconsider your sourcing? It could free up a ton of our time, part of which could be used to take better care of you."

The room became silent. The idea was provocative, but in this context, it needed more time to settle.

Lupe finally spoke, "I guess we should look at that, Rena. Let's park it for now, and we'll revisit it after we've had a chance to study it through."

Debbie seemed a little rattled, so an associate, Nora, took over. "After we've decided on a source, we order the items, and then we track them to be absolutely sure they get here on time. If you don't receive a T-shirt, no one cares, but if you don't receive a textbook, there will be a classroom full of angry students, not to mention the professor. You can bet we'll hear about it."

Joe was getting restless, and it was clear that he had something to say. "Nora, I know you guys are in a BIG hurry to get that stuff in, but sometimes the orders are phoned in and then no one takes the time to get the order into the computer. When those books get here, we have no idea what's going on. In any given week, we're tracking upwards of thirty orders received with no purchase order. Heck, I suspect that violates every rule in the book. But the real reason I'm bringing this up is that it requires so much effort to track you down and to get the matter fixed. That's obviously time neither of us has."

If looks could kill, Joe would have been a goner. "I thought we were here to help you fix your service problems, not to take potshots at our purchasing processes," Nora countered.

Lupe was quick to respond. "I'm sorry, Nora. We don't mean to be pushy with any of this. Frankly, I know you have a legitimate beef on the phone calls and e-mails. Someone commented on the questionnaire that we don't get back to you in a timely way. You've got to be anxious to verify that the books are here, especially as we get close to the beginning of a term. Can you shed any light on that?"

Chuck finally spoke. "There's not much to share, Lupe. That's just a fact. We feel like we're at the bottom of your list of priorities. The phone, e-mail, voice mail, everything becomes snail mail with you guys. What's the story?"

This exchange catapulted Ed into the discussion. "Wait just a minute, Chuck. We're at peak production for four months of the year and all these other distractions leave us just a tad overworked and underappreciated. Besides, half the time we just look at the same computer records that you have. The records are accurate as of the time the receiving is posted."

"But that's my point, Ed." Chuck continued. "We don't know how long it will take you to get these orders posted. I have been told that if there is a problem with a shipment it gets set aside for days, sometimes even weeks, until you have time to deal with it. How can we know that our special orders are not caught up in the delay? You force us to call to find out, and then you don't answer the phone."

Again, there was an uncomfortable silence. Yet Lupe was inwardly excited. They had already pinpointed fruitful ideas for consolidating sourcing and making sure that the purchase orders got registered in the computer. Simple changes like that could save a great deal of time. On the human side, well, at least these people were talking. "That's a real issue, Chuck, she said. I promise you right here and now that we'll change it. If your poor rating on the receiving service was in part tied to sluggishness in posting, we need to change the workflow and track receiving turnaround times. If we could guarantee that the receiving would be completed and posted within forty-eight hours, would that improve service to you and make most of those calls unnecessary?"

"No doubt about it," replied Gary, who had been thoughtfully taking notes. "And in return, we'll check out the suggestions that have come up so far. Frankly, the pressure is on us to figure out how to ratchet up our productivity as well. It would be best for both the company and our teams to make some of these changes."

Gary's endorsement seemed to cement their resolve to mend fences as the conversation progressed through the remaining interactions required in the receiving function.

As the meeting drew to a close, Lupe summarized the sentiments of most. "Ladies and gentlemen, I think we've come a long way today. It's interesting to note that each of our departments rated the other quite poorly on the human factors of accessibility, friendliness, and responsiveness. After today's discussion that's not hard to understand. We have two very busy teams working through very intense business cycles. That alone would stress any operation, but we seem to be adding to it by not working together as well as we might to streamline common processes. No one took me to task when I omitted our final corporate value at the start of this meeting. As you know, it is integrity. In a sense, integrity is the most important value of all. It presumes that we will do what we say in all the other values. It requires accountability, and accountability requires measurement. Let's commit to keeping this group together and holding ourselves accountable to measured improvement. Let's move forward step by step from the measurement of our opinions to the measurement of agreed-upon performance specifications. If we define *timely receiving* to be within forty-eight hours, we will track that. If we define *accurate receiving* to be error rates of under 0.1 percent, we can track that. If we define *cost-effective receiving* as progressively improving the ratio of orders received per hour worked, we can track that as well. By agreeing on standards like these, we can remove some of the subjectivity around the assessment so that next year you will be able to rate us in a more informed way, and we hope we will have deserved higher ratings. You are our customers. As we shared at the outset, we have targeted a minimum rating of 4.0 for next year, and for our part we promise to do everything necessary to make that happen."

It was then that Gary stood. As he looked at the DC representatives, he concluded by saying, "Lupe, Rena, Ed, Pat, Jim, and Joe, thank you for starting us down this path. I have been with this company for over a decade and, to be frank, I think we have lost our way. Nowhere has that been more disturbing than witnessing how poorly my own shop has been working with you folks. You have my word that we will do our part. In fact, we'd like to see your ratings of us reach at least 4.5 by next year at this time." The group chuckled at Gary's response of friendly competition. "Well, the pizza is in the break room, folks. I'm just glad we didn't start this meeting with lunch. We might have ended in a food fight. Thanks again, Lupe, for getting the ball rolling."

Summary

Because the delivery of value to customers is central to the purpose of all organizations, some have even claimed that customers must come first. Despite widespread awareness of the importance of pleasing customers, it is surprising to observe that most organizations continue to operate without effective feedback systems. Effective systems measure the value exchange, both customer satisfaction and customer contribution.

The dearth of customer feedback within work teams is even more alarming. Few teams understand corporate customer strategy and priority. Fewer still clearly define and measure the satisfaction and contribution of their own customers. Assessing customer satisfaction in work teams requires answering three commonsense questions.

Who Are They?

Workers' typical answers, ranging from "no one" to "everyone," reveal alarming naïveté. Yet everyone has customers. They are the people served. They are the next links in the value chain. They are the recipients of value created by the team. Defining this finite set of customers as real people for whom the team's efforts are expended sets the foundation for customer measurement.

Some teams serve primarily internal clients; others serve external ones. Some of these customers are important to the purpose of the team; others are not. Typically a relatively small segment of customers has a disproportionate impact on the team's success in fulfilling its unique mission. These customers deserve priority and focused attention. Measurement systems must differentiate between these important customers and everyone else.

What Do Customers Value and Expect from Work Teams?

Teams have three common approaches to getting answers. Asking the team is easy, inexpensive, and effective, and it fosters buy-in and support for service improvement. Asking the experts taps the considerable insight already amassed by others who have conscientiously studied the subject. But ultimately work teams must validate and edit these ideas by asking their customers.

Customers value reliability most highly in getting the core product or service. But because it is expected, they are rarely impressed when they do receive it, and when these baseline expectations are not met, customers become very displeased. The real differentiation comes from consistently giving customers more than they expect. Four approaches to exceeding expectation are to deliver these core products and services faster, to make them better, to make them cheaper, and to make them easier to access and use.

How Is the Work Team Doing at Meeting Expectations?

Only when a team has clearly defined who its customers are and what they value can it measure how well it is doing. Ideally, it should measure perceptions of both importance and performance. Elements that are rated high in importance but low in performance become priorities for attention, particularly when they are integral to the value package envisioned in the company's strategy. Elements that are rated high in importance and performance define successes and point to core competencies that deserve to be acknowledged, developed, and promoted. *The real goal should be not satisfaction on the part of the customer but surprise, delight, and loyalty.* To achieve that goal requires consistently exceeding customer expectations on strategic value elements, those intended to distinguish the company and its workers.

The customer's perceptions of value received are subjective and sometimes wrong. One way to assess whether the perceptions are accurate and to manage perceptions over time is to convert customer expectations into specifications that can be measured. For example, if customers value friendly service and friendly service is defined by behaviors like smiling, greeting, and offering assistance, it becomes possible to measure the frequency of these friendly behaviors. Similar specifications can be defined for most other value attributes, such as speed, quality, and price.

What Does the Work Team Value and Expect from the Customer?

Organizations and their work teams value customers that align with the corporate purpose; that fit with mission, vision, and strategy. Organizations can ask if customers are in the population targeted for service and to what degree they contribute to the success of the firm. In the private sector, this contribution would include the customer's direct contribution to profitability. Companies also value a willingness of customers to partner with them by providing feedback and in other ways supporting corporate efforts to improve and succeed.

How Well Is the Customer Doing at Meeting or Exceeding These Expectations?

A team can use a simple questionnaire to gather feedback, asking team members to assess corporate interests in each customer or customer group around major value elements. By rating both importance and performance, the questionnaire can direct attention to priority actions. As before, other measures may apply and be more appropriate. For example, in the case of external customers in the private sector, customer profitability may be quantifiable.

Managing the winning exchange of value requires measuring value delivered and value received. This measurement is most powerfully employed in the narrowly focused context of work teams where mutual expectations can be concretely defined and tracked.

4

Employees Come First

Exchanging Value with Employees

Companies must put their people, not their customers, first.
—HAL ROSENBLUTH

A peevish old fellow boarded a crowded bus. After occupying a prime seat near the front, he tried to reserve another for himself by placing his luggage on it. Just before the vehicle started, a teenage boy came running up and jumped aboard. "This bus is full," said the man irritably. "That seat next to me is reserved for a friend of mine who has put his bag there."

The youth paid no attention but sat down, saying, "All right, I'll just stay here until he comes." He placed the suitcase on his knee while the elderly man glared at him in vain. Of course, the friend didn't appear, and soon the bus began to move. As it pulled past the stop, the young fellow tossed the bag through the open window, remarking, "Apparently your friend has missed the bus. We wouldn't want him to lose his luggage too!"[1]

To outsiders owners seem to occupy a favored position among stakeholders because they made investments and took risks in pursuit of the purpose of their choosing. Owners seem to control all the seats on the bus. But experience shows that like the old fellow on the bus, those who would abuse their squatters' rights end up losing luggage. This is because there is a human equivalent to the law of the harvest: we reap what we sow, only multiplied.

Employees often treat customers and owners in the same way that they perceive themselves to be treated. Treat them poorly and reap the consequences of surly and rude service, resentment and cynicism in the workplace, theft of time and materials. But treat good people well, with respect and proactive concern to meet their reasonable expectations, and repayment will be multiplied in kind. It is this core insight that has caused some, like Hal Rosenbluth, to suggest that companies must put employees first, placing the value exchange between a company and its people at the very center of corporate strategy.

Although this golden rule has lasted millennia in the wisdom literature, it admittedly falls short in important ways. Some have correctly noted that to treat others in the same way that you would wish to be treated fails to recognize that others may be different from us. They possess different competencies with which to contribute, and they value different benefits from their work experience. Would it not be better to treat others the way they most appreciate? Some go further, observing that sometimes employees misunderstand their own interests. In such circumstances supervisors must play a role more akin to Plato's philosopher king, exercising their authority with wisdom for the common good. Both observations add insight, perhaps giving rise to some higher standard. However, lest we run amuck in semantics, the enduring point is that *understanding and delivering what employees value is fundamental to achieving corporate purpose.*

One obvious reason to pay attention to employees is that employees exercise considerable discretion at work. They choose how they will serve customers and represent owners. Such choices occur dozens of times in a single day in responsibilities undertaken or ignored, vital feedback offered freely or withheld, services cheerfully rendered or gruffly dispensed. The cumulative impact of all these choices may add up to the difference between excellence and mediocrity, or even between the organization's success or failure. Although most organizations understand this principle, many offer their workers little more than platitudes. Their walls, newsletters, and uniforms are peppered with snappy slogans like

"Our people are our greatest resource!" or "We are people commit-ted to quality!" But if there is no conscientious effort to manage the value exchange with employees, such words ring hollow. Few are deceived. Where delivering value to employees really matters, it is systematically measured and acted upon. Among organizations, this is rare!

Organization-wide efforts to assess employee perceptions through periodic climate checks are useful and have their place. But companies don't have one climate, they have many. Like the proverbial blind men feeling the elephant, an individual's work-related experiences are substantially influenced by a relatively few co-workers interacting together with a common supervisor and sharing in a focused purpose. They create a cultural cocoon limit-ing employee perceptions to largely local circumstances in the team and, to a lesser extent, the departments within which they function.

As with the other core stakeholders, measuring both the em-ployee's satisfaction with value received and the company's satis-faction with value returned will inform mutually beneficial efforts to improve. In doing so, the same questions apply. Who are they? What do they value and expect from their work experience? How well is the organization doing at meeting or exceeding their legiti-mate expectations? Conversely, what does the company value in re-turn, and how well are these employees doing at meeting or exceeding its expectations?

Who Are Our Employees?

On the surface, answering the question Who are our employees? for a work team of two dozen or less would appear about as insight-ful as observing that water is wet. Of course we know who they are! They show up every day. Their job descriptions and personnel records are on file. Although the temporary and part-time workers may come and go in relative anonymity, we can at least claim to know the workforce, albeit only by name, rank, and résumé. How-ever, effective supervision requires more.

Decades ago it was commonplace in business to view management mechanistically. One textbook characteristically defined it to be "the achievement of organizational objectives through the efficient and effective combination of human and material resources." By implication, good managers were akin to corporate chefs following a recipe, blending people and things together with just the right timing. Within this framework employees are resources, their competencies are interchangeable, and the productive process is a rational closed system. Managers manage and workers work. This style of management had undeniable successes, especially in manufacturing, where business could be conducted in a relatively controlled context. But even there many have argued that the failure to fully tap human potential left money on the table.

Today, circumstances have undeniably changed. More than 86 percent of our jobs are in the services sector, where value is often created and delivered in real time. When services are knowledgeable, friendly, efficient, and responsive, customers pay more and they come back again. Add this to a business context of rapid change driven by discovery, innovation, and intensifying competition. Employees at all levels are increasingly the source of competitive advantage. If this potential to contribute is to be fully tapped, they must be better understood.

The practical and business benefits of understanding customers in a more personal way are widely recognized. Some organizations are investing heavily to learn customers' backgrounds, needs, and behaviors in order to inform deliberate efforts to nurture and manage relationships. The reason for all this attention is an unflappable conviction that these people are essential to corporate purpose. Are employees any less so? Why would we not also aspire to manage *lifelong* employee relationships, *one to one*, with the same rigor and care invested in our very best customers? What would it mean to know them in this way? How might that understanding contribute to improving both their satisfaction and their contribution?

While few would deny that understanding individual differences among employees is strategic, underlying models of human nature to foster this understanding vary markedly. People can be Type A or Type B, left-brained or right-brained, introverts or extroverts, Theory X or Theory Y workers. More complex perspectives classify people with greater care. For example, the BEST system (also called the Medicine Wheel) suggests two dimensions of differentiation, a continuum from "bold" to "sympathetic," describing the task-relationship mix and from "expressive" to "technical" describing cognitive leanings. The *Myers-Briggs Type Indicator®* personality inventory goes further still by distinguishing four primary human dimensions. Whether based on a simple or complex model, whether conscious or unconscious, the view of human behavior that all supervisors bring into the workplace substantially influences how they treat others.

In his most recent book, *The 8th Habit: From Effectiveness to Greatness,* Stephen Covey advances a model for understanding people that both hearkens back to ancient wisdom literature and remains consistent with the latest research. *Whole people are a blend of mind, heart, body, and spirit. Each person possesses specific mental, emotional, physical, and spiritual intelligences. Individuality is manifested as people employ their respective bents in the form of personal vision, passion, discipline, and conscience.* Whatever model is used, understanding these differences informs and leverages the supervisor's effort to put the right people in the right roles.

People also differ with respect to circumstances. Some commute long distances. Others have small children or live-in parents to care for. Still others have special stresses related to their finances, habits, or health. And the list goes on. These circumstances change, and with those changes come both joy and grief. *Knowing employees as people will inform the supervisor's efforts to deploy them as resources in mutually advantageous ways. It will also afford opportunity to demonstrate genuine interest, care, and concern in ways that evoke appreciation and engender trust.* Conscientious efforts to learn more about them, such as the one proposed in Exercise 7, will nurture that kind of relationship.

Who Are Our Employees?

> **Directions:** List team members and support staff in the left column, and record comments about each in the right column.
>
> Each individual brings a unique combination of mental, emotional, physical, and spiritual needs and competencies to the workplace. Knowing employees as people will inform the effort to deploy them as resources by equipping you to better match people to purpose. Add any observations about each employee's life circumstances that might create special workplace needs.

Core member of team	Description of team member

Member of support staff*	Description of member of support staff

* For example, part-time or temporary worker

Value Delivered: Employee Satisfaction

As they do with owners and customers, organizations routinely exchange value with their employees (as illustrated in Figure 13). The value they deliver includes not only material benefits like the compensation package but also a host of experiential benefits, including appreciation, involvement, and teamwork, that make work fulfilling. In return, organizations expect their people to fully contribute to the pursuit of corporate purpose. In effect, they value the people-to-purpose fit that fosters the highest possible standards of stewardship. These bilateral expectations must be carefully defined, monitored, and refined over time to develop and sustain winning relationships. Let's examine that process more carefully.

FIGURE 13

Employee Value Exchange

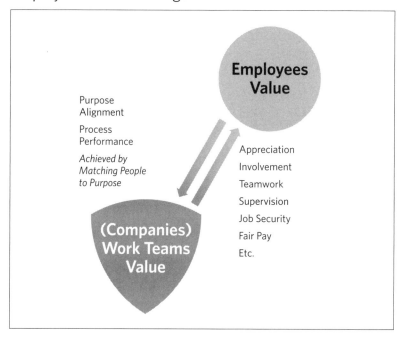

Purpose
Alignment

Process
Performance

*Achieved by
Matching People
to Purpose*

**Employees
Value**

Appreciation

Involvement

Teamwork

Supervision

Job Security

Fair Pay

Etc.

**(Companies)
Work Teams
Value**

What Do Employees Value and Expect of Company/Teams?

Few subjects have been studied more thoroughly, and findings point to a number of commonly shared values from the work experience. Considering these findings can provide a helpful starting point in preparing a team's list of what they value and expect in their work experience. For example, most lists include:

- appreciation for work well done

- caring and competent supervision

- involvement in decision making that affects the individual or the team

- encouragement of teamwork

- fair compensation

- the opportunity for professional development

- the opportunity for advancement

- job security

- a feeling of being a part of something visionary and worthwhile

- feedback on performance

- honest and open communication

- a fun workplace

These and other factors will differ in importance by individual team members and may even differ over time as an individual's personal circumstances change.

Any of these elements can be described in greater detail. "Caring and competent supervision," for example, can be broken down into one to two dozen specific attributes. Does the supervisor clearly define expectations? Does he provide adequate support in achieving them? Does he listen well? Does he maintain confidences? In the same fashion, teamwork can be examined much more closely. Chapters 7 and 8 offer specific tools to do that. However, in getting started gathering baseline feedback, remember that employees are accessible, and more details can be garnered quickly, easily, and inexpensively. Proceeding promptly with a thoughtful list of core value elements is better than interminable delay. Do it. Then improve it.

Although this exchange of value between workers and the company is fundamental to corporate purpose, it is rarely discussed in work teams. Imagine this setting: The supervisor calls the team together and says, "We want to better understand what you value here, and we want to hold ourselves accountable for meeting or even exceeding reasonable expectations that you might have of us." Handing the team members a list such as the one developed in Exercise 8, he asks, "Is this the right list? We would also like to help you understand what we value from you and would like to discuss ideas that will enable everyone to get more from our work together." *Amazingly, most organizations do not measure what employees value on a regular schedule. It is rarer still that results are openly discussed and systematically acted upon within work teams.*

How Is the Company/Team Doing?

There is but one way to find out. Ask! Ask in open-ended, informal, loosely structured formats, perhaps over a cup of coffee or as a discussion topic in staff meetings. Ask also in formal settings such as performance reviews, goal-setting sessions, or meetings with individual employees to plan their future roles in the company. Doing so will transform those discussions into the pursuit of winning relationships.

Another structured way to ask is by conducting periodic perception surveys akin to those described in Chapter 3 to gather customer feedback. For example, in exploring the team's assessment of any value element, the survey instrument would include:

EXERCISE 8
What Do Our Employees Value and Expect?

Directions: Use the following methods to determine what employees value and expect from your team:

Ask the experts. Review information available from books, professional associations, Web sites, and other resources to gain insight regarding what employees value most.

Ask the employees. Validate and edit this list through discussions with your team members.

Record your findings below, describing each element as clearly and succinctly as possible. Adapt the length of the list to your needs.

What do employees value and expect?

1. _____
_____

2. _____
_____

3. _____

4. _____
_____

5. _____

6. _____

7. _____
_____

8. _____
_____

9. _____
_____

10. _____
_____

11. _____

12. _____
_____

- **Definition:** A clear, concise, and easily understood description of the factors valued by team members.

- **Importance:** An assessment of how important each element is. As before, responses will range from 1 = Not at all important to 5 = Extremely important.

- **Performance:** An assessment of the workplace experience. To what degree is this organization meeting the employees' expectations in providing the value described? Framing the performance question around expec-tations is actionable. Wherever there are responses that fall below expectations, attention is immediately directed to either lowering expectations to more realistic levels or improving performance in delivering that value.

- **Explanation:** Wherever ratings are unusually high or low, brief anecdotal explanations should be actively solicited. The explanations are instrumental in understanding the rating and often point out opportunities to improve.

As with the customer perception questionnaire, results can also be presented graphically by plotting the averages, with importance on the Y-axis and performance on the X-axis. Where results are positive, this measured excellence creates a credible basis for acknowledgment and celebration. Where results are negative, targeted actions can be defined to better understand and then act on these perceived problems. Exercise 9 provides a worksheet to guide these efforts.

Measures of perceived performance often lead to other clarifying measurements. For example, in Figure 14 (page 141), seven of ten employees rated "fair pay" below expectations when compared to that paid at other organizations for similar work and experience. Even if the team's perception is wrong, this is a problem that demands attention. However, it is first necessary to understand whether the perception is right or wrong. This requires a different kind of measurement. In this instance, a comparison of the team's wage rates and productivity levels to the overall marketplace for similar work could determine whether the team's perceptions are

EXERCISE 9

How Is the Company Doing at Meeting or Exceeding Employee Expectations?

Work Team—Employee Questionnaire

Employee classification questions: When collecting feedback from work teams, it may prove helpful to gather information that will help you categorize responses.

Help us serve you better. Complete the survey by filling in the circle below that best describes your function and then follow the directions below.

○ Supervisor _____   ○ _____

Directions: Please circle the number to score each element, focusing on the *importance* to you and your *rating* of how we're doing. Please explain high or low ratings.

Value Elements

Clearly define each value (see Exercise 9). Examples of factors commonly valued by employees are appreciation, involvement, job security, fair pay, and opportunity to advance.

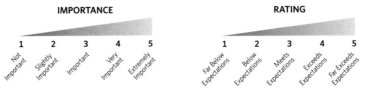

Explanation: Actively solicit explanations for all responses that are rated above or below expectations.

Open-ended questions: Add open-ended questions that give employees the opportunity to share strongly held views or their core advice on what or how to improve. Examples:

What can we change that would most improve your work experience?

What should the management know that members of the team might not otherwise be inclined to share?

What can we do to become a better team?

FIGURE 14
Sample Employee Survey

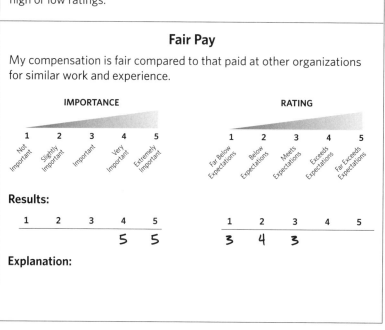

Directions: Please circle the number to score each service, focusing on the *importance* to you and your *rating* of how we're doing. Please explain high or low ratings.

Fair Pay

My compensation is fair compared to that paid at other organizations for similar work and experience.

IMPORTANCE

1	2	3	4	5
Not Important	Slightly Important	Important	Very Important	Extremely Important

RATING

1	2	3	4	5
Far Below Expectations	Below Expectations	Meets Expectations	Exceeds Expectations	Far Exceeds Expectations

Results:

1	2	3	4	5		1	2	3	4	5
			5	5				3	4	3

Explanation:

accurate. This more objective measurement will not automatically bring perceptions into alignment, but it can help by shifting the discussion away from the exchange of opinions from biased parties to a common and collaborative search for truth intended to foster joint interests. Most elements valued by employees can be specified in this way. "Job security" might be presented as the number of lost jobs in the last several fiscal periods, perhaps accompanied by an assessment of what became of these workers. "Opportunity to advance" might be described as the percentage of internal candidates promoted. Even "appreciation" could be indexed as the number of times in the given period individuals have received expressions of appreciation. In this way, *perceived value can be validated or corrected by other indicators.*

Employee Contribution: Value Received

As we have said before, value creation is a two-way street. The company must also be satisfied with value received. To assess that value, it behooves employees to understand what it is that the company values from them and how well they are doing at providing it.

What Does the Company/Team Value or Expect from Its Employees?

More than anything else, companies value furthering of their purpose, the fulfillment of mission, vision, and strategy in a way that is consistent with their value systems. To succeed, they require an effective match of *people to purpose,* a match that aligns the fit of uniquely gifted individuals to the specialized work required. We make two practical observations about corporate fitness intended to clarify the desired ends and inform decisions. *First, there are limits within which one can craft a better fit either by changing the person or reframing the purposes assigned. Second, people bring their minds, hearts, spirits, and bodies to work with them. Their full potential will not be tapped unless whole people are matched to whole positions.*

The range of change

In a recent book summarizing Gallup poll feedback from eighty thousand "great managers," Buckingham and Coffman make the provocative claim that because "people don't change that much," managers shouldn't "waste time trying to put in what was left out." They deem it wiser to "draw out what was put in." *The key to excellent performance, they observe, is to match talents with roles.*[2] They define talents as encompassing all "recurring patterns of thought, feeling, or behavior" that come as natural extensions of one's individuality. The underlying assumption is that who we are is substantially determined well before we reach the working world. The primary duty of effective supervision is therefore to be a matchmaker, linking people to the work they are most naturally gifted to do. In this sense, *talents both equip and limit people.* Effective salespeople are assertive, effective health care providers are compassionate, effective engineers are technically minded. These attributes derive from individual personality, more akin to fixed firmware than changeable software. Matching for temperament, interests, aptitudes, and other core aspects of human individuality requires that supervisors apply a different filter. By implication, no aspect of employee strategy will prove more critical to a winning exchange of value with the company than matching these innate internal competencies to work roles. Of course, people can and do change. Employees develop new competencies, and supervisors make a difference in creating a context for productivity. But there are limitations and costs. In this brave new world, we find ourselves stumbling about, mumbling, "God grant me the serenity to accept the things I cannot change, the courage to change the things I can, and the wisdom to know the difference."

Corporate fitness through better fit

The notion of matching people to purpose is hardly revolutionary. Both job postings and résumés have always described qualifications intended to put the right people in the required roles. The problem is twofold. This kind of superficial match leaves whole dimensions of human and organizational uniqueness unexplored and unconnected. First, do the corporate vision and the position spark a passion for the work? Are the corporate culture and value system congruent with those of the individual? Second, once an individual is hired, there is a widespread lack of commitment to improve the match over time. Returning to Covey's whole person model as an example, a more complete match would need to encompass mind, heart, body, and spirit. Table 7 illustrates a broader range of questions that can be asked.

How Well Are the Employees Doing?

At the risk of belaboring the obvious, organizations want their employees to be doing the right things in the right ways. Clearly defined expectations are essential to assessing how well they are doing in both respects. Expectations must be carefully aligned from

TABLE 7

Corporate Fitness: The People-to-Purpose Fit

	People (Qualifications of the individual employee)	Purpose (Requirements of the position, role, task, or objective to be accomplished)
Mental Fitness	• Does the person have the aptitude (natural talent) to accomplish this purpose? • Has the person had the life experience (educational, work-related, and other) necessary to develop the knowledge and skills to be competent in performing this purpose?	
Emotional Fitness	• Does the person have the temperament or personality to accomplish this purpose? • Does the person demonstrate passion and enthusiasm for this purpose?	
Physical Fitness	• Does the person meet all physical requirements to succeed in accomplishing this purpose?	
Spiritual Fitness	• Does the person share compatible values with this organization? • Does the person find both the corporate and personal purposes inspiring, worthy, and fulfilling?	

the corporate level through divisional and departmental levels to work teams and individuals. *Clear expectations create the plumb line against which measurement becomes possible and meaningful.*

We discussed in Chapter 2 assessing the work team's performance in achieving purpose alignment and process efficiency. However, employees' expectations must also be defined and assessed individually. Informal and anecdotal feedback is useful and powerful. Good supervisors invest the time to place themselves where they can witness positive or negative behaviors firsthand, where they can coach, mentor, and engage people. Formal and structured individual feedback systems are also necessary. These tools are well known but often poorly used. They include the following.

- **Job descriptions:** Eyes glaze over at the mere mention of the words. For most supervisors, job descriptions get dusted off every few years when a vacancy occurs, a disciplinary procedure is initiated, or a request for upgrade comes through. They are rarely used as a strategic tool with which to match people to purpose. Yet that is what they are intended to do. They define corporate needs by laying out job duties and activities and the expected distribution of effort to accomplish them. They also define individual requirements by delineating core competencies and backgrounds. Ongoing review creates both an opportunity to redefine the work and an equitable way to assess the worker.

- **Objectives:** In some positions, written objectives provide a useful mechanism to define expectations more specifically. These objectives reflect the immediate purposeful priorities entrusted to the individual. Objectives are generally few in number, unambiguous, and specific; they also generally include a timetable and spell out resources required to accomplish the work.

- **Productivity indicators:** In circumstances where companies can link value created to individual performance, they are well positioned to monitor and reward personal productivity. Examples include salespeople on commission, manufacturing employees on piecework, and executives with incentives tied to share value. When these links are not practical, team metrics can and should be included in assessing individual team members.

- **Supervisor assessment:** Institution-wide performance assessment instruments tend to describe generic skills. Even so, they provide a baseline framework for defining expectations and assessing performance. They might include assessments on living up to corporate values as well as on widely valued attributes like ability to communicate, service-mindedness, stewardship, motivation, job knowledge, inclusiveness, adaptability, and self-development.

Two-way assessment and winning agreements

Many organizations require an annual performance review. The reviews are top-down and one-way assessments. Where the supervisor's expectations have not been clearly determined in advance, they devolve into subjective judgments that are easily and often justifiably judged to be unfair. We will see in Chapter 9 that they need not be so. *Performance reviews can be dialogues, two-way assessments deliberately designed to evaluate and improve the exchange of value between individuals and the company.* However, to serve that purpose both the supervisor and the employee must come prepared with information essential to inform the discussion. See Table 8 for suggestions.

The intent of this process is to assess and improve the people-to-purpose fit by refining the winning agreement binding the company to its individual employees at all levels. The process entails a review and edit of the source materials described in Table 8 intended to define and assess performance in meeting mutual expectations. Success in fulfilling corporate expectations is supported by whatever documents define them, including the job description, objectives, productivity metrics, and the supervisor's assessment. The employee might respond in kind with a review of his personal assessment of the company performance, similar to a personal response to the questionnaire in Exercise 9 (page 140). The process then calls for both assessing past performance and setting future expectations, with explicit intent to improve this value-for-value exchange. A dialogue informed by two-way assessments such as these raises fundamental questions: "Is this a good match? Is this a fair exchange; are both parties winning? If not, why not? What needs to change? Can this change be economically accomplished through training or motivation? If it is a mismatch that cannot be remedied, what must be done? *This conscious refinement of definitions and alignment of expectations is the very foundation of employee relationship management, but it is clearly not common practice.*

A classic fairy tale in Western culture describes a vain emperor who had been duped into thinking that he had commissioned the finest garments ever made, so finely woven in fact that only the

TABLE 8

Performance Dialogues

	Evaluate Last Year's Performance	Define Next Year's Expectations
Company Satisfaction	Compare - Job description - Objectives - Performance metrics - Supervisor assessment	Prepare - Job description - Objectives - Productivity metrics
Employee Satisfaction	Compare - Employee assessment	Prepare - Development plan

wisest and most perceptive people could see them. The royal court responded with effusive praise and flattery, none wanting to be the first to confess that he lacked the necessary sagacity to see and appreciate such artistry. On a grand day, with much pomp and circumstance, the emperor strutted into the courtyard in the buff. You may recall that it was an innocent youth who finally cried out, "Why does the emperor have no clothes?" Only then did the crowd awaken to the truth, to the great chagrin of their potentate. There is a striking parallel in organizational life as it pertains to employee strategy. Not surprisingly, it begins in the executive ranks, where corporate purpose is best understood and where employee plans are formulated as part of a grander scheme to advance a greater good. Such plans include strategic competencies required, along with approaches to acquire, retain, and develop just the right employees. Corporate purpose must then be dissected and delegated, cascading from top to bottom and eventually trickling down to implementation-level work teams and individual workers. But, for most, by the time it reaches its destination it is diluted and vague, incomplete and impersonal. But only where purpose is clear can human resources be effectively matched. Only when purpose is converted into measured expectation can there be accountability.

Ad hoc climate surveys, perfunctory job descriptions, bureaucratic one-way performance assessments, and unbalanced measurement systems may be sufficient to lead some to suggest that they have artistically crafted a finely woven garment that only the most astute can perceive. To the contrary, the emperor has no clothes! As a matter of practice, most organizations remain naked.

First Bookstore Case Study: Employees

Let us return to our fictional case study of the distribution center at First Bookstore. First, Lupe must understand who the employees are, then how the company is doing at meeting their expectations. Finally, she must look at what the company values and expects in return.

Who Are They?

Lupe was the sort of supervisor who wasn't afraid to get her hands dirty. It wasn't unusual to find her pitching in to unload a truck, shelve products, or even make the campus deliveries. Doing some of the work kept her in touch with day-to-day operations as few other things could. Besides that, it endeared her to her team of nine. Most of them had worked together for more than a decade. Along the way, they had come to know each other pretty well, a fact that had all sorts of positive and practical implications. For example, Lupe realized that Rena needed to be out by 4 p.m. on weekdays to pick up her two grandchildren from day care. She knew that Dave often became stressed and impatient when unexpected things came up. She knew that Joe was having problems at home that occasionally affected his concentration at work. Ed, a senior member of the team, was a nice guy, but he was clearly feeling the weight of his years. Lupe tried to spare him from the most physically challenging work. On the other hand, twenty-five-year-old Merritt was a weight lifter and bodybuilder. He seemed to delight in bench-pressing the seventy-pound book cartons before tossing them into the racks. Harvey was working his way through night classes at the local community college and needed to leave early on Mondays and Wednesdays. For him, the DC was a way to pay the bills while en route to bigger and better things in accounting. Even though team members rarely socialized outside work hours, Lupe made it a priority to know them, even keeping a diary (see Sample of Exercise 7) to keep their needs and circumstances in view. (See page 134 for the blank Exercise 7.) This closeness made working together more relaxed, even though everyone knew that Lupe took the job seriously and expected others to do so as well.

What Do the Employees Value and Expect?

The last few years had been tough on the whole business. Sales were down, and attention throughout the firm had shifted to cost control, especially in backstage operations like the DC's. Cost control had become the overarching company priority, and everyone knew it. What Lupe didn't know was how all of this was being internalized by her people. Did they really understand what the company was up against? Apart from casual conversation about the company's fortunes at the watercooler or in the break room, she had never used more structured feedback such as questionnaires. The whole idea seemed foreign to working folk like hers; they were a small team, and they were doers.

With growing pressure to cut costs and an awareness that nearly all of her costs were tied up in staffing, this was no time for business as usual. Besides that, there was growing evidence that the team's newly implemented changes to improve customer service and refine their processes would result in a big boost in productivity. If that turned out to be true, their work would no longer require a staff of ten. What a thought! Lupe's mind also returned to Jon Levine's founding vision, a vision that included a fulfilling work experience for employees. Lupe knew that any hope of mutually advantageous change would require that she better understand what her people valued from their work and how well the company was providing it. That had prompted her visit with the HR manager last week. Together they had developed an initial list that could be used to jump-start a conversation with the team that in-

Who Are Our Employees? Extract from Lupe's Diary

Directions: List team members and support staff in the left column, and record comments about each in the right column.

Each individual brings a unique combination of mental, emotional, physical, and spiritual needs and competencies to the workplace. Knowing employees as people will inform the effort to deploy them as resources by equipping you to better match people to purpose. Add any observations about the employee's life circumstances that might create special workplace needs.

Core member of team	Description of team member
Rena Casden	Rena has two young grandchildren. She's an early starter, generally here by 7 a.m., but needs to leave by 4 p.m. to do child care.
Dave Weidman	Dave is a hard worker. He seems to be a perfectionist. Wants everything just so. Seems impatient.
Joe Switzer	Joe has problems at home, and they are affecting his work. He seems preoccupied, is making more mistakes. Is irritable.
Ed McGiff	Ed can handle the job standard minimums, but he is slowing down and having trouble with the pace and physical demands of the job.
Merritt McMurty	A bodybuilder. Macho. Seems to loves physical activity and the outdoors.
Harvey Watson	Is attending night school in hopes of becoming an accountant. Needs to leave early Mondays and Wednesdays.
Pete Doran	. . .
Jason Ditzell	. . .
Pat Callahan	. . .

Member of support staff	Description of member of support staff
Generally unknown group to both Lupe and the team	I don't know much about the temps and part-timers.

cluded most of the basics, such as "appreciation for work well done," "caring and competent supervision," "involvement in decision making," "encouragement of teamwork," "fair compensation," and several others.

Lupe decided to use the Monday morning stand-up meeting to ask whether this was in fact the right list. "Is this what you really value from working here?" she asked.

There was an initial silence that would have been uncomfortable were it not for the kinship within this team. Finally Lupe broke through. "Hey, Dave what's up with you guys? Did I say something politically incorrect?"

"Nope," Dave responded. "I guess we're just a bit shell-shocked. In the fifteen years I've been here, no one ever asked that before. There was that survey done years back, something about the weather. Oh, yeah, they called it a "climate survey." It took six months to get it done, and we never did hear how it turned out. Besides, I work here in this DC, and if it's cloudy here, what difference does it make to me that the sun is shining somewhere else. You know what I mean?"

"Yeah, Lupe," said Rena. "I couldn't agree more. As a practical matter, we work here in this warehouse, not some other part of the company. But let's get back to this list you have here. I think it's basically OK. I doubt if anyone here would remove anything. However, some of the categories are awfully broad. Most of us appreciate "good teamwork," but it seems that you'd want to spell that out more. I mean, what does "good teamwork" really mean? The same could be said of "caring and competent supervision." You're a pretty good boss, but you're sure not perfect. Wouldn't we want a little more detail with some of these?"

"You're right about that, Rena, especially about my being a good boss," Lupe laughed. "But if this is a reasonable starting list, perhaps we can just begin here. It would seem that the best way to go is to check in with you guys a bit more formally at least once a year. Besides that, I know that there are questionnaires about some of these other things like teamwork and supervision. Maybe we can use them if there is any hint of a problem."

From there on the discussion was pretty animated. After all, as Larry said, "they're finally asking us what we value right here in the distribution center. That's a first. Now let's see if anything happens to it." Lupe was careful to record their feedback on Sample of Exercise 8. (The blank form is on page 138.)

How Is the Company Doing at Meeting Expectations?

Lupe was encouraged. She headed back to the HR department where they used her list defined in the Sample of Exercise 8 to craft the simple questionnaire shown in the Sample of Exercise 9. (See page 140 for the reproducible form.) It included a clear, concise statement to describe each element on the list. These words conveyed not only what her team valued but also what her company might reasonably be expected to provide. Next the DC team could be asked to assess both how important each factor was and to rate the company in fulfilling their expectations at providing it. Whenever a rating was especially high or low, they were also requested to explain their response.

The following week, Lupe used her meeting time to gather responses. It was easy. Before starting, she carefully explained each value element, making sure that the whole team clearly understood what they were assessing. She then took special care to explain the difference between ratings of importance and performance. She found that doing this face-to-face was especially helpful in clearing up confusion about definitions. It also gave her a chance to stress how critical it was that they explain the high and low ratings so that she might be able to better understand why they felt the way they did.

On the one hand, she knew that feedback specific to her team would be far more helpful than anything commingled with other operating units within the company. On the other, confidentiality was important, especially if an individual lacked trust. With only ten responses (including her own), some of the feedback might be muted by such concerns. Still, on balance, Lupe moved forward, assuring her team that the results were intended to be used to help

SAMPLE OF EXERCISE 8

What Do Our Employees Value and Expect?

Directions: Use the following methods to determine what employees value and expect from your team:

Ask the experts. Review information available from books, professional associations, Web sites, and other resources to gain insight regarding what employees value most.

Ask the employees. Validate and edit this list through discussions with employees.

Record your findings below, describing each element as clearly and succinctly as possible. Adapt the length of the list to your needs.

What do employees value and expect?

1. *Fair Pay. My compensation is fair compared to that paid at other organizations for similar work and experience.*

2. *Appreciation. My work is appreciated, especially when I go above and beyond the norm.*

3. *Involvement. I am involved in decisions that affect my work.*

4. *Teamwork. Our team works well together. We get along well, and we are productive.*

5. *Supervision. My boss is a caring and competent supervisor.*

6. *Professional Development. The firm invests enough in developing my skills.*

7. *Opportunity for Advancement. The firm offers adequate opportunity for advancement.*

8. *Job Security. If I work hard and am productive, the company will do its best to find a place for me.*

9. *Direction, Vision, and Fit. The direction and vision of our company is clear, and I understand how I (and my team) fit in it.*

10. *Measurement. I understand how my (and my team's) work is measured.*

11. *Fun. I enjoy my work. It is fulfilling and productive.*

12. *Communication. Communication is sufficient, clear, timely, and complete.*

SAMPLE OF EXERCISE 9

How Is the Company Doing at Meeting or Exceeding Expectations?

Distribution Center—Employee Questionnaire

As part of our desire to nurture a productive and fulfilling work experience, we want to rightly understand and continuously improve those aspects of the work experience that you value most. Please help us by completing the questionnaire below,

Directions: Please circle the number to score each element, focusing on the *importance* to you and your *rating* of how we're doing. Please explain high or low ratings.

Fair Pay

My compensation is fair compared to that paid at other organizations for similar work and experience.

Explanation:

Appreciation

My work is appreciated, especially when I go above and beyond the norm.

Explanation:

SAMPLE OF EXERCISE 9 cont'd

Distribution Center—Employee Questionnaire

Involvement

I am involved in decisions that affect my work.

Explanation:

Teamwork

Our work team works well together. We get along well, and we are productive.

Explanation:

Supervision

My boss is a caring and competent supervisor.

Explanation:

SAMPLE OF EXERCISE 9 cont'd

Distribution Center—Employee Questionnaire

Professional Development

The firm invests enough in developing my skills.

IMPORTANCE   RATING

Explanation:

Opportunity for Advancement

The firm offers adequate opportunity to advance.

IMPORTANCE   RATING

Explanation:

Job Security

If I work hard and am productive, the company will do its best to find a place for me.

IMPORTANCE   RATING

Explanation:

SAMPLE OF EXERCISE 9 cont'd

Distribution Center—Employee Questionnaire

Direction, Vision, and Fit

The direction and vision of our company is clear, and I understand how I (and my team) fit in it.

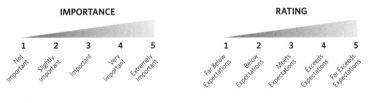

Explanation:

Measurement

I understand how my (and my team's) work is measured.

Explanation:

Fun

I enjoy my work. It is fulfilling and productive.

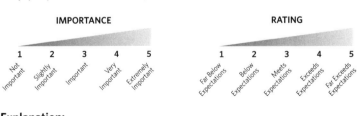

Explanation:

SAMPLE OF EXERCISE 9 cont'd

Distribution Center—Employee Questionnaire

Communication

Communication is sufficient, clear, timely, and complete.

IMPORTANCE	RATING

1   2   3   4   5   1   2   3   4   5

Not Important   Slightly Important   Important   Very Important   Extremely Important   Far Below Expectations   Below Expectations   Meets Expectations   Exceeds Expectations   Far Exceeds Expectations

Explanation:

Overall

I find this to be a fulfilling work experience.

IMPORTANCE	RATING

1   2   3   4   5   1   2   3   4   5

Not Important   Slightly Important   Important   Very Important   Extremely Important   Far Below Expectations   Below Expectations   Meets Expectations   Exceeds Expectations   Far Exceeds Expectations

Explanation:

What can we do to become a better team?

_____

_____

_____

What should management know that employees might not otherwise be inclined to share?

_____

_____

_____

her define and deliver more of what they valued most. Just as with the customer data, the feedback was easily tabulated, by transcribing hash marks onto a master copy of the questionnaire as shown in Figure 14 (page 141), a portion of Sample of Exercise 9. For ease of presentation, Lupe computed and graphed the averages and plotted the results. In less than an hour the results were powerfully presented in Figure 15.

As Lupe scanned the results, she was gratified to see that several of her team's successes clustered around categories that she directly influenced. For the most part, their expectations were being exceeded as it related to involvement, teamwork, and especially appreciation and supervision. The explanations added further weight to her theory. "We're really a pretty good team," one wrote. "Lupe always gets us into the act when it's going to have a major impact on us." "Lupe's the greatest," wrote another.

But other comments left Lupe somewhat concerned. For example, measurement didn't seem to matter much to the team, even though it mattered a great deal to Jim and the owners. She knew that this was the sort of disconnect that was bound to create some conflicts downstream unless she made them aware of its true importance.

She was completely blindsided by the magnitude of what appeared to be a cluster of related problems. Concerns for job security had penetrated to nearly everyone on the team. Lupe knew that flat sales, operating losses, and the prospect of new competition meant that there would be growing pressure to reduce staff, but she had not anticipated that this would be so widely understood. Of course, communication is one of the toughest areas to meet expectations. Lupe really worked hard on that one; she rarely skipped the weekly stand-up meetings, and she made sure she got plenty of informal one-on-one time with the team members. However, concerns about job security may well have been leaving people thirsty for far more information and perhaps of a different sort altogether. No doubt this situation, if left unattended, would also make working a whole lot less fun.

FIGURE 15

Distribution Center Team Employee Rating

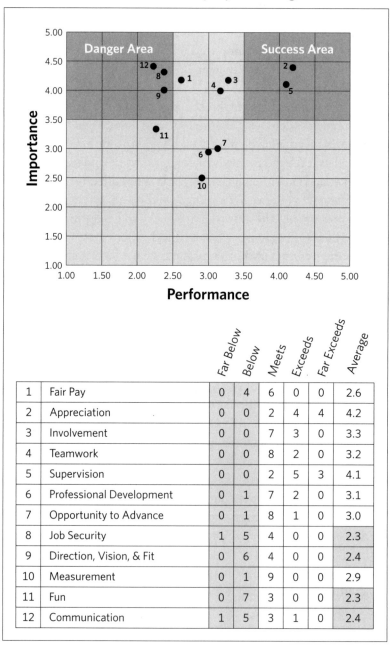

		Far Below	Below	Meets	Exceeds	Far Exceeds	Average
1	Fair Pay	0	4	6	0	0	2.6
2	Appreciation	0	0	2	4	4	4.2
3	Involvement	0	0	7	3	0	3.3
4	Teamwork	0	0	8	2	0	3.2
5	Supervision	0	0	2	5	3	4.1
6	Professional Development	0	1	7	2	0	3.1
7	Opportunity to Advance	0	1	8	1	0	3.0
8	Job Security	1	5	4	0	0	2.3
9	Direction, Vision, & Fit	0	6	4	0	0	2.4
10	Measurement	0	1	9	0	0	2.9
11	Fun	0	7	3	0	0	2.3
12	Communication	1	5	3	1	0	2.4

Lupe knew that the founder's original vision and direction had pretty much evaporated over the years. She was stunned, however, to see that the team noticed the problem too. From their comments it was clear that they didn't understand the company's overall plan and direction, how they fit in to it, or how the company intended to accomplish it. In uncertain times like these, this lack of direction seemed to be taking its toll. One person wrote, "With all our problems, how are we going to get out of this mess?" Another wrote, "Are we even going to be here next year?" And, in what seemed a complete disconnect, several of the staff perceived that they were unfairly compensated. Again, the comments helped a little, although no one noted anything specific; they just had this sense that pay and benefits were low, especially after the last three years of pitifully small pay increases.

These were pretty sizable gaps, places where the company rated well below their expectations. Lupe couldn't help thinking that those beliefs, if truly held, would negatively affect team members' attitudes and efforts at work. Despite the potential for conflict, she was almost eager to get them together, this time for an extended session to get a fuller understanding of why they felt this way. For the first time ever, she felt that she knew what her people valued and how well their work experience was meeting their expectations. She also had some ideas about how to better understand why they felt as they did. What an opportunity!

The meeting began differently from the routine weekly sessions. For one thing, Lupe had taken a twenty-minute detour on her way to work to get fresh doughnuts; even the coffee was flavored. Everyone was invited to sit down around two long fold-out tables in one corner of the production floor while Lupe handed out copies of Figure 15 (page 160). Apart from an occasional slurp of coffee, everyone seemed engrossed in the information; after all, it was theirs.

After a few minutes Lupe called for everyone's attention. "I realize that you don't need anyone to explain this chart. It pretty much speaks for itself, and it has quite a lot to say about how we're doing at meeting your expectations. That's why we won't be able to get through it all in one meeting. But I want to promise you that everything you have said will be discussed. No doubt, we will need to make some changes to do better. I hope that there will also be times when we can get some more facts that may change your point of view. And sometimes we will simply not agree, but we will at least disagree agreeably. For today, then, let's tune in to what appear to be our core successes and problems."

"I always thought we got along pretty well together," said Dave, "and, frankly, these numbers seem to confirm that."

"I agree," said Ed. "My friends sometimes tell me about how things go for them at work. Although most of us have been here long enough that we take it for granted, we probably have it better than most."

"And that's in no small measure due to you, Lupe," said Rena. "You're a pretty good boss."

"I'm not fishing for a compliment, Rena, but can anyone explain what that means? Knowing what you value can help me make sure I do more of it." For several minutes the room filled with chatter as people shot out their ideas:

- "You work with us, Lupe, rather than us just working for you."

- "You know the job."

- "You're not on a power trip. I've seen a lot of ego among bosses."

- "You make sure the people upstairs know how we're doing and what we need to do our work better."

- "You appreciate it when somebody goes out of their way to meet a deadline or do something extra."

- "More than that, Lupe, you know us personally, and that makes a big difference to me."

- "You help us find the work we do best."

- "You care, and it can't be said any better than that."

The conversation went on for another five minutes while Lupe jotted down notes feverishly.

"Guys, as much as I would like to keep this going all day, our data indicated that there were still some pretty serious problems elsewhere. First, let me say that there were four people who felt that the pay is unfair. When we feel that way, it's easy to grow almost cynical at work. That's why I will take this one very seriously. If you don't mind, I will ask that we delay that discussion until I can work with HR to gather some market data on pay rates. Then we'll talk it through with these additional facts in front of us. After that, if anyone is still unhappy we can look at your specific situation.

"My biggest concern from this feedback was that the scores were very low on job security, communication, and understanding where our company is going and how we fit into the big picture. From a careful read of your explanations, it really seemed as though they were substantially linked to the hard times that our company is facing right now and the uncertainty that creates for us. Am I off base?"

"You're right on the money," said Merritt. "Most of us can't afford to be unemployed. We have kids, mortgages, and car payments. If we're in trouble here, we want to know about it, not get a pink slip on a Friday afternoon."

"Yeah, having this cloud hanging over our head stinks," said Larry. "I'd rather know the bad news now. At least give us the time to bail out and land on our feet."

"Besides that, the company seems to be asking us to help it automate, streamline, and cut out work that isn't mission-critical," said Rena. "Good grief, we're going to make the inevitable happen even faster if we do that."

"But what happens if we hunker down and resist?" said Lupe, "If you ask me, that's one sure way to fail."

The room became completely quiet as everyone pondered the gravity of the issue and its obvious conclusions. At the very least, this team would have to work smarter. That meant that familiar and comfortable patterns would have to change for everyone at the table. But, as Rena feared, that also virtually ensured that the team would also have to get smaller.

"I wish I could say what we all want to hear: We are good people, and we do good work. Keep up the good work. Nothing needs to change," said Lupe. "But that's just not honest. We do need to change, not just because it is critical to the very competitiveness of our company but because we believe in excellence, because we all signed up to 'be the best.' The crazy thing is that this kind of commitment to excellence is the only real job security."

Joe had hardly participated until now, but the pressure was too great. "Wait just a minute, Lupe. That's OK for those who get to stay, but it's not so great for the guys that get canned. What about them? For that matter, it could be me. This is like Russian roulette. We get to pull the trigger every time we make another layoff possible by making our work go away."

"That's a fair point, Joe, and if we can't address it honestly all this win-win talk is pure smoke. But why should we assume that everyone in this room wants to continue working here? And even if we all want to stay and that's not possible, why should we assume that we couldn't work together to find someone a solid opportunity somewhere else?"

Ed looked up slowly from his position at the end of the table. "You all know that I have kind of done my time already. I'm slowing down. Besides that, Martha and I have already bought an RV. Like a lot of people our age, we want to spend time with the grandkids, do some traveling, and putter and play a bit while we still can. Sometime soon, I will be ready to go. Maybe that can help."

"Me, too," said Harvey. "I have spent the last six years working part-time on my degree in accounting. You're all great, but, heck, as soon as I can, I'm out of here."

"Thanks, Ed, and you, too, Harvey. I knew you both had plans, but we all appreciate your sharing them now. It's not always this easy, and we may need to cut even another position or two before we're done. But know this; we will work it out together. We have to. I promise. The communication is going to get better from here on out, and the first thing to discuss is this big fat elephant in the room. It's job security. It is the future of the company and how we fit in to it. That's why I have asked the boss to join us after the break, to begin that discussion. I also asked him to share more about what he values and expects from us during this time of transition."

As a leader, Jim was low-key and thoughtful, not the sort of person who would make people uncomfortable. But the thought of seeing the president and general manager created some angst as the tall, solemn looking executive walked into the room and took his place at the table. It helped a little that he smiled and greeted each person by name.

"Thanks for coming, Jim," said Lupe. "We know how busy you are, especially now. But to be quite candid, we need to hear from you. Our data indicate that there is more than a little concern here about job security. We know that we can work smarter. We know that the company is pressing to cut costs. Because most of our costs are tied up in personnel, that will mean that we'll have to make some tough decisions in the next few months. What we don't know is where you see this company going. Is this a short-term dip or a long-term spiral into the abyss? And if there is a future for the company, where do we fit, and what can we do to help along the way?"

"First, Lupe, let me say how much I appreciate what you and your team are doing. You are facing the situation head-on, by clearly defining what's expected and making your own changes. I also have to confess that the very fact that you all have these questions is a pretty poor reflection on me, and that's embarrassing. In my early years as CEO I probably took too much for granted, and the past two years have been the hardest I've ever experienced. The competition is coming from all directions. Some of it caught me by surprise. In the short term, we have had no other choices than to cut margins and costs at the same time we increase services. That will not change in the next eighteen to twenty-four months. That is why I have asked every department head to come up with a plan to work smarter and, yes, to cut staff wherever that makes sense. I honestly think Jon Levine would have done it in the same forthright way. In fact, he would have also held us accountable to finding a winning way to do it, one that took care of everyone."

"Where does it end, Jim?" asked Lupe. "That's what's on every-one's mind. Can we beat this thing, or are we destined to death by a thousand cuts?"

"No, Lupe, the future really is getting brighter. A new strategy is about to roll out. You see, we are privileged to serve a special popu-lation here. The thousands of people who come through our doors are young, technologically literate, upwardly mobile, future leaders of our society. We're birthing a new lifelong relationship manage-ment plan that begins with expanded products and services here, but then uses the Internet to stay close to students when they leave campus for bigger and better things. This whole endeavor requires partnering with several key players. We'll need some pretty sophis-ticated technology tools, some different skills internally, and new partners to make it all work. It will take us five years to get there. Along the way, we just need to figure out how to work smarter."

As Jim paused for breath, the room once again became silent. No one had even had a clue that such a strategy was under devel-opment. As usual, Rena was one of the first to comment. "Jim, you can't imagine how encouraging it is just to know that something positive is in the wings. That gives us hope. But in the world you describe, where I assume we will sell more on the Web and sell more types of things in the store, what will that mean for us?"

"Plenty," Jim replied. "Of course, there will be a wider assort-ment of products being received here. There's no way to be com-petitive in these businesses unless our systems and processes are solid. We'll have to expand the outgoing mail operation to respond to the Web services, and we'll extend the range of sales floor ser-vices; that's almost certainly going to demand more support from the DC."

The strain on their faces began to ease as Jim went on to de-scribe the new vision and strategy in greater detail. As Lupe watched, she was struck by the mounting sense of urgency—an ur-gency driven both by the inescapable demand to change now and the opportunities that this change might bring later. She was also struck by how essential it is to make corporate plans meaningful to the rank-and-file employees expected to implement those plans and how easy it is to overlook the people at the bottom.

What Does the Company Value and Expect?

"Jim, thank you," said Lupe. "This has meant a lot. You know that in the first part of our time together we have been talking about matters of employee satisfaction and what our team values from the company as well as how well the company is doing at delivering it. One reason we asked you here is that we value knowing where the company is going and how we fit. But before you leave, we need your help on something else. Winning change also requires a commitment from us. What does the company value from us individually, especially in the months ahead?"

"I'm sure you all realize that the company asks the same of individuals as it asks of its work teams: *do only that which contributes to our purpose and do it well.* Our values determine how we pursue our purpose. We need people of character who will understand and live by our values. We need competent people, well-suited to the work asked of them. That's a whole lot more than just being motivated. It requires a good fit between people's natural talents and the jobs they are asked to do for us. You might say it requires a people-to-purpose fit that is good enough."

"Good enough for what?" responded Lupe.

"At minimum it must be good enough to enable us to remain competitive. But I guess if old Jon Levine were here, he'd set the sights a whole lot higher. We need to be good enough to deliver legendary service to our prime customers, to provide a fulfilling work experience to high-performing people like you, and to rank among the best practices in our business, outperforming our industry peers in substantial ways. Now that's a pretty tall order. But it's also a job worth coming to work for," said Jim.

Just then Jim's cell rang, summoning him to an urgent priority, and three trucks pulled in to the lot almost on cue. The meeting was unceremoniously adjourned as everyone scrambled to his or her various duties. But the climate in the DC had notably changed that morning. A ray of sunshine seemed to be peering through the clouds. Maybe, things were going to turn out all right after all.

As Lupe looked back on her team's assessment, she began to realize that the employees rated job security, communication, and understanding organizational direction in the danger zone. It soon became clear that this resulted in large part from present uncertainty in the business, combined with being left pretty much in the dark about future prospects and assuming the worst. As the conversation progressed, team members learned that although staff reduction seemed inevitable, two employees were nearly ready to move on, and the leadership expected a future period of growth that would include a significant role for their team.

As the following story illustrates, sometimes surprise comes even as we pursue commonsense steps to understand and pursue winning agreements. In the third century BC, the king of Syracuse commissioned a golden crown. On receiving the crown, he grew concerned that the goldsmith might have cheated him by mixing the gold with baser metals such as silver or even by using another metal and gilding it. As the story goes, he commissioned none other than Archimedes to determine whether the crown was solid gold, but to do so without damaging it. Archimedes thought and thought over this. Still pondering the problem as he sat down in his bath one day, the water overflowed. In that moment he experienced an epiphany.

He realized that the rise of the water level was proportional to the volume of the object submerged. That would mean he could measure the volume of the crown by dipping it in water and, knowing the volume, determine the density and composition. As the story goes, he was so thrilled that he jumped from his bath, running naked through the streets of Syracuse yelling, "Eureka! . . . I have discovered it!"

Discovery sometimes comes to us that way, in a blinding flash of insight that becomes instantly obvious. Eureka! Organizations and employees depend on each other to get what each values most. In most companies the relationship is governed more by inertia than intent and by long years of evolution, not thoughtful design. We can do better by crafting a conscious and explicit exchange of value based on measured employee satisfaction with value delivered and company satisfaction with value received in return. We can mutually commit to a winning agreement designed to match people to purpose. The common sense is compelling. The methods are simple. The scope is manageable.

Summary

There is a human equivalent to the law of the harvest: we reap what we sow, only multiplied. Employees tend to treat both customers and owners in the same way that they perceive themselves to be treated. While this golden rule falls short in some respects, it remains substantially the case that understanding and delivering what employees value is integral to achieving corporate purpose. Where delivering value to employees really matters, it is systematically measured and acted upon. Among organizations, this is rare.

Who Are They?

Knowing employees as people is essential if supervisors are to effectively match people to purpose. But this match requires more than the baseline familiarity found in a typical job description or résumé. Employees are whole people, a complex blend of mind, heart, spirit, and body. Each individual is uniquely equipped for a finite range of work. Employees also differ with respect to circumstances. Knowing employees as people requires this more inclusive understanding. This knowledge will inform efforts to productively deploy them as resources in mutually advantageous ways.

What Do Employees Value and Expect?

Despite differences among employees, studies show that workers tend to value many common elements, such as appreciation for work well done, involvement in decisions affecting their work, and fair pay. For obvious reasons the employees themselves must define what it is that they value. Any lists developed using outside sources must be validated and edited by the team. The discussion itself can also be empowering and positive.

How Is the Company (Team) Doing at Meeting or Exceeding Expectations?

To find out how the company and team are doing, employees must be asked. The process of asking should include informal and unstructured forums as well as formal methods such as performance reviews, goal-setting meetings, and the value questionnaire. The questionnaire seeks to clearly define each value element. It then asks employees to assess both importance and performance and to explain high and low ratings. High and low ratings on important value elements become de facto priorities for the team's development effort. Summary results that are high or low often lead to more fact-finding, including more detailed perception questionnaires and other types of indicators.

Employee Contribution

We should not presume that companies always get what they value from their employees—they often do not. More than anything, they value employees who are well matched to the work and to the workplace culture. Instruments organizations use to define and measure their expectations for individual purpose include job descriptions, performance assessments, objectives, and performance metrics.

When traditional feedback discussions are converted into dialogues, mutual expectations can be clearly defined, monitored, and refined over time into winning agreements intended to continually improve the match of people to purpose.

5

Stakeholders Come First

The Winning Exchange of Value

> *An implicit universal mission statement would read some-*
> *thing like this: "To improve the economic well-being and*
> *quality of life of all stakeholders".* —STEPHEN COVEY

Pepe Rodriguez, one of the most notorious bank robbers in the
early settling of the West, lived just south of the border in Mexico.
He regularly crept into Texas towns to rob banks, returning to
Mexico before the Texas Rangers could catch him.

The frustrated rangers were so embarrassed by this that they il-
legally crossed the border into Mexico. Eventually, they cornered
Pepe in a Mexican bar that he frequented. Unfortunately, Pepe
couldn't speak any English, so the rangers asked the bartender to
translate for them.

The Texas Rangers, with their guns drawn, told the bartender
to ask Pepe where he had hidden all the money he had stolen from
the Texas banks. "Tell him that if he doesn't tell us where the
money is right now, we're going to shoot him dead on the spot."

The bartender translated all this for Pepe. Immediately, Pepe
explained in Spanish that the money was hidden in the town well.
They could find it by counting down seven stones from the handle,
and behind the seventh stone was all the loot he had stolen.

The bartender then turned to the rangers and said in English, "Pepe is a very brave man. He says that you are a bunch of stinking pigs, and he is not afraid to die!"[1]

Sending in the Posse

A company will often send in a posse of managers and consultants, guns drawn, to conduct a "performance audit." The perceived, albeit unspoken, message to the work team is that "you have worked neither hard enough nor smart enough. Through acts both committed and omitted, you have stolen our gold." The click of the hammer is almost audible. "Tell us now, where have you hidden the process improvement, or else!"

Finally, someone blurts out what everyone knows. "It's the receiving process! Most of the equipment was purchased before the combustion engine was invented. The facilities are laid out like the obstacle course at Marine boot camp. The computers are so slow that the screen savers come on during each update. Every product has to be handled two or more times, and three of the twelve steps we go through are altogether unnecessary. Besides that, our company policy manual must have been inspired by the Byzantine Empire; we can't procure a widget without a five-part form and the patience of Mother Theresa."

Like the bartender, the performance posse translates the team's feedback into a plan of action for senior management. The plan captures every point but one, the source. A few months later reorganization is announced, reengineering is implemented, and pink slips are dispatched to the four least senior members of the team. And so it goes, at least in the minds of many directly impacted by corporate unit reviews. Workers are understandably cautious when speaking about process improvement, realizing instinctively that what they say can be used against them. At best, it puts those impacted out of their comfort zone. At worst, it leads to the unemployment office. *Without trust, what rational being would voluntarily cooperate? For that matter, what rational being would not actively resist?*

Engendering Trust among Stakeholders

There is a better way, one that engenders trust over time by deliberately aligning the legitimate interests of all core stakeholders with the company's interests (see Figure 16 on page 176). It requires a more inclusive purpose, incorporating explicit and balanced commitment to all stakeholders, but especially to customers, employees, and owners. It requires bilateral accountability based on measured feedback to inform ongoing assessment and improvement in the value exchange with the company. It requires that this process be repeated at every level, in every work team and, ultimately, with every individual. It is within this framework that ALL stakeholders must be treated as though they come first.

Owners

Few would deny that owners come first. After all, they are typically the founders, the funders, and the risk takers. Whether motivated by the pursuit of wealth or by some worthy social calling, they created and even now sustain and direct the organization. Aligning the efforts of work teams to more fully achieve their carefully prescribed purpose and improving efficiency is how owners win. In return, work teams rightly expect that this collective purpose be made clear and that resources with which to pursue it are sufficient.

Customers

But customers must also come first. Central to all organizational purpose is the creation of goods and services that customers value. Meeting or exceeding customers' expectations is mission-critical. The work team's customers, who are often internal to the organization, are the recipients of the team's products and services. They win when the team reliably delivers its products and services. But they are pleasantly surprised when the team provides them faster, better, or cheaper service. In return, the organization rightly expects its customers to support its mission, provide necessary resources, and partner in meaningful ways.

Employees

Even employees must come first. It is only through their efforts that customers are served and corporate purpose is pursued. This is doubly true today in an economy that is increasingly service and knowledge based. Employees value many things from their work experience, including appreciation, involvement, fair pay, and the feeling of being part of a worthy purpose. Employees win by getting more of what they value. In return, organizations value and expect employees to be productively engaged in mission-critical corporate priorities.

For most organizations today, these stakeholders exercise substantial and increasing discretion in their work and business dealings. Customers determine where to purchase; employees decide not only where they work but also how they work; owners, of course, choose not only how much to invest but often whether to continue placing their resources at risk in an enterprise at all. *To the full extent that stakeholders have choices, it is a universal corporate purpose that organizations foster the winning exchange of value among core stakeholders.*

Stakeholder Alignment in Work Teams

In the final analysis it is the front line that produces the bottom line. Corporate purpose, while primarily crafted at the top, is largely implemented at the bottom in natural work teams (a supervisor and direct reports) and in project teams (a team leader and team members). It is here, in this corporate microcosm, that we find common supervision, common purpose, and common stakeholders. It is here that most of the organization's resources are expended. It is also here that activities are most easily understood, measured, managed, and improved. Each team is a discrete link in a value chain. Each team has clearly definable stakeholders—customers, employees, and owners—with overlapping interests. Alignment re-

quires that the team assess both stakeholder satisfaction and contribution by answering the following core questions:

1. Who are they?

2. What do they value and expect from the team?

3. How well is the team doing at delivering it?

4. What does the team value in return?

5. How well is the stakeholder doing at delivering it?

These questions focus attention on what matters most and
what must be measured. Such measures are not complete and all-
encompassing, but they do come first. They are simple, intuitive,
and actionable. *Winning change requires that the team understand
what constitutes a win for its stakeholders. Only then is it possible to
define a strategically targeted value proposition for each and align
the collective effort to accomplish it.*

From a distance this may appear naive or impractical. Some will
say, "People will abuse so generous a spirit. Why give up more than
you have to? Besides, an organization's allegiance to people cannot
be made explicit without becoming unduly restrictive." Other critics observe that there are times when win-lose must be an option;
at the end of the day the corporate interests must come first. Good
managers must act accordingly, especially when dealing with people out there and over there and down there. Individuals must be
expendable. No one promised more. No one expects more. While
few would be quite so blunt, this perspective is both understandable and commonplace among management. The dilemma, then, is
this: a corporate me-first mind-set will prove corrosive to trust and
cooperation in the long term, and a we-first mind-set may appear
restrictive in the short term.

Yet down deep everyone realizes that stakeholder alignment is
essential (as shown in Figure 16). Failure to substantially deliver
what stakeholders value over time will sabotage virtually any

FIGURE 16
The Universal Purpose

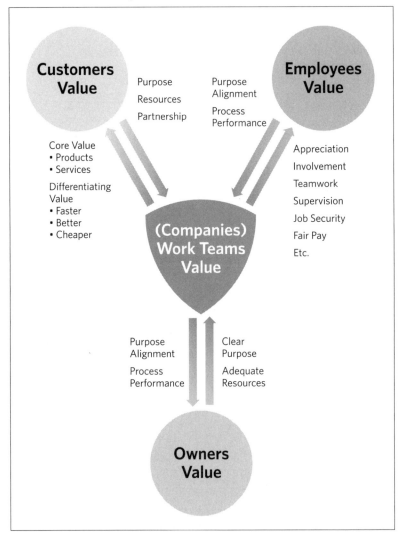

corporate purpose; channeling the collective energy in pursuit of the mutually advantageous exchange of value makes the collective purpose far more achievable. Nowhere is it more practical to apply these insights than in work teams. We will see how as we conclude the First Bookstore case study.

The First Bookstore Case Study: All Stakeholders

Almost a year had passed since Lupe's initial meeting with Jim. Much had been accomplished during that time. The DC had already managed to capture an annual net savings of more than four hundred thousand dollars, a full two hundred thousand dollars more than was required. Savings were brought about primarily by reductions in staffing expenses, including cuts of four full-time positions and a significant cut in the seasonal payroll for temporary staff. Even more impressive, these accomplishments had the full involvement and commitment of the team. As anticipated, Ed had retired. After completing his degree, Harvey had transferred into the business office as the assistant manager to pursue a new career in accounting. Joe and Merritt had also moved on; Joe transferred to the sales floor, and Merritt took a position as route manager when the DC's campus deliveries had been outsourced. The most recent survey feedback from the remaining six staffers showed measured improvement. There was a growing confidence that the company would succeed and a sense of pride at all the team had accomplished.

Even the customers were happy. Lupe's efforts to engage them had prompted months of close collaboration to get to the root of several key problems. Amazingly, Gary's team of buyers, with an average rating of 4.5, now topped the charts. Life was different now. Less was taken for granted. Outcomes were measured, making successes all the sweeter. These accomplishments had prompted Jim to request Lupe to share her secrets in the upcoming department managers' meeting.

Lupe had been looking forward to this. Spirits were high as the meeting began, with the management team in full attendance and at full attention. Gary was present representing his buyers. Shelly, who headed the retail operations team, had arrived five minutes early. Susan, the office manager, was eyeing one of the chocolate éclairs as she took her seat. And the two assistant store managers, Orlando and Kevin, hurriedly entered the room just as Jim called the meeting to order.

"Colleagues," said Jim, "It's not every day that we can have a session like this. About a year ago now, Lupe came to me with some pretty tough questions to try to get ahead of the curve on what our business needs were going to mean for her unit. She not only met with me but she also gathered feedback from her primary customers, including some of you in this room, as well as from her staff. To be frank, I didn't expect all that much to come of it. But results speak for themselves. She has pulled off a miracle down there in the DC. That's why I've asked her to explain it for us this morning. If we can't clone her, we must at least clone her formula. So, Lupe, we're all ears."

"Look guys," Lupe grinned, "I know three things about meetings. One, you don't really want me to come here crowing about how clever we are. Two, the thing you'd value most is something that you can actually use in your own shops. And, three, the average attention span doesn't last much longer than fifteen minutes. You've already received our full report, including all the exercises you need to make the same changes in your own unit, so our team pulled together yesterday to come up with our short list of surprises. The surprises convey that sense of "Eureka" that occurs when you come across something that turns out to be common sense but is not common practice.

"I guess the biggest insight is that *all of our core stakeholders come first*. We have three. The owners are represented primarily by Jim, and he was pressing us for immediate cost cutting. Our customers are represented by Gary, Shelly, and Susan, and they were calling for better service. At the same time, our employees were scared to death, not knowing whether the company would solve its problems by dumping them on the street without warning or concern for their welfare. From the beginning we made it clear that we were targeting a winning result, something good for everybody. We earned a lot of trust by approaching the problem that way and, believe me, we needed it."

"But, Lupe," said Kevin, "How could you know that a mutual win would even be possible? Weren't you concerned that you might not be able to make good on the promise?"

Lupe responded without hesitation. "The truth is that we couldn't promise more than we could control. But we did promise to make a mutual win the target for our efforts, Kevin. Everyone seemed to understand that.

"But the real surprise was in the synergy. That's what I wanted to call your attention to. After we had gathered feedback from all three stakeholders, we found several things. *Many times the elements valued by a given stakeholder were interconnected with each other.* By that I mean that the stakeholder's happiness or dissatisfaction with one factor seemed to overflow into others. For example, our team's fears about job security seemed to indicate a need for more communication so they could get a clear read on where the company was headed and how they fit into that future. In effect, there was a common problem under the surface.

"We also found that in some cases problems with a stakeholder's *satisfaction were directly linked to problems with that stakeholder's contribution.* You can vouch for that can't you, Gary? It turned out that many of our deficiencies in serving our customers were caused in part by their behaviors, such as unneeded phone calls or e-mails, failure to follow policies, or choices to source goods in ways that created tons of extra work. Because of our customers' actions, our staff ended up having less time to take care of them in other areas. In effect, our failure to meet their expectations tied directly to their failure to meet ours."

"That's a good point, Lupe," responded Gary. "In fact, you rated us as poorly as we rated you. We just needed to define and address some deeper problems where there was a mutual benefit."

"But the biggest insight for us," said Lupe, "was that *our stakeholders had overlapping goals.* Our customers wanted our services to be faster, better, and cheaper. It seemed counterintuitive at first, but that was remarkably consistent with Jim's goal that we cut costs and make operations more productive. It turned out that doing things right the first time allowed us to satisfy both."

"This whole thing sounds pretty impressive." said Orlando. "You pulled all of this off without a hitch. I mean, the only thing missing here is the part where you all sing songs around the campfire. Was it really that harmonious?"

"Absolutely not," grimaced Lupe. "Actually, that was our last point, Orlando. *Conflicts are inevitable.* Stakeholder feedback can be pretty offensive at first. It tends to bring the toughest questions to the surface, pointing out our biggest problems. Frankly, we were not all that pleased to hear that much bad news, and there were times when we needed a referee to get through those meetings. Facing facts and marshalling the courage to act is tough. But we found that if you don't get defensive, you can go a long way toward finding a winning solution.

"Well, my fifteen minutes are up. I know that the average audience forgets 85 percent of what it hears within an hour. But remember this much. *As stakeholders, we depend on each other.* It doesn't take an industrial engineer to see that delivering value to core stakeholders matters to everyone. If we're going to manage that exchange of value we certainly need to define and measure it."

"That's the point, Lupe. And it's time that we followed your lead." Turning to the other managers, Jim ended with a request and a promise. "If you will all commit to completing those exercises that Lupe included in her report, it certainly looks to me as though this same process would work company-wide. And while you're doing that, I'll have to fill some gaps by leading an effort to collectively redefine our corporate purpose, making sure that ALL of our stakeholders get the attention they deserve.

"Jon Levine must be smiling on us today. After being lost for more than a decade, I think we are finally finding our way back home. It was always his philosophy since founding First Bookstore to place all stakeholders first."

Getting Started

There is a human equivalent to the law of inertia. Absent an outside force, both people and things tend to continue doing what they are doing. There are understandable inclinations to resist, to deny, and to rationalize, even aside from the fear of change. Getting started requires introducing a new force, one great enough to overcome organizational inertia. As a supervisor, you are that force. However, you are well advised to enlist additional support wherever possible. This should include *your boss*. Work with management to develop common expectations and commitments for the effort, commitments that include the resources needed. Also search out a *workflow process adviser*. Expertise in work process management can be helpful, and most organizations have these skills at hand. Finally, seek out a *people process adviser*. Together, these professionals can assist both in managing staff concerns and in creatively assisting to find winning opportunities to transition. An overview of one approach to work team review is captured in Table 9.

Universal Purpose

An organization in Montana offered a bounty of five thousand dollars for every wolf captured alive as part of a relocation program. Two hunters named Sam and Jed decided to head for the hills and make some money capturing wolves. Day and night they scoured the mountains and forests searching for their prey. Exhausted after three days of hunting without any success, they both fell asleep.

During the night Sam suddenly woke up to find that he and Jed were surrounded by a pack of fifty wolves with flaming red eyes and bared teeth, snarling at the two hunters and preparing to pounce.

Sam nudged Jed and said, "Hey, wake up, Jed! We're gonna be rich!"[2]

Like most unsuccessful managers, Sam had become so focused on what they wanted that he had forgotten to ask, what's in it for the wolf? The answer appears to be a night out for a delicious meal with the pack. This selfish streak takes many forms and in varying degrees is a part of all of us. At times people treat others like things, taken for granted, manipulated, disrespected, or ignored. It has caused no end of woes. The vision of riches will fade quickly as the reality sets in that in most markets, long-term success requires the cooperation and support of others. It requires what might be termed a we-first, not a me-first, perspective.

TABLE 9

Management Process

Step One: Stakeholder Data Gathering
Using exercises provided in Chapters 2, 3, and 4, gather baseline information describing the work team's current performance in providing what customers, employees, and owners value.

Step Two: Assessment
Use the stakeholder data to evaluate the team's operations. Where appropriate, obtain additional feedback or ask trusted outsiders to help review the team's operations. Define and prioritize needed changes.

Step Three: Implement Priority Changes
Implement changes, giving preference to those that can have the greatest impact on improving stakeholder value and can most easily and inexpensively be acted upon.

Step Four: Internalize Changes
Train the team in the use of measured feedback on stakeholder satisfaction on an ongoing basis. Help team members acquire any skills needed with new processes.

Step Five: Recognition
Pay attention to ongoing feedback from stakeholders. Recognize and reward measured improvements.

To the degree that stakeholders have choices, their organizations are bound by a common universal purpose to foster the winning exchange of value. In such a world, stakeholder value is the coin of the realm. Managing the value exchange requires clear definition, ongoing measurement, and continuous improvement.

Summary

Part 1 of this book has been dedicated to creating a simple stakeholder feedback model. In the end, stakeholders matter most. Satisfying them is integral to the purpose of all organizational effort. Measuring the exchange of value with them is foundational to continous improvement.

In Part 2 we now turn our attention to power tools to measure what matters. They include instruments to gather data, case studies to understand it, and topical inquiries that will collectively improve your stakeholder feedback system. Chapter 6 picks up where we end here, exploring trust and ways to measure and manage it. In Chapter 7, we use the case study for Jake to demonstrate the potential of a simple and easy-to-use 360-degree feedback instrument to improve leadership competencies. Chapter 8 then introduces a well-tested teamwork feedback instrument, which is explained in another case study format. In Chapter 9, we take on performance assessment, advocating a two-way instrument that supports dialogue and clearly defined expectations. Finally in Chapter 10, we seek to enrich the insight pertaining to owner feedback using an actual case focusing on two vital indicators. Collectively, these instruments allow work teams to self-diagnose and to better align people with purpose.

Part Two

Power Tools
for Management

6

Trust Matters

The Key to Organizational Change

Trust can only arise where people have deep, intense interest in each other. They must be able to distinguish one another's qualities, to know which aspects of one another are special and worth trusting. —PETER SENGE

This chapter is about understanding the many dimensions of trust and how to facilitate that understanding through the use of simply applied metrics that you can use with your team or organization.[1] There is a myth that gathering useful data demands a sophisticated understanding of metrics, statistics, and other areas of related knowledge. The truth is that 90 percent of all the data useful in business requires no such grasp of these complexities. Rather, what is required are a couple of straightforward actions. First is a clear understanding of what you wish to measure and a willingness to ask the tough questions that may lay bare the underbelly of the issue being explored. Second is the ability to establish a structure and climate so that those engaged in assessing the issue or providing the feedback feel safe and, as a result, will provide the most honest information possible. We have chosen to measure trust as a vehicle for demonstrating how to create a useful instrument that can provide a meaningful set of metrics to help those gathering the data deal with issues that influence the life of their organization.

Fitting Trust into the Equation of Change

Building trust is, indeed, a major factor for leaders involved with initiating change or establishing a climate of work conducive to honesty, candor, risk taking, and overall positive morale. When trust does not exist in a team or organization, everyone knows it, and over time that knowledge will influence everything, from morale and productivity to relationships and decision making.

For example, planning is something that occurs—with favorable results or not—in nearly every organization. The notion of trust is assumed in most strategic planning. Leaders assume that people will tell the truth, respond in light of what is best for the organization, and put aside their own self-interest and personal agendas so that the organization can move forward in a manner that maximizes its mission and its position in the marketplace. However idealistic and reasonable this may sound, implied trust is, quite simply, not sufficient for this to occur.

To ensure the benefits of a positive planning process, leaders commonly hire qualified experts to help them formulate a well-defined linear planning process. They build their plans by defining the goals they wish to accomplish in relation to values, mission statements, and institutional vision. They gather metrics from broad-ranging constituencies and eventually formulate an implementation plan. Finally, more often than not, little happens. Disappointment by the hopeful, and skepticism by critics, can fuel a profound disillusionment that can undermine the morale of an entire institution. Failure to build trust at the front end of such a change effort will more than likely result in resistance at the point of implementation. Mistrust from years of avoiding conflict, poor communications, political intrigue, and the silo nature of conducting business can thwart meaningful change. The question is not whether mistrust will occur but rather how.

Because a lack of understanding of how to establish trust in a team or organization is common, we can predict that the mere suggestion of a need to build trust within the planning process will lead to strong denials and the demand "Let's just get on with the planning." The deterioration of trust brought about by an ineffective planning effort will only further poison future initiatives of this kind. Who wants to invest additional monies, time, and mental energy in what people will see as another predictable failure? Even though successful planning is a rather rare accomplishment, few leaders will understand that a long-standing and underlying lack of trust had anything to do with the failure of the concrete and often elegantly laid out planning strategy. In fact, most people have difficulty comprehending the concept of trust itself.

Reframing Our View of Trust

Years ago, Sarah Engel, a former graduate student and now a professional colleague of ours, came to us excited about an insight she had gained in relation to one of the least understood concepts of management—trust. Like us, she had been perplexed by the fact that almost regardless of the type of organization for which she worked, trust was nearly always identified as a factor inhibiting both management effectiveness and the implementation of various change initiatives. Our experience with small and large businesses, colleges and universities, retail stores, the military, and even convents only reinforced this sense of Sarah's reality. Trust is an essential ingredient in organizational effectiveness, and the degree to which it is present will have an influence on many aspects of organizational life. Ask people in an organization, large or small, about trust, and they seldom equivocate. People know when trust is present and when it is not, even if it has never been carefully defined. It is a litmus test for relationships between individuals, groups, administrators, and workers. What separates trust from other factors in the management equation is that *trust is treated, almost universally, as a problem.* In fact, *trust represents an outcome* based on the influence of a wide range of other factors. Unless these factors are discovered and addressed, trust will continue to be difficult to grasp and all but impossible to strengthen. This is why the use of metrics can be so useful: *we must first know the nature of these underlying influences that affect trust.*

Trust as Outcome

Factors that make up communication, while complex, can be broken down into identifiable parts. These can then be systematically attacked by a leader or team that is bent on improving communication—either within the team or with other stakeholders. For example, the failure to share information is a particular kind of communication problem that can be solved. The failure to solicit feedback from critical constituents is another difficult but quite manageable problem under the communication umbrella. Trust, however, cuts across a wide variety of issues that can prove difficult to identify, let alone solve. Engel and her colleagues changed trust from being thought of in an oversimplified way, as a problem, to being thought of as an outcome. Further, she realized that many of the critical variables that pose the greatest threat to trust could be identified. Then she began to use these factors as part of a systematic diagnosis and, later, as part of a purposeful problem-solving process. By attempting to isolate the most critical factors that reduce trust, we can begin to initiate strategies that can bolster trust between individuals, within a team, or in an organization.

A leader's effectiveness is, in part, predicated on how willing he or she is to identify sources of mistrust and then to intervene proactively in an effort to reduce the consequences of these negative factors. Engel's excitement was about having isolated some of these quite manageable variables that, if addressed, can have a positive effect on morale and even productivity. Over the years, we have taken these initial ideas and expanded them so that any leader can identify areas that create mistrust and, at the same time by utilizing specific design interventions, can improve overall trust. To know the source is to know the answers. We have broken these factors into three main categories:

- Content or product knowledge and skills

- Management structure and discipline

- Process or maintenance skills and behaviors

Content or Product Knowledge and Skills

In our culture, bottom-line objectives are predictably determined by the ability of individuals to generate an effective product. It matters little if such an outcome represents completing a complex laboratory experiment, conducting a conference, or carrying out an extensive program evaluation. Therefore, we would expect an inordinate amount of attention to be focused on the task dimensions of producing that product. This demands two kinds of knowledge and related skills—first is *content knowledge* and, second, is *technical knowledge*. We estimate that 90 percent of leadership energy is focused on these two vital areas. Without competence in them, there is little hope that success will result. Content knowledge has to do with the intellectual understanding of the product itself and the essential information necessary to create it. Such knowledge separates competitors. It can be vital in determining whether a good idea is translatable into a successful result. For example, recent competition in the field of biotechnology has only heightened the importance of such intellectual knowledge and the competition surrounding it. Trust in an institution or in a particular department is partly based on the ability to predict the quality and value of the product and to distinguish it from the competition. Without such intellectual capital, and the consistent ability to move from idea to product, both confidence and trust are diminished. A lack of confidence and trust can result in a reduced willingness to invest time, money, or other resources in pursuit of the product and ultimately decreases the chances of achieving the desired outcome.

On an individual management level, the same holds true. A new team manager, vice president, or even president must create an impression with key constituencies that she has a broad-based understanding of widely varying subject matter in addition to recognized content knowledge within her field of expertise. For many, this is the starting point of trust and helps determine whether they will be willing to be led. Technical knowledge and skills in support of the product represent a wide range of activities and understandings without which even the best ideas might languish. Building efficient production cycles, innovative marketing, and sales strategies, as well as taking advantage of some of the new communications technologies, can all have a positive effect on trust. In an increasingly competitive business climate, the capacity to translate technology into efficiencies can provide a competitive edge and increase both confidence and trust.

Management Structure and Discipline

Whether people within an organization believe that work can be accomplished effectively because of competent organization, decision making, planning, and the efficient utilization of resources can weigh heavily on their ability to trust. Clearly, having great competence in areas of content or technical understanding will go only so far. Without the ability to organize work efficiently, all the skills and knowledge will be of little avail. As organizations grow, the ability to manage increasing complexities and at the same time expand capacity to allow growth becomes a critical challenge for management. Providing sufficient structure in areas such as roles, goals, levels of authority, and communication can provide members of the organization with a sense of security. Some of the variables within this category that influence trust are the following:

1. **Clearly defined goals** represent one of the foundations of organizational trust. They guide what we do, where we're going, and how success will ultimately be measured. Our experience suggests that goals are often unclear and poorly defined at the organization, group, and individual levels.

2. **Role clarity** ties naturally into goal-related issues. When individuals know what they are supposed to do and how that

function fits into the complexities of the organization, their level of trust goes up. When individuals are unclear and roles bleed across areas or between individuals, their trust goes down and competition or other dysfunctional behaviors are likely to increase.

3. **Well-defined authority** theoretically represents one of the benefits of a highly structured hierarchical and bureaucratic organization. Historically, as organizations grew in structural complexity, conflict was supposed to be reduced dramatically. In such bureaucratic organizations, lines of authority were generally clear, and people knew what authority was theirs and what lay in the hands of others. In modern management there is a need for greater interdependence; the hierarchies are broken down and rigid silos done away with, and lines of authority can become hazy at best. People accustomed to clear authority and marked territories often become confused and agitated when such expectations are cloudy and ill defined. And in a matrix-based organization where individuals often report to multiple bosses, the difficulties are compounded as issues of unclear authority, competition, and personal interests can undermine trust at many levels and in many ways.

4. **Rewards and recognition** can impair interpersonal and organizational trust through the way rewards are distributed and recognition is applied. In many of the organizations where we serve as consultants, favoritism has appeared as a factor influencing morale. Often it happens unintentionally, as a few people are recognized for their successes. However well earned such recognition is, others critical to the organization's success—and equally deserving—may be left feeling unappreciated. Even worse, financial rewards can be felt to be arbitrarily defined—based on who you know or what you have done lately—rather than as a result of achieving clearly defined goals and agreed-upon outcomes.

5. **Measured accountability** is at the heart of any good performance management process. The discipline necessary to build and maintain a fair and equitable system of performance management—especially in organizations that are crisis-reactive—is, in our experience, rare.

   Without the structure and discipline ensured by measured accountability, people will feel unprotected and at the whims of their bosses. The last fifty years' history of labor unions has been about unfairness and distrust in this area more than in any other. By ensuring clearly defined parameters and predictability of pay and promotion, trust tends to increase. Recognizing individuals for exceptional work on an organization or group level can be a minefield unless the criteria and method of selection are absolutely clear. Sadly, this rarely occurs—leaving mistrust and jealousy in its all-too-familiar wake. Most people wish for nothing more in this regard than to believe that they are protected and that fairness will prevail in the way they are evaluated and rewarded.

6. **Effective communication** is essential to ensure trust across units and the entire organization. While new technologies make much more information available than ever before, individuals still have the ability to maintain power and control through the withholding or selective distribution of information. Having effective structures and processes for ensuring access and distribution of information is central to maintaining trust at all levels. Put plainly, if people have information, they are likely to make better choices than if they don't. In a highly fluid and changing organization, leadership is obliged to assess options continually and to create alternatives for moving the organization forward. In organizations not known for openness or for the transparency of ideas across departments, committees, or with their boards, fluidity of communications will be rare. What is communicated often rests in the hands of a few, who determine what access others should have. One would expect high levels of mistrust.

Process or Maintenance Skills and Behaviors

As we have discussed, most of the focus of organizations has traditionally been on the content or task dimensions of work. Little training or time is regularly devoted to the process or maintenance skills that influence organizational life. There is no question that it is easier to comprehend the more concrete concepts, the clearly achievable goals, or the measurable outcomes of specific projects. The more ephemeral process domain has traditionally received little attention or training. Yet it is critical to understanding how work is accomplished, because it is here that much of the foundation for trust is laid.

Many leaders dismiss trust building as a waste of time. Nevertheless, research supports what many have intuitively understood all along: how people are treated and the feelings that result drive morale. In turn, morale has a direct impact on productivity, absenteeism, and efficiency. At the core of building greater trust is the maintenance of relationships among those who are dependent on one another and who must increasingly rely on shared information and mutual problem solving. The heart of effective team building lies in those elements that directly influence how much trust exists. The process or maintenance domain is the mortar that holds together both the intellectual ideas and the critical relationships that are necessary for success.

The central goal of the process domain is to define *how* work is accomplished. We need to ask how we can remove barriers for those who are working and help them accomplish organizational tasks as effectively as possible, while at the same time maintaining positive relationships, morale, and high levels of productivity. Here is where the human element is factored in to the work of the organization. Following are eight process or behavioral skills that have been found to help establish mutual trust.

Establish a climate of collaboration and participation

Collaboration and participation are at the heart of trust building within any organization or team. A well-known rule of thumb is that if people are going to be directly affected by an action, they should have the opportunity to influence the decisions surrounding it.

Create an atmosphere of support

This is an important step toward reducing the typical adversarial relationships spawned by the natural competition found in most work settings. At an organization level, breaking down the influence of autonomous silos can be a major step. At a practical level, leaders can reduce such natural divisiveness by establishing ground rules and working norms that contribute to a positive atmosphere, one that is driven by ideas and the search for common ground rather than by criticism and judgments.

Develop conflict resolution skills

If people are to begin trusting that they can speak the truth, deal with real differences, and not fear retribution, they need to understand how to resolve conflict. When people fear conflict, the best and most necessary conversations will never reach the table. This is not to say that conflict should be avoided. Rather, it needs to be encouraged and managed through the development of basic tools for effective listening, problem solving, and decision making. Trust is increased when participants realize that they can survive and even prosper in the face of a variety of healthy conflicts that are bound to arise. In the win-lose climate that prevails in many business settings, humiliation and intimidation often outweigh thoughtful listening and effective problem solving so that conflict is either denied or taken underground, never to see the light of rational conflict management techniques.

Improve listening skills

Listening is often a skill in search of an audience, because winning a point is often more important than exploring all the dimensions of a new idea. But listening is a critical skill for fostering trust. By establishing simple ground rules and structures so that all those involved have their say and, equally important, believe they have been heard, trust is almost immediately enhanced. Research shows that within a typical group of ten participants in an open discussion, three people will tend to dominate the discussion. Put the same people in another group, and they will tend to dominate again, regardless of the change in topic. The result will be that other voices, also with ideas of value, will withdraw from the discussion. The result will be disillusionment about the quality of decisions made by the group and, for that matter, by the organization. The first job of any facilitator wishing to build ideas or open a discussion is to equalize participation and to utilize the brainpower in the room. More often than not, this is a design issue where a little structure can counteract ineffective group norms or procedures, personal needs, or overzealous individuals.

The problem, of course, is that the few individuals who have been accustomed to dominating discussions will give up their control without a fight. However, something as simple as the use of a *nominal technique* can completely shift the dynamics of a group, ensuring full participation of all individuals and raising the listening quotient significantly. In this technique, participants are asked to write down their ideas on a topic in advance of any discussion. These ideas are then solicited one at a time around the group with each idea being posted on chart paper. Unlike traditional brainstorming, the quickest thinkers don't "win" and leave other participants in the dust. Once all ideas have been gleaned from the group, an open discussion can be encouraged and new ideas added to the list. Listening becomes one of the important outcomes of the discussion.

A second example of structure that promotes listening is to suggest that individuals cannot express a second idea until every person in the group has had the opportunity to respond to the first idea raised. Such a simple structure requires little facilitation, demands greater listening, and at the same time can foster greater involvement. All of this has a direct influence on levels of trust.

Develop effective feedback skills

Without feedback, change is perceptibly more difficult. Feedback is the key to individual and organizational knowledge of factors that block organizational effectiveness. It not only enables us to identify hindrances to progress but helps us monitor whether progress is in fact occurring. Without it there can be no accountability. When members of the organization witness people soliciting and then utilizing feedback, the credibility of the organization's leadership and the trust so essential to any change management effort are enhanced. But feedback is a teachable skill set that must be modeled consistently by leaders who respond openly and nondefensively to the feedback that arises. It is relatively rare that organizations make a commitment to training and the patient cultivating of trust so that individuals will risk providing the feedback that is needed and available.

Understand the willingness of people to take risks

Risk taking is a measure of individuals' openness to engage new ideas, of their level of concern with the judgments of others, and of their willingness to explore the future. At the heart of risk taking is the degree to which the individual's fear of failure or rejection inhibits the group's ability to engage novel ideas and to hear the truth, even when the idea might not be popular. Risk taking demands that individuals trust themselves sufficiently to test their ideas. It presupposes that they will be judged for their ideas rather than for their person—an assumption often heard verbalized but one that all too often is not observed.

Treat people with respect

The level of mutual respect people feel will determine whether they will give feedback, speak the truth, or share their ideas. If individuals can't trust that they will be treated with respect, the organization will find it difficult to solicit information or to explore the kinds of process issues influencing either productivity or morale. We find that the majority of organizations with which we work have issues around gaps in status, pay, perceived contributions, and entitlements. Yet if treating people with respect is not highly valued, exploration of any of these issues will be difficult.

Generate affection for the organization and its members
The affection an individual feels for another person, the team, or the institution can be a catalyst for the development of trust. The old saw "I don't have to like you to work with you" is probably true. However, when we like to be around people, enjoy their company and their style, and care about them as individuals, we will be more inclined to trust them. Similarly, having fun, responding to humor, and acknowledging people's good work can create channels through which affection and ultimately trust flow. Such affection can occur naturally as people of goodwill learn to appreciate one another through hard work and good intentions. Sensitive leaders find ways to celebrate, have fun, and build positive relationships on a regular basis. The dividends for building trust can be palpable.

These eight processes or behavioral attributes are among many others that help leaders establish or build mutual trust at the process level. As can be seen, they are interdependent, and most build on others. Listening, feedback, and respect tend to go together, as do conflict management skills and the ability to collaborate. Low scores in one attribute will tend to generate low scores in the other. Generating data and exploring the resulting patterns can be highly instructive for a team leader. Responding to such information will go a long way toward achieving higher trust levels and, in turn, better morale.

Trust Is Relative, Not Absolute

When we speak of trust being the outcome of a wide variety of independent variables, we imply that trust is difficult to define. There are quite literally hundreds of specific factors that can undermine one's personal effort to build trust with an individual, on a team, or within a larger organization. We have identified only a few of these. Which of these factors is responsible for actions such as initiating a malicious rumor or using sarcasm as a weapon to minimize an individual's contribution or being unwilling to own a mistake? We want to increase your awareness of how conscious a leader must be of the influence trust can have on the process of effective management and on such particular areas as planning or change management. The very fact that trust is such a complex concept suggests that organizations don't suddenly get trust, and they certainly are never able to mandate it. Instead, it is an ever-changing reality earned over time, one that they must nurture and attend to continually.

A sensitive team leader, a manager, or a CEO should be dealing with many of these variables influencing trust on a regular basis. He should be tuned in to pressure as it builds and then purposefully intervene so the general level of trust is not damaged. As in many aspects of the leader's role, well-conceived and well-placed metrics can provide insight and ultimately choices allowing leaders to act in a proactive rather than a reactive manner.

Measuring Trust in Your Organization

Having identified a range of variables that can influence the development of trust in a team or organization, we can relatively easily move to determining which of these factors are present and in what amounts in a particular organization. Because the complexities surrounding the establishment of trust can hardly be replicated, we are not particularly interested in comparing such scores to those of other organizations. After all, a tyrannical boss, blatant favoritism, a history of fear and intimidation by supervisors, or any of a number of other variables can alter any "neat" template defining trust. However, what follows is an instrument that can cast a powerful light on some of the variables known to influence trust. By asking a number of questions about the variables that determine the level of trust, you can get clues to the organizational culture and behaviors that impede the development of trust. Armed with such specific information, you will be able to design interventions that can begin to alter identified dysfunctional norms and the specific behaviors that can deter trust.

By carving out a set of meaningful questions based on observable behaviors, you create categories that can act as benchmarks, which can be graphed and can reveal measured improvement over time. As you will note, for this to occur, the questions must be behaviorally defined in a manner that allows the respondents to witness such behaviors in action. This does not demand a Ph.D. in psychometrics. It merely requires that the desired behaviors be observable and be defined in specific terms.

The Trust Survey

The Trust Survey (see Exercise 10) is a way of measuring the factors or behaviors that determine the level of trust in your organization. You may desire to measure only the process variables, or you may find that twelve of the items have more value to you and your particular organization. The great thing about using metrics is that if you know the desired outcome and what it looks like in action, you have within your grasp the means to measure it. This does not imply manipulating the outcome so that it matches what you desire. It assumes truth in advertising—a search for the truth by leaders who desire to improve the current state of affairs.

We should note that while any such list can be expanded or reduced based on the unique factors present in a team or the organization, the questions in this survey have proved to be particularly valuable within a wide range of organizations.

Scoring instructions and interpretation

Using such scaled item questionnaires for gathering metrics within an organization is often criticized because different people have different standards—some "grade" hard and others easy. However, the general patterns and trends of the metrics are usually consistent. By having a 10-point scale, the person responding is encouraged to state his feelings/opinion as strongly as he can. Most people seem to agree that items scored in the 7 to 10 range reflect strong positive scores, while a score of 6 becomes less acceptable and scores of 5 or below become more problematic. Few would deny that items scored in the 1, 2, 3, or 4 range on a 10-point scale reflect areas that may well require attention. The tendency is for those who score everything high to be offset by individuals who

The Trust Survey

Directions: Each of the following items reflects an aspect of trust. Determine the degree to which each behavior is present in your team or organization and **rate it on a scale of 1 to 10** in the space to the left of each statement (with **10 the highest,** suggesting an ample supply of the quality, and **1 the lowest,** suggesting a lack of the quality).

To what degree does your team or organization . . .

___ 1. Have the content knowledge necessary to meet the goals that will define its success?

___ 2. Have the technology necessary to provide optimal service to its members and clients?

___ 3. Have clearly defined and attainable goals by which to measure its success?

___ 4. Have clearly defined roles among the individuals who are responsible for leading it to success?

___ 5. Establish well-defined responsibilities for members and give them the requisite authority to successfully attain their goals?

___ 6. Reward and recognize its members for their efforts and particular achievements?

___ 7. Hold individuals measurably accountable for meeting their agreed-upon personal goals?

___ 8. Accomplish the tasks to which it has committed (to achieve its mission and goals)?

___ 9. Communicate effectively to various stakeholders and members what is expected of them?

___ 10. Communicate successful accomplishments and updates to progress being made?

___ 11. Engage essential constituents in collaborative problem solving and feedback in areas important to them?

___ 12. Create a climate of support and cooperation that minimizes self-interest and silo thinking?

___ 13. Have both the skills and the will needed to deal with past and present conflicts that influence trust?

___ 14. Demonstrate the skills of effective listening so that participants truly feel heard?

EXERCISE 10 cont'd

_____15. Have both the ability and desire to use feedback?

_____16. Exhibit openness in responding to the ideas of both members and clients alike?

_____17. Create a climate that promotes risk taking (that is, one that allows participants to speak the truth or initiate new ideas without fear of retribution)?

_____18. Establish a climate that demands that respect is shown to all participants?

_____19. Provide the opportunity for the kinds of celebration, fun, and play that build affection and care across various stakeholder groups?

20. In light of the questions above, what factor or factors need to be addressed if trust is to increase substantially in your team or organization? Please be specific and suggest why.

_____

_____

_____

_____

_____

---

tend to be supercritical and score most items lower than the average person. The key is to look at patterns of responses, choosing those in which the data appear consistent and there is little room for equivocation.

When scoring scaled items, try not to overanalyze or overinterpret the resulting data. When you lay out the results across a line, "what you see is usually what you get." Quite often the information will raise additional questions, which should be tracked, much like a hunter in search of game. You can do this through some carefully crafted interview questions or a focused open-ended questionnaire. The goal is to understand what people mean from the data provided and to get them to elaborate with specific examples whenever possible.

An example using the Trust Survey

The Trust Survey provides leaders a first look at the level of trust that exists in their group or organization at a particular time. It can be used as a general check of the overall climate or, for example, just prior to undertaking a change management or strategic planning initiative. As we have suggested, it is not meant to be a definitive analysis. Rather, it can help to focus on particular areas that need addressing. As our example will illustrate, it is not unusual for three or four of the responses to be scored relatively high (suggesting an abundance of those particular qualities) as well as three or four that are scored low (suggesting a less than desirable amount of those particular qualities). For example, imagine the following array of scores from a twenty-nine-person staff of a division embarking on a process to reorganize their current management structure. In such an effort, one would hope that both listening and the willingness to risk would be high. Yet item 17 should give pause to the leadership team.

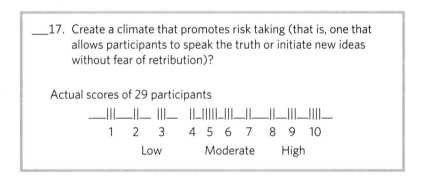

___17. Create a climate that promotes risk taking (that is, one that allows participants to speak the truth or initiate new ideas without fear of retribution)?

Actual scores of 29 participants

—|||—||— |||— ||—|||||—|||—||—||—|||—||||—
 1 2 3   4 5 6 7 8 9 10
    Low   Moderate   High

If we were to take an average of the scores shown (5.9), we would probably not be very worried. However, if we look at the distribution of scores across the line, we can easily see that more than a third of the participants responded with scores of 4 or below. Apparently they do not feel safe, and that fear of retribution—for whatever current or historic reasons—is influencing their responses. Compare this with a nearly equal number who registered very high scores (7–10). We can only imagine the tension that might exist between the two groups and the repercussion such scores would have for the necessary dialogues that need to occur if the reorganization effort is to be successful. This pattern is underscored when we look at the array of scores for item 14, relating to listening. Again, although the mean score of the twenty-nine respondents is 5.7, fourteen individuals scored between 7 and 10, while more than one-third scored between 1 and 4. Obviously for a significant number of individuals the climate is not only unsafe but they do not feel heard. Typically, the response of these individuals would be to withdraw from the process and eventually to not buy in to whatever decisions result from the change efforts.

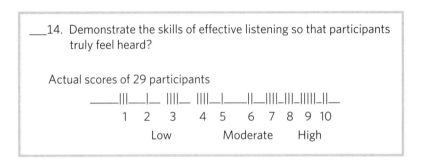

Similar patterns were found in item 16 (Exhibit openness in responding to the ideas of both members and clients alike?) and in item 12 (Create a climate of support and cooperation that minimizes self-interest and silo thinking?). Taking these four items and assessing elements common to them all, it becomes clear that a significant number in the twenty-nine-person group perceive the work climate as one in which they are free to share their opinions and in which their ideas are heard and, in general, valued. The problem is that nearly 50 percent feel differently, a significant number of them quite differently. Why this result occurred and what to do about it would be important if the key leaders seek to gain full participation and eventual ownership of the decisions that evolve from the change management process and their effort to restructure their organization. They will need to seek more information and then commit to change in the process or maintenance domain, since not doing so may have strong implications for the future morale and bottom-line productivity of the organization.

Not all of the metrics reflected this kind of problem for this organization. The responses for the majority of the nineteen items were skewed toward the positive end of the continuum. For example, the first four items (relating to content and product aspects of the management process) averaged more than 7, with half of the respondents in the 8–10 range. In fact, the responses to item 3, related to clearly defined and obtainable goals, appeared as follows:

Actual scores of 29 participants

1 2 3 4 5 6 7 8 9 10
Low   Moderate   High

For the organization's leaders the results overall were obviously good news, bad news. The organization was apparently making good progress within the task/product domain and was falling short in some areas of organization. However, more important, in areas relating to how the work was being accomplished, the leaders now had real choices. If the leaders decided there was value in improving the process or maintenance dimension, the explicit nature of the low-scored items would provide insight they did not have previously. Question 20 (the open-ended question) provided some further information that was useful. Following are some examples of the comments:

- Four individuals suggested in different ways that the key leadership group of four acted like a cabal of like-minded people for whom collaboration was a pretense used only to placate the larger group. They said they believed that many of the decisions had already been made and implied that unless the leaders were serious about collaboration, they shouldn't bother with the charade of participation.

- Three individuals commented on the boss's unwillingness to listen to others.

- Three people alluded to favoritism that they felt needed attention.

- Two people indicated that there was no time for dealing with interpersonal issues because there were always deadlines to meet in such a fast-paced and competitive marketplace.

- Five individuals said they had few issues, and things were just fine as they were.

While these various responses mirrored the concerns or lack of concerns identified in the scaled-item questions, the specificity of the comments added an important dimension to the scaled-item data. Clearly there were strong differences in the division, at the very time the restructuring was intended to pull the group together.

Since this diagnostic metric (the Trust Survey), is not meant to provide more than a sense of the factors influencing trust, it probably raised more questions than it answered. However, what the leaders of this division did learn was that they had a problem brewing among a significant group of people engaged in the process of restructuring their organization. It would make sense to probe further and ask more questions, but *only if they were prepared to deal with the issues being driven to the surface.* To not act in an open, nondefensive, and responsive manner would send a clear message to the group that such feedback was not being valued or taken seriously. In this case, the leaders decided it was important to move ahead and take a hard look at their issues. They agreed that a few additional open-ended questions would help in their deliberations.

In this case, they felt that additional anonymous information would add clarity to the data from the Trust Survey and allow them to move more intelligently into a problem-solving mode. After all of the data had been presented to the group during an all-staff meeting, the additional questions were generated by the divisional vice president and three representatives of the group of twenty-nine. They realized that if trust were to increase, the vice president and his leadership group would have to become more transparent in how they generated and analyzed such information. By utilizing people from the group of twenty-nine, the effort represented a first step in reducing the perception that collaboration was a charade and that solutions (probably including the view that the restructuring was already predetermined) were fabricated in advance of such large-group sessions. It reflects nothing more complicated than an attempt to bring clarity to several of the scaled items. The results of the effort to gather additional metrics are shown in Exercise 11.

Follow-Up to the Trust Survey

Directions: Based on the summarized data from the Trust Survey we shared with you, please respond to the following questions so that we can be better prepared to address some of your issues during our next planning meeting.

1. Please suggest three things you would do to increase our ability to listen to one another as we work together in our restructuring efforts and in the future.

   a._____

   b._____

   c._____

2. What factors do you believe hinder people in our division from being willing to take risks? Please be specific.

   a._____

   b._____

3. In the recent Trust Survey, half the members of this group indicated that we have problems of self-interest influencing our decision making and that we remain territorial in our work together. What would you do to address this issue that exists for so many of your peers?

   a._____

   _____

   b._____

   _____

4. Please circle the number on the scale below to indicate the degree to which you believe that favoritism gets in the way of our working together in this division.

1	2	3	4	5	6	7	8	9	10
Little favoritism				Some favoritism			A great deal of favoritism		

5. If you believe favoritism does get in the way (you scored it 6 or above), how does it manifest itself? Please be specific

   _____

   _____

   _____

Bringing Truth and Rationality to Management

The leadership team did three things by undertaking this brief follow-up questionnaire. First, they demonstrated to the division that they were taking the original information seriously and were committed to working in a highly visible manner, owning the problems and working toward their solution. Second, they used the information gathering, analysis, interpretation, and eventual problem solving in a manner that would model a greater degree of collaboration by involving more of the membership in all phases of the process. Third, they used information from the second questionnaire to help create a more open meeting by initiating specific suggestions for ensuring more effective listening in the meetings themselves and by crediting the staff for ideas gleaned from the questionnaire.

Their lesson was that building metrics into their restructuring initiative would only be as valuable as the information was trusted. The follow-up was perceived as reflecting a real effort at collaboration. The leadership team recognized that utilizing easily gathered data could add credibility to the management process and become a vehicle for helping to establish a more open and trusted relationship with their staff.

This simple example demonstrates that *measuring what matters* is at the heart of good management. The first step is being conscious enough to ask the right questions. Next is having the courage to act on the information in an open and transparent manner. No one likes to learn, as in this case, that nearly a third of your organization is disgruntled and that large numbers of individuals mistrust management's intentions. Nor is it easy to put yourself and your leadership team under the scrutiny of your peers and direct reports. In this situation, the benefits of taking this kind of risk had almost immediate value because of how the data were gathered, how the resulting information was distributed, and, finally, how the information was dealt with. The questionnaires that were developed, the data that were shared, and the issues that were engaged all reflected work in the process domain which, in fact, was the source of many of the issues that were identified. It is also the area that traditionally receives the least attention because of the focus elsewhere, on getting the work done. The long-term consequences on morale and productivity are seldom factored in.

For this division, the exploration into the process domain uncovered a variety of issues during the next year. As trust increased, so did candor and the willingness to risk. The leadership discovered that it had been isolated from the truth, with surprising consequences that very likely would not have gained visibility had the leaders not been willing to utilize their simple metrics. They made the following discoveries:

1. Well-intentioned leaders had, over the years, created a culture of dependency resulting from their control of all critical decisions. One consequence was an increasingly passive staff, some of whom resented the dependency and some of whom welcomed it (the reason for the split on the scaled-item questions).

2. This dependency also fostered an increasing aversion to conflict of any kind because problems, if they were to be dealt with at all, were resolved by the leadership team—so why bother?

3. The lack of faith in collaboration centered on the leaders wanting things done their way, a perception that resulted in increased passivity, decreasing initiative, and little risk taking—but increasing resentment.

4. The result was that individuals built loyalties in their subgroups (the division was divided into four departments) and showed little inclination to go out of their way for the good of the larger division or for the organization as a whole.

Summary

Using metrics is an organic process in which seeds (in this case good, tough questions) are planted and a crop (information) is cultivated. The way in which the garden is tended will determine the kind of crop that is harvested. In the case we have looked at, the leadership team began to harvest new choices for themselves in their division, including a greater level of trust, more openness and collaboration, and a more highly empowered workforce. Initial skepticism, along with a show-me attitude, gave way to an increasing belief that management was committed to greater transparency and collaboration.

This turnaround occurred because the leaders were willing to look beyond the bottom-line concerns that had driven them for so long. The leaders began by asking questions about the process or *how* work was being accomplished. While it seemed simple and straightforward, this group joined the ranks of the few, since such exploration is uncommon in most organizations. The following questions could be used as a filter when considering task and process issues of a team or organization.

How often does a committee or task force undertake a highly charged assignment among a group of individuals with long-standing differences and a history of mistrust?

How often does the organization undertake a planning initiative when there is a palpable mistrust among the leaders who are expected to lead the process, with no effort to resolve the unfinished business?

How often do the participants in a major change effort lack the requisite skills for engaging the community of individuals who will be influenced by the outcomes?

How often do our leaders show disrespect toward those with whom they work—often in public settings—without repercussions or accountability?

In all human relationships if we don't take steps to resolve tensions, conflict, and aberrant behaviors, things will get worse before they get better. The limited time individuals have when pushed to maximum performance leaves virtually no room for asking the hard questions raised here or for actually dealing with the underlying tensions that can influence productivity and morale. The result is a rush to problem solving and decision making before individuals or the group have the opportunity to buy in to the outcome. As a result, all too often at the point of implementation, the apparent agreement disintegrates.

The danger is not that the intelligent participants of goodwill cannot generate good ideas in a short amount of time. Rather, it is that time will not be taken to generate sufficient trust among those same individuals to ensure successful implementation of the ideas. In many ways, idea generation is the easiest part. What is challenging is creating a climate where candor, feedback, and the expression of real differences can occur with skill, and where people feel heard and respected even for their expressions of divergent views.

Our goal has been to show how simple, straightforward questions can open a team, a department, or a division to its reality. Done well, the process outlined here will result in greater objectivity on the part of leaders when undertaking challenging tasks that demand cooperation and trust to accomplish. The metrics generated can be a litmus test for a group and a means of keeping them focused on the kinds of issues that can have an indelible influence on the life of any organization.

7

Leadership Matters

A Case Study of a Manager

*Bless those who challenge us, for they remind us of the doors
we have closed and those we have yet to open. They are big
medicine.* —NAVAJO PRAYER

Earlier we told of the peevish old man who self-righteously protected the seat next to him on the bus for what turned out to be an imaginary friend. The brash young man who called his bluff and sat unceremoniously in the seat placing the old man's suitcase on his lap was willing to wait until the friend showed up. All too often the old man's behavior would be rewarded, actually reinforced, because no one would hold him accountable for being so rude, intimidating, and obnoxious. How stunned he must have been watching his suitcase sail out the window—a real consequence for his selfish and controlling behavior.

This chapter is about how metrics that are simple to develop and easy to use can gain the attention of difficult employees who, perhaps for years, have manipulated those around them and become known as problems. They exist in nearly every organization, these long-term contributors turned pain in the neck. They are often redlined, shunted into nonessential jobs or simply tolerated for fear that firing them would lead to difficult lawsuits, with their records showing they had been systematically rewarded over the years.

A Reluctant Jake

Recently, a client took me aside and said, " I am confused by a problem that places me between a rock and a hard place. I have a twenty-five-year veteran who has been a manager for half that time, and he's not getting with the program. He's paying lip service to the new values and changes we're introducing."

I asked him to continue, but I could see what was coming: another case of a long-term employee not adapting to the new demands of a changing organization. After years of loyalty, this person couldn't just be discarded. As the client continued, I learned that the situation was worse than that. "In the past, Jake has always done exactly what was expected. He is demanding, highly controlling, and often insensitive; he intimidates most of his employees and will not tolerate disagreement or his authority being questioned. Over time he's become even less tolerant, he periodically flies off the handle, and he has been known to humiliate his subordinates in public.

"When getting the job done was the sole definition of management, he was often acknowledged for putting in long hours and never complaining. Put plainly, management never had to worry about his area. But, now, with our 'new day' management style, his approach strikes at the heart of two of our core values—cooperation and participation. I don't know what to do about him. The complaints keep pouring in, but people are afraid to confront him directly because he has a reputation of getting even if you ever get on his bad side."

My client painted a picture that is almost a classic in modern-day mismanagement. It suggested that the following may have happened:

- Management had not developed a balanced process of supervision in which product or outcome goals were to some degree balanced by attention to process or maintenance goals. In other words, there had been little or no recognition that how one manages, deals with people, and builds morale has any value when compared with the more easily measured outcome-based goals of upper management. Such a short-term mentality is losing favor by increasing numbers who recognize there are measurable bottom-line payoffs from attention to *how* such work is accomplished over time.

- Because Jake's bosses over the years didn't have to worry about him—and there were few outward signs of trouble—they simply let him alone. They even joked about how "there was never any trouble in Jake's area," while they winked at his obvious tyrannical behavior.

- As he became more abrasive, and even arrogant, Jake's supervisors didn't know what to do with him. He had always been rewarded for the exact behaviors that were no longer acceptable. In fact, during his management career, hardly a year went by in which Jake had not been given a larger-than-average raise. If Jake were fired (which most of my client's peers were suggesting), he might, with good reason, sue the proverbial pants off the organization.

- The supervisors who managed Jake and other managers in the organization were not only averse to conflict but simply lacking in the skills to deal with many others in the organization who had been ignored and not dealt with over the years.

One of the secrets rarely discussed concerning the downsizing and reengineering trends of the 1980s and early 1990s was management's desire to get rid of employees who had long been rewarded for their abrasive and autocratic management styles or who, for whatever reasons, no longer fit into management's plans.

Supervisory Incompetence

On the one hand, upper management was guilty of gross negligence—not providing certain managers with feedback, education, or disciplinary action for blatant acts of hostile and aggressive behavior toward their employees. They had not held their managers accountable and were just as much to blame as are the Jakes of the world who have been systematically rewarded and reinforced for obnoxious and often destructive behaviors. Then, Jake stood to *suffer the consequences for their failure to deal effectively with such obviously improper management behavior.*

On the other hand, the rewards system seduced Jake and others like him into believing that they were "the best" because they had been tolerated, patronized, or ignored for so long. In this organization, Jake and others inferred that lack of attention indicated support for their behavior and their overall approach to management. The lack of supervision reinforced dysfunctional behavior.

Predictably, when Bob, Jake's boss, finally gave him the feedback he needed, Jake was outraged. He fumed that he felt betrayed after being praised for his approach to management for so long. "What have I done wrong?" he bellowed. Hadn't he done everything he had been asked? After all, he had never heard anything about being too aggressive, belligerent, hostile, or any of the other criticisms that were now being hurled in his direction.

Certainly, he had been tough, but the job demanded that he be tough. "And besides," he queried, "who are these individuals suddenly attacking my reputation? Let them accuse me to my face. If they are afraid, they don't deserve to be listened to."

So, my client asked, "What is the antidote for this very real and difficult problem?" While he recognized that he and others were guilty of their own supervisory misconduct, he was more interested in quick action that would turn around a rapidly deteriorating situation with Jake and, presumably, others. He faced an uncomfortable question of ethics on the one hand and practical problem solving on the other.

From a systems perspective it was essential that management recognize that Jake was a symptom and not the problem. Clearly, it was going to be much more difficult to *implement* the concepts of collaboration, cooperation, and participative management than to understand them.

One problem of this "new management" perspective is that the words are so easily spoken and so difficult, without proper training, to make meaningful. The values of domination, control, and intimidation appeared to be deeply ingrained in the system, just as the norm of not really supervising or not holding people accountable for their negative management behaviors had been acceptable. Meaningful change would require time, financial commitment, and retraining so that the spoken values aligned themselves with the skills and behaviors of the new management practices that were now in vogue.

Above all, change would require upper management to model more positive and effective behaviors. Top managers had to first be willing to own their part of the problem. They had consistently focused their attention on short-term results at the expense of long-term morale and productivity. Historically their response to such a predicament would be to "fix" those representing the problem or symptoms. They failed to comprehend how, over time, they had colluded to both create and maintain the problem.

As for Jake and others like him, something had to occur soon because continuing to condone his abusive attitude made any efforts at meaningful change a joke in the eyes of the employees. While the system change might take years, the issue of Jake had to be addressed immediately. People were, in fact, waiting to see if the new initiatives by management had teeth. Dealing with Jake would prove to be a highly visible and critical first step.

360-Degree Feedback: A Response to Jake and His Manager's Dilemma

Most of the time, firing someone represents a last straw after tolerating ineffective behavior for years. It's the angry response of "I've finally had all I can take of so and so's attitude." As with Jake, where people had long hoped that he would somehow get the message through osmosis or some other magical act, there had been little feedback, and no reeducation through appropriate courses or mentoring. The process known as 360-degree feedback provides a decisive, positive, and ethical response to Jake. But it demands that management acknowledge that they are part of the problem and that Jake deserves a real opportunity to change and get with the program. The underlying assumption is that it is unfair to expect quick change after years of tolerating and reinforcing his abusive approach to management.

This approach *cannot* be an insidious ploy on the part of management to prove their case against Jake so they can get rid of him and not be sued. Without belief that he and others like him are capable of change and deserve the opportunity, the effort will result in a self-fulfilling prophecy: failure for Jake and the sad realization by management and others that they knew all along he couldn't be saved. Going through the motions is not acceptable—real effort to save Jake is essential. Put simply, he is a victim of management's negligence.

For his part, Jake would have a tough challenge ahead. Change of this magnitude is never easy, especially when it deals with long-standing habits and previously supported behaviors. But, it needs to be noted, *we are not attempting to change the essence of who Jake is, only how he chooses to behave toward those who report to him.*

This distinction is critical and is built on the premise that Jake, as is the case with the old man on the bus, knew exactly what he was doing when he chose to be abusive, intimidating, or controlling. It also assumes that, at fifty-two and with nearly thirteen years to go before retirement, he had considerable incentive to alter his style and general approach to management.

Too often we are led to believe that someone is a lost cause because his particular behavior as a leader is inherent in his *nature,* that some immutable, genetically implanted pattern conditioned him at an early age and is impossible to change. But people behave in ways that are easy, comfortable, and rewarding. If such behaviors are no longer deemed acceptable and new behaviors are rewarded, they can change. Also, if the consequences for continuing in old behaviors are potentially negative enough, the chance of real change occurring goes up.

If Jake was required to alter his management behavior to maintain his positive job performance ratings, and ultimately to keep his job, the chances for real change occurring would increase dramati-

cally. Measuring change on Jake's part is at the heart of this process.

The feedback we've been speaking about could help Jake take his situation seriously and focus his attention on what it took to be successful. Specific action steps could follow; they could be bench-marked to track his success and to determine whether his response warranted further support and, if so, what kind.

The Origins of Data-Based 360-Degree Feedback

In 1975, our small consulting firm in Philadelphia developed the first approach to what is now known as 360-degree feedback. We were not trying to help leaders in trouble survive; rather, our program focused on helping good leaders use their time more effectively, motivate others, conduct better meetings, deal with conflict, or handle specific troubling problems. We called the process "Executive Role Counseling," and it was built on the following assumptions:

- Most of us have difficulty understanding our impact on others. We are literally too close to ourselves and lack the objectivity to perceive ourselves dispassionately and accurately.

- We need descriptive data to help us be rational as we attempt to scope out our leadership reality and increase our effectiveness.

- When most people begin to understand the consequences of their behavior—and are provided specific help and strategies to overcome what they and others perceive as negative results—they will be motivated to improve their own performance.

- Most astounding is what happens to people when they realize that there are few secrets. The hard reality is that others know us well, warts and all. The 360-degree feedback process, through systematically gathering candid information from those we influence, reveals just how transparent we are.

- If we assume that others really know our frailties and foibles, we can begin to address these shortcomings more directly and honestly. Knowing them truly changes the game of life for many and reduces the need to continue fooling both ourselves and others.

Over the years, the truth of these assumptions has been translated into an entire movement within modern management.[1] By offering ineffective leaders like Jake periodic assessments of their actual management behavior, management supervisors can help them work toward behavioral improvements that can dramatically influence the quality of both their leadership and their individual effectiveness.

In the rest of this chapter, we will see the detailed strategy we used to help Jake turn around and become a more effective leader at the age of fifty-two. The process is neither costly nor complex and is within the capacity of any boss who has the patience, commitment, and sensitivity to help an employee save his job. It is a reflection of what is best about the new management strategies being pursued within organizations.

A 360-Degree Turnaround

After Jake's typically defensive response to the idea that he might be a less-than-perfect manager, rather than attacking his behavior and obvious denial, Bob suggested to him that he had a dilemma. While he didn't want to put undue weight on hearsay, if people were afraid and intimidated, he needed to ascertain the issues and try to correct them. Bob believed that Jake would want the truth. That meant he would require additional information. He suggested that he and Jake develop a number of questions to describe the behaviors they each valued most in a leader within the organization. They would then decide who among those familiar with Jake as a boss, colleague, or friend could best respond to the agreed-upon questions. Eventually, the two of them would decide if Jake should address any issues suggested by the data; if necessary, they would create action strategies that they could monitor together. He noted that even if the data for some reason turned out to be less than positive, the process would be perceived as a developmental intervention, providing new choices for Jake and the opportunity to improve his effectiveness.

Jake grudgingly accepted the process. He admitted that during his entire career he had received virtually no feedback except for discussions about salary increases and an occasional pat on the back when he completed a project. Still, he had concerns and wondered why he was being singled out in this instance when there were lots more like him. He was suspicious, but he couldn't resist a procedure that would potentially disprove critics who were tarnishing his good name.

Bob asked him to list ten to fifteen leadership behaviors he thought were important to his being a competent leader, giving special attention to those values that the leadership team supported and that represented the newly directed shift in management practices. As his boss, Bob would also think of an equal number of values and behavioral characteristics; then they would negotiate a satisfactory list of between twelve and twenty questions based on these behaviors. The two lists were as follows:

Jake's List

1. Is organized
2. Is goal directed
3. Maintains control
4. Commands respect
5. Communicates well
6. Takes charge
7. Disciplines people fairly
8. Holds people accountable
9. Has a sense of humor
10. Treats people equally
11. Gives clear directions
12. Runs an efficient meeting
13. Is open to new ideas

Bob's List

1. Listens well
2. Works well with people
3. Delegates effectively
4. Is well organized
5. Collaborates effectively
6. Holds people accountable
7. Communicates clearly
8. Is easy to approach
9. Problem-solves effectively
10. Plans effectively
11. Is good at conflict resolution
12. Is patient and calm
13. Is a good meeting facilitator
14. Is open to feedback
15. Treats people fairly

Jake and Bob agreed that they could each choose five of the criteria from their own lists and that these criteria would eventually be laid out as items on a ten-point scale. Then they would agree on as many others as they could, up to twenty.

It was obvious from the outset that Jake and Bob were approaching management from "slightly" different points of view. As might be expected, Jake's list leaned toward behaviors that were control oriented. Bob, on the other hand, clearly aware of other issues, focused more on process—on Jake's relationships with those working for him. The ensuing discussion enabled Bob to explain his own view of management and why he felt some items were important to him. Similarly, Jake was able to articulate his own views. Leadership Development Assessment, Part 1, is the eventual measurement instrument they built for Jake. (See Figure 17.)

The assessment instrument was designed to reveal many of Jake's strengths and limitations. Jake was to buy in on all the items, and there was to be a clear understanding why the particular items were being chosen over others. The intent was not to paint Jake into a corner and slight his many strengths. However, it was also evident that some of his strengths had been taken to extremes, and they were no longer proving to be assets to him.

In addition, not all aspects of Jake's leadership that were causing problems for employees were identified in the fourteen agreed-upon scaled items. Many of the issues that were not identified would be uncovered in the second part of the assessment. With this in mind, Jake and Bob agreed on a number of open-ended questions that would allow for an even more telling picture of his management style. The questions were designed to provide specific examples of how he diluted or enhanced his effectiveness.

Finally, Jake was asked to answer both the open-ended questions and the scaled items from two perspectives: first, as he saw himself in his role at the time and, second, as he believed those responding—on average—would perceive him. In a sense, he would try to predict what the responses would be from those whose opinions he was seeking. Because he had had so little feedback over the years, there would inevitably be areas of discrepancy that would

FIGURE 17
Leadership Development Assessment, Part 1

Indicate your relationship to Jake:
____friend or family ____ employee ____ colleague ____ other

Directions: Please respond to each of the following items relating to my behavior as a leader based on your personal knowledge of me. I am attempting to assess my own effectiveness and would appreciate your being as honest and straightforward as possible. Return your anonymous evaluation in the attached envelope to the outside resource, who will tabulate and interpret your responses. I will then be given the results and will use them as part of an ongoing leadership development process. Thank you.

For each item, circle the number on a scale of 1 to 10 that best suggests Jake's usual behavior. In number 1, for example, 1 = most disorganized and 10 = most organized.

1.　1　2　3　4　5　6　7　8　9　10
IS DISORGANIZED　　　　　　　　IS WELL ORGANIZED

2.　1　2　3　4　5　6　7　8　9　10
IS DIFFICULT TO APPROACH　　　　IS EASY TO APPROACH

3.　1　2　3　4　5　6　7　8　9　10
DOES NOT LISTEN　　　　　　　　LISTENS WELL

4.　1　2　3　4　5　6　7　8　9　10
DOES NOT SET GOALS　　　　　　SETS CLEAR GOALS

5.　1　2　3　4　5　6　7　8　9　10
DOES NOT HOLD PEOPLE ACCOUNTABLE　　HOLDS PEOPLE ACCOUNTABLE

6.　1　2　3　4　5　6　7　8　9　10
RUNS INEFFECTIVE MEETINGS　　RUNS EFFECTIVE, ENGAGING MEETINGS

7.　1　2　3　4　5　6　7　8　9　10
IS A POOR COMMUNICATOR　　　IS AN EFFECTIVE COMMUNICATOR

8.　1　2　3　4　5　6　7　8　9　10
USES LITTLE OR NEGATIVE HUMOR　　USES HUMOR EFFECTIVELY

FIGURE 17 cont'd
Leadership Development Assessment, Part 1

9.	1	2	3	4	5	6	7	8	9	10
	TREATS PEOPLE UNFAIRLY						TREATS PEOPLE FAIRLY			
10.	1	2	3	4	5	6	7	8	9	10
	DOES NOT COLLABORATE EFFECTIVELY						COLLABORATES EFFECTIVELY			
11.	1	2	3	4	5	6	7	8	9	10
	IS NOT OPEN TO FEEDBACK						IS OPEN TO FEEDBACK			
12.	1	2	3	4	5	6	7	8	9	10
	FINDS DELEGATING DIFFICULT						DELEGATES EFFECTIVELY			
13.	1	2	3	4	5	6	7	8	9	10
	HANDLES CONFLICT POORLY						HANDLES CONFLICT WITH EASE			
14.	1	2	3	4	5	6	7	8	9	10
	IS OFTEN IMPATIENT OR REACTIVE						IS PATIENT AND CALM			

contribute to his understanding of his own leadership. By estimating what he believed others would say and comparing these responses to his own view—as well as to those of his supervisor, Bob—he could ascertain how in touch he was with reality. Further, he would learn if and where his own perceptions had been flawed.

The Leadership Development Assessment, Part 2 (see Figure 18), is the second instrument Jake and Bob agreed to. Again, the questions are simple, direct, and potentially useful for gathering information.

Laying the Groundwork for 360-Degree Feedback

Part of the success of the 360-degree experience would depend on how believable Jake was in convincing the respondents that he

FIGURE 18
Leadership Development Assessment, Part 2

Indicate your relationship to Jake:
_____friend or family _____ employee _____ colleague _____ other

Directions: Please answer each of the following questions in the space provided. Specific examples will be greatly appreciated and will enable Jake to focus on areas of needed development.

Question 1: Please indicate Jake's three greatest strengths or assets he has as a leader that you believe he should maintain.

1._____

2._____

3._____

Question 2: When you see Jake approaching, what are the three strongest feelings or thoughts that come to your mind?

1. _____   2. _____   3. _____

Question 3: What are the three behaviors that are most critical in blocking Jake from being as effective a leader as he could be?

1._____

2._____

3._____

Question 4: If you could give Jake two pieces of advice that would help him in his role but that, for whatever reason, you might be afraid to give him, what would they be? (Again, please be specific.)

1._____
_____

2._____
_____

Question 5: If you were Jake, in his role as leader, what would you do immediately to improve morale and productivity? Please be specific and assume no change in personnel and no large windfall of money in your budget.

1._____
_____

2._____
_____

3._____
_____

seriously intended to take a hard look at his own behavior. As far as his employees were concerned—many of whom had problems with him—they not only had to believe in his good intentions but they also had to feel secure in their anonymity.

We cannot overestimate how fearful people become when their careers can be jeopardized. This was especially true with Jake, who had often retaliated against those who crossed him. To make matters worse, his defensive attitude and pattern of denial offered little reason to expect much from his initial efforts. For many respondents the question was, Why should I risk potential negative consequences for telling the truth? Again, building safety and confidentiality into the process was essential, as was the need for Jake to show his enthusiasm for the process itself.

Orienting Jake and His Employees

In the first meeting between Jake and Bob, something unexpected happened that helped to create a more positive attitude. After hearing the concerns over his behavior and management style—especially given the direction the organization was taking—Jake had responded in a typical fashion. He had blustered and attacked his accuser. He suggested that Bob was unfair and that he had never heard any of these concerns previously. Instead of rolling over and passively accepting his outrageous and intimidating behavior, Bob said calmly, "This appears to be exactly what people have been talking about, and it's no longer acceptable. Your typical response to someone who differs from your opinion or way of thinking is to attack, deny, and overpower. If you did it to me, a person with some authority over you, I can only imagine what you would do to one of your direct reports.

"Let's face it, you can be threatening and overbearing. I don't need much more than your present reaction to validate much of what people are saying. However, to be fair, and in order not to judge you prematurely, I'm going to suggest a means of approaching the data so that we can develop a clear picture of your true situation as objectively as possible."

Bob then laid out the fundamentals of 360-degree feedback and what it would take to make it work.[2] He expected that Jake would engage the process fully and openly, and that, based on what the data revealed, he and Jake would spend the next few months working to get him on track.

After perhaps three months, they would review the results of the action plans based on the 360-degree data and take a more definitive look at Jake's future. What made Jake all of a sudden so conscientious and open was that at some level he knew that the game was up and that he would have to begin taking a serious look at his own management style as well as at the new ideas advanced by upper management. And it was also clear that Bob's own behavior and his attention to Jake, who had been a simmering problem for a long time, was changing as Bob's own skills and attitudes began to reflect the new direction of management.

As a result, after some coaching from Bob, Jake discussed the situation with his nine employees. He asked for their help in his self-improvement program by filling out two questionnaires. He told them that he had heard some unsettling information and wanted a better picture of reality. He even stated that he was prepared to review the results with the group. He indicated that he was also asking his boss, Bob, and six to ten others (from outside the workplace) who knew him well to complete the questionnaires. He also mentioned that he would compare the collected data with his own assessment of himself and what he thought they and others would say.

He then distributed the two assessment questionnaires, along with envelopes addressed to an external professional previously used by the division. The consultant would tally and interpret the data and ensure confidentiality. Because he was interested in each person's *individual* response, he requested that the members of the group sit some distance apart.

Finally, he told the group that they would be working closely with his own boss to understand the data and to build specific action plans. He said that he would probably ask them to respond to the questionnaires again in six months to evaluate his progress; he emphasized that it was important for them to be candid because the current information would be used to benchmark his improvement. He emphasized that what he was doing was consistent with management's new emphasis on data-based inquiry. Although the process would be challenging, he saw it as essential to his growth and hoped that he could count on their candor and cooperation.

Analysis and Interpretation of 360-Degree Feedback

Even though the two instruments were designed for simplicity and cost effectiveness, they generated a huge amount of data that could be used to support Jake in his efforts at self-improvement. As always, with a sample of only twenty respondents, including himself, the results should be accepted with reservations. Nevertheless, the fourteen questions in the Leadership Development Assessment, Part 1, would predictably generate some valuable and irrefutable patterns of behavior.

The data from Jake's nine employees could be taken alone and would be extremely helpful. The added data from family, friends, and colleagues, however, would make more apparent the areas of strength and needed development. Furthermore, the potential discrepancies between Jake's perceptions and others', including Bob's, could provide additional useful information. Once one begins to ask the right questions and probe the obvious relationships, reviewing such data is not difficult. But since we rarely do this, the following approach should prove helpful.

The Great Reversal Approach

The first rule of all data analysis and interpretation is that it matters little how valid, reliable, and objective the results are if the individual or organization doesn't own them. The challenge for Jake, as it would be for anyone receiving such information, was for him to consider it a gift, perhaps a once-in-a-lifetime opportunity to take a hard look at himself and move forward as a more effective leader.

Most of us rarely if ever receive quality feedback that reflects who we are to others and how we affect them. It is little wonder, then, that our misperceptions are rampant. Because Jake pushed people away, intimidated those around him, and controlled the information he received, he heard what he wanted to hear and virtually never received anything but positive feedback. Realizing that it would be difficult for Jake to hear what could be uncomfortable information, Bob had him take the tallied information overnight, without any accompanying interpretation. He instructed Jake in great detail how he might begin to draw implications for his role as a leader. In addition, he asked Jake to consider what forces in his early development, as well as in later adult years, had shaped his current values and approach to leadership.

To help Jake gain some distance and objectivity, Bob suggested that he attempt to act as though he, Jake, was a consultant who was asked to answer some of the following questions about Jake the leader, person, friend, and family man. Having responded to these questions as fully as possible, he would then return to Bob, who would act as if he were Jake the client, and they would engage in a dialogue. He would ask questions to clarify Jake's interpretation so that they could both understand as much as possible from the data.

Clearly, Jake knew considerably more about the results, their historical roots, and implications than anyone else, and it was hoped that by encouraging him to view the data as a consultant he would develop the distance necessary to be a more dispassionate interpreter. Since Jake realized that Bob was prepared to study the same results and would familiarize himself with their nuances, it was to his advantage to be as open and forthcoming as possible; otherwise, he might appear ignorant, insensitive, or both.

By now, it would have become evident to Jake that this undertaking was serious business and that it connoted a very different approach to him, his job, and, quite possibly, his career. Reviewing the results in this light would make it much more difficult for Jake to deny or avoid many of the implications from the data. Bob provided Jake with twelve questions to guide him in his role as "consultant to himself."

1. Among the fourteen scaled items in Part 1, which of the scores appear in the good to excellent range, usually defined as between 8 and 10 on the ten-point scale? (Most people will find scores from 5 to 7 in the acceptable range, even though when asked whether they would be acceptable for those working for them, the answer is usually no.)

2. Usually, scores are clustered in obvious patterns. What do the patterns tell you about Jake's leadership effectiveness? Which behaviors seem to be most effective and which are *least effective*? Are those behaviors in which Jake scored low in any way related? For example, suppose he scored low in listening and in communicating and low in being open to feedback. This result would begin to raise new questions and problems because the behaviors tend to be so interdependent. As Jake attempts to understand how to become more effective in his leadership, what are the implications of such large patterns?

3. Looking at the four different categories of responses—from family and friends, employees, colleagues, and others—do you find consistent patterns? For instance, is a split among the employee group predictable across the various questions? Do most of them respond together while a few others seem to disagree consistently? Why might this be, and what might be the consequences—if any—for morale and productivity? Or is there a consistent difference between how colleagues score compared to employees or family and friends? Given what you know about Jake (his entire role and behavior) and some of the issues he needs to address as a leader, try to explain why these patterns occur.

4. Are there interesting discrepancies between Jake's view of himself (x on Figure 19, page 233) and the various groups'

perceptions of him? Do the employees consistently score Jake's behavior well above or below what he predicted they would on average (xo)? What causes such differences? Ask the same questions in relation to how Jake's family and colleagues scored his behavior.

5. Are there discrepancies between Jake's scores (x) and the way I (Bob) see him (s)? Imagine what I will say as to why we differ.

6. Are there significant or consistent differences between how Jake thought the other groups would perceive him on the scaled items (xo) and the way they actually perceived him? Why would this be?

7. In theory, the open-ended data should explain why people scored high or low on many of the scaled items. What consistencies—either high or low—do you see in the responses to any of the scaled items? What consistencies do you see between high or low scores Jake received on the scaled items and the answers to the five open-ended questions ?

8. How did Jake's early upbringing or experiences influence some of the behavior patterns revealed in the responses, both positive and negative?

9. What in Jake's education, training, or earlier work experience helps to explain his particular approach to leadership, the kinds of success he's had, and some of the behaviors that, according to the responses, keep him from being as effective as he might be?

10. Based on your (as Jake the consultant) interpretation of the data, what specific concerns should Jake have concerning his leadership, and what areas appear to deserve greater attention?

11. Are there particular areas of knowledge, skill, or experience that Jake could use to help improve his current leadership effectiveness?

12. What areas of identified strengths, which have always been helpful to Jake, may have become overused or excessive and are no longer as beneficial?

The data Jake received, without interpretation, are summarized in Figure 19, for Part 1, and in the next section, for Part 2. You, the reader, might want to assess the implications of the scaled and open-ended questions. You could ask most of the same questions Jake was asked to answer as if he were a consultant to himself. Then compare your analysis and interpretations to those following the data summaries. In fact, most of the data summaries represent the raw data spread out on a line (in the case of scaled items) and the categorized responses—using direct quotations as much as possible—for the open-ended questions. The questionnaires were sent to a consultant primarily to ensure confidentiality and to protect those responding.

Jake's Open-Ended Data Summary from Part 2

Below are responses to the five questions in Part 2 of the Leadership Development Assessment. (Similar attributes or behaviors have been clustered, with occasional quotes that appear characteristic. The numbers in parentheses denote the number of additional responses that used that term or a similar one.)

Question 1: Please indicate Jake's three greatest strengths or assets he has as a leader that you believe he should maintain.

What *respondents said* **were Jake's strengths:**
(There were no apparent differences across the various groups.)
Strong (7)
Direct (3) • No bullshit • With Jake you know where you are.
In charge (1) • In control • Takes control of a situation.
Organized (3) • Gets things done.

FIGURE 19

Leadership Development Assessment, Part 1 (Responses)

Indicate your relationship to Jake: _____friend or family _____ employee _____ colleague _____ other

Directions: For each item, circle the number on a scale of 1 to 10 that suggests Jake's usual behavior:

		cxo	I	If	IIffc	IIIfcs	Icx	I	
1.	1	2	3	4	5	6	7	8	9	10

IS DISORGANIZED   IS WELL ORGANIZED

	III	I	I	c	IIfcs	ffxo	fc	IIx	fc	
2.	1	2	3	4	5	6	7	8	9	10

IS DIFFICULT TO APPROACH   IS EASY TO APPROACH

	III	IIIIf	fc	c	Ifxos	c	Ifcx	IIx	fc	
3.	1	2	3	4	5	6	7	8	9	10

DOES NOT LISTEN   LISTENS WELL

				I	If	f	Ifc	IIIIfcc	Ixos	Icx
4.	1	2	3	4	5	6	7	8	9	10

DOES NOT SET GOALS   SETS CLEAR GOALS

				If		IIIcc	IIIc	Ixos	Icx
5.	1	2	3	4	5	6	7	8	9	10

DOES NOT HOLD PEOPLE ACCOUNTABLE   HOLDS PEOPLE ACCOUNTABLE

	I	Iff	IIIfc		IIcc	Ifs	cxo	x		
6.	1	2	3	4	5	6	7	8	9	10

RUNS INEFFECTIVE MEETINGS   RUNS EFFECTIVE, ENGAGING MEETINGS

	III	If	I	fs	IIfc	ccxo	fcx	I	I	
7.	1	2	3	4	5	6	7	8	9	10

IS A POOR COMMUNICATOR   IS AN EFFECTIVE COMMUNICATOR

	I	Ifc	II	IIcs	c	I	x, xo	Iffc	If	
8.	1	2	3	4	5	6	7	8	9	10

USES LITTLE OR NEGATIVE HUMOR   USES HUMOR EFFECTIVELY

	II	IIIIf	Ic	fcs	fcxo	If	cx	I		
9.	1	2	3	4	5	6	7	8	9	10

TREATS PEOPLE UNFAIRLY   TREATS PEOPLE FAIRLY

FIGURE 19 cont'd
Leadership Development Assessment, Part 1 (Responses)

	llf	ll	ls	llfc	ls	fcxo	lf	cx		
10.	1	2	3	4	5	6	7	8	9	10

DOES NOT COLLABORATE EFFECTIVELY　　　COLLABORATES EFFECTIVELY

	lll	llfc	lll	ffxo	lfcx	cs	c			
11.	1	2	3	4	5	6	7	8	9	10

IS NOT OPEN TO FEEDBACK　　　IS OPEN TO FEEDBACK

			llll	l	cs	l	fccx	llfcxo	lf	f
12.	1	2	3	4	5	6	7	8	9	10

FINDS DELEGATING DIFFICULT　　　DELEGATES EFFECTIVELY

	ll	lffcs	lllc	lfc	fxo	cx	l	l		
13.	1	2	3	4	5	6	7	8	9	10

HANDLES CONFLICT POORLY　　　HANDLES CONFLICT WITH EASE

	ll	slffcc	llxo	llfcx	lc	l	f			l
14.	1	2	3	4	5	6	7	8	9	10

IS OFTEN IMPATIENT OR REACTIVE　　　IS PATIENT AND CALM

Note: The following symbols were used to denote the source of each response: direct report/employee = l; Jake's score = x; what Jake thought others would, on average, say = xo; family = f; other = o; colleague = c; supervisor (Bob) = s.

Dependable (2) • Does what he says he'll do. • You can be sure the job will get done.
Politically aware
Sense of humor
Holds people accountable (3) • You can't get away with anything with Jake.
Loyal (3) • Dedicated to the organization.
Not afraid of conflict.
Competent • Knows his job
Clear goals (2) • Goal-directed
Determined (1) • Tenacious

What *Jake thought* **were his greatest strengths (x):**
Will get the job done
Loyal
Knows the organization in order to make things happen

What *Jake thought* **others would say (xo):**

Will get the job done
Tough but fair
Honest

What Bob, *Jake's supervisor,* **said were Jake's greatest strengths (s):**

Dependable
Well organized
Loyal to the organization

Question 2: When you see Jake approaching, what are the three strongest feelings or thoughts that come to your mind?

Afraid (3)	Hey, big guy	Nothing
Get ready for a quip	Watch out (1)	Fun
No comment (6)	Caution	Go the other way
Be careful	Good guy	Loyal
Hostile	Rigid, inflexible	The Eagles (football friend)
Tough (2)	Friend	The boss (2)
All business	Here comes the enemy	Mr. Trouble, trouble
Friendly (2)	Angry, unfriendly (3)	Know-it-all
Stay on his good side	He's unconscious	How can I not be noticed?
The rock	Bully	Positive
Controlling		

Each of these items was evaluated as being positive, negative, or neutral. The percentages were calculated based only on actual comments made.

Percentage of positive words or comments used: 23
Percentage of neutral words or comments used: 17
Percentage of negative words or comments used: 60

Question 3: What are the three behaviors that are most critical in blocking Jake from being as effective a leader as he could be?

He gives little thanks (3). • Will take you for granted • Shows little appreciation for work well done • Dominant (9) • Overbearing • Controlling
He has to get over believing he is the only person who can be right.
Not a good listener (3)
Even when he listens you don't get the feeling he hears you.
Intimidating (6) • Uses threatening behavior to control people

He will ask for your opinion and then rebuff you publicly when he doesn't agree; he actually shouts when he's angry and it works because people just show up and go through the motions.
Rigid (3) • Inflexible
Treats those he doesn't like like shit.
Plays favorites (2) • If he likes you, it's fat city.
If you're on his good side everything is fine, but cross him or make a mistake and you'll know it for years.

Uses negative humor (2) put-downs, sarcasm • With Jake, humor is always at the expense of someone.
Temper (2) and anger (2) get in the way.
His temper is legendary—he blows and people run.
He doesn't allow a climate of trust to develop.
Poor communication (2) • One way he controls people is to hold information that he could share close to the vest.
Boring meetings
Needs to delegate (2)

What Jake thought were his greatest blocks (x):
Needs to delegate more
Sometimes my opinions are too strong.
I need to communicate more with those reporting to me.

What Jake thought others would say (xo):
He's too demanding.
He can be threatening, too controlling.
Needs to delegate more

What Bob, Jake's supervisor, believes are his blocks:
Too controlling, needs to let go more (i.e., delegate)
Has many people afraid because of his physical size and temper
People need to feel valued more—morale appears low.

Question 4: If you could give Jake two pieces of advice that would help him in his role but that, for whatever reason, you might be afraid to give him, what would they be? Please be specific. (The following are direct quotes from those participating in the survey.)

1. Spread opportunities and recognition around, everyone needs them.

2. People resent seeing you treat your boss and peers with loving kindness and those who report to you like pieces of nothing—like the difference between sharecroppers and owners.

3. It feels as though you live by three words: Control, Control, and Control. It makes people crazy.

4. Stop abusing people. You seem to be doing it less, but you still use your temper as a weapon, and it can hurt.

5. Relax! Enjoy your job so we can enjoy ours.

6. You take everything so seriously. I've never seen you have fun.

7. You are a tough but usually fair boss, but you need to admit your own mistakes and stop acting as if you're so perfect.

8. I and others feel left out in your meetings. It would help if you stopped talking "at" people and involved them more.

9. Try the golden rule on for size.

10. Stop being a bully. Because you're the boss, people can't fight back or even disagree with you. It makes people not want to come to work.

11. Lighten up!

12. You have lots of nice qualities. Let people see them more often.

13. You want people to respond immediately to every suggestion you make, yet you seem totally closed to any feedback. Try it, you'll probably like it.

14. You get a lot of respect for knowing your job well, but you can easily blow it when you are insensitive.

15. Relax!

16. Listen more—people have good things to say.

17. Some people are underutilized, and others are used all the time. Try to spread out the work and goodies more evenly.

18. Recognize that some people actually work as hard as you, and need praise and recognition even if you don't.

19. Try not to push so much. People will do great work if you get out of the way.

20. How can someone so well organized dress like a slob?

21. People aren't machines. Don't treat them like that.

22. It feels as if you are a bit behind in relation to some of the new management stuff they're asking of others. Why not try it? Things like more participation would work in our area.

23. Take it easy. People make mistakes and so do you. It doesn't have to be a source of anger.

24. Stop acting like a marine all the time. It's even going out of style in the marines.

25. I'd suggest that you try giving people more authority and control over what they do. You give lots of responsibility and tend to keep too much authority.

26. All work and no play makes Jake a dull boy.

27. This exercise gives me a glimmer of hope that you may have begun to listen to those who can help you.

What Jake's advice to himself was (x):
Stop taking myself so seriously.
Listen to people more.
Use my time more efficiently.

What Jake thought was the advice others would give him:
Delegate more—spread the work around.
Don't be so hard on people.
Listen.

What Bob, Jake's supervisor, gave him as advice:
Involve more people in decisions that matter to them.
Let some of the "nice guy" part of you out; I see it when you relate to upper management. (Also with your family.)
Listen hard to those who work in your area.

Question 5: If you were Jake, and in his role as leader, what would you do immediately to improve morale and productivity? Assume no change in personnel and no large windfall of money in your budget. (The following are all direct quotes.)

1. I'd meet with my direct reports regularly and begin to act more like a coach and guide rather than a cop or a dictator. I'd try to know each individual as a person.

2. I'd let those working for me have more responsibility and the authority to go with it so they could do their jobs without always waiting to check everything out.

3. I'd stop playing favorites—it kills morale and creates an atmosphere of tension and jealousy.

4. The first thing would be to begin talking to people civilly and without the feeling that everything is a crisis. The constant sense of urgency leaves people on edge and feeling exhausted.

5. I'd reorganize our area and redistribute the workload. It's all out of whack with some people doing so much more than others. As part of this, I would start to manage more and stop getting involved in everything. People can handle it.

6. I'd take a vacation and let people know on my return that there would be a "new day," and I'd begin to treat the people at work with more respect and dignity.

7. The first thing would be to try and build a team. Let's face it, morale sucks, and a lot of things would have to get out on the table. The most important thing would be to create a sense of "we" instead of him and us.

8. There's a lot of talk about reengineering. Well I'd assess every person's role and interests and skills, see where we overlap and where we do unnecessary activity, and then have us reapportion our workloads so that we have to work with each other more.

9. I'd start treating people fairly.

10. I'd bring in an outsider and do some intense team building where we could work together, play together, and have some much-needed fun.

11. I'd have a long conversation with all members of our group and try to help them believe that we can do more, that we can be more cooperative and less competitive, and agree how to work together more. As of now we all do our own (or Jake's) thing and it's everyone for himself or herself.

12. Get Jake some training in how to work together with people.

13. I'd do something to work on trust in our work group. It feels as if everyone is at everyone all the time.

14. I'd have a big pizza and beer party as the first in a series of "fun things" we'd do every month to celebrate ourselves as a group.

15. We should go away for two or three days and agree on a plan. A means of getting on the same page. Sort of starting over with some common goals and ways we might help each other get there.

What Jake's response was (x):
Bring the group together to develop some common goals so we have some reason to talk together.

What Jake thought others would say (xo):
Deal with the personality differences and unresolved conflicts in the group—probably with a facilitator of some kind who could also teach us how to work better together.

How Bob, Jake's supervisor, responded to the questions (s):
There appears to be considerable tension in the group that needs to be resolved. The first step would be to create an activity or event that would allow everyone to experience some success together as a group doing something that would be meaningful (solve a problem, develop mutual values, create a common mission or vision).

Jake's Response to the Data

As both Jake and his supervisor reported, Jake was stunned by the amount, consistency, and predominantly negative flavor of the information he received. There was no room for denial or excuses. When he had agreed to undertake the 360-degree feedback, it had mainly been a practical decision to placate Bob. Jake later admitted that he thought he could probably blow off the negative data no matter what they suggested.

He decided to cooperate with what he viewed as a charade because, in his twenty-some years with the organization, he had never lost a skirmish, let alone a match. True, he paid a heavy price for his stubbornness and overbearing attitude. Over the years, upper management had begun to see him as a liability and had redlined him in his present role. Nevertheless, they kept rewarding him as a highly effective supervisor who met deadlines and, most important, controlled his employees.

Jake is a perfect example of organizational codependency. Management colluded by knowingly ignoring Jake's destructive behaviors; doing so made life easier for them, though Jake's employees suffered. And, on a different level, the employees also colluded (acted codependently) when they protected themselves from his wrath. They accepted his abuse silently, did not confront him, and did not report his indiscretions to upper management—except through informal complaints.

They found it easier to endure the pain because the consequences of telling and being found out were intolerable. They preferred to live with the enemy they knew and hold on to their jobs until something better came along, or until Jake was promoted out of their lives. While management and employees lived in silence, their behavior encouraged Jake to act boldly and actually reinforced his destructive behaviors, which took an increasingly larger toll.

Jake's shock and dismay turned quickly to fear and trepidation. How could he possibly keep his job with such heavily weighted negative data? And, even if he could, was it possible to change? Weren't they asking him to be something that he could not be? But to their credit, management believed he deserved the opportunity to change, given the collusion that had reinforced his deleterious style. Management also assumed that people *can* change if they are no longer rewarded for destructive behaviors and have the opportunity to learn and practice more appropriate ones. Though most gave Jake little chance to overcome his old reactive patterns, they were determined to give him an honest shot at real change.

Following is a summary of the information Jake gleaned from the two questionnaires, along with Bob's own interpretations that added balance and insight. Regarding the scaled items, Jake agreed that scores of 8, 9, and 10 were preferred, 7 was borderline but acceptable, 5 and 6 needed definite attention, and anything below 5 required immediate resuscitation. Jake also agreed to share the results with his employees and to develop a specific action plan.

Areas of Strength

Of the fourteen scaled items representing behaviors he valued as a leader, Jake found only four items in the acceptable range, and one of those was suspect. Most of the respondents agreed that he was well organized. Most people, including Jake himself and Bob, scored him at 8 or above; when asked if he were goal directed, he received similar ratings. He was scored lowest on organization and goal-directedness by his family, where in a relationship with a strong and demanding wife, he apparently is more laissez-faire.

Holding people accountable was his highest score. One can see why management supported him all those years: organization, accountability, and goal-directedness were highly ranked, and having good interpersonal relations and maintenance behaviors received little or no reinforcement from management.

The data took on considerable credibility for Jake when he saw that he was given kudos in areas he knew were his strengths. He couldn't easily deny the negatives if people had credited him with many positives. Obviously, there was no vendetta; people who disliked him didn't simply give low scores across the board. (This is consistent with our experience: people tend to be incredibly fair and will give even the most brutish lout their honest opinion if they have any hope that things will get better and he may improve.)

The final positive score among the scaled items was on item 12, delegation. Of the twenty possible scores, twelve were at 7 or above. The problem was that of his nine direct reports, six had scored him 6 or below, with four clustered at 3. In the eyes of friends, family, colleagues, and even his supervisor, he was seen as effective at delegating. Jake placed himself on the borderline at 7. Even a superficial analysis hinted at possible trouble in this area for Jake. Delegation would be one of the areas he would most likely have to address.

More Strengths

Jake wasn't kept around for so many years without other redeeming qualities. The words people used to describe his strengths rang loud and clear: strong, direct, tenacious, determined, get the job done, no bullshit, dependable, and loyal.

The agreement was uniform across all groups. For management, who valued production and control, Jake was perfect. Throw in loyalty, and you had someone you could count on to get the job done, take initiative, and not be pushed around by troublesome employees. And it worked, until the fallout accumulated and began getting in the way of (1) productivity, (2) morale, and (3) the new philosophy ushered in by the quality management movement.

Strengths Becoming Weaknesses

One of the diagnostic questions Bob asked Jake to consider was whether he had strengths that over time had become impediments. When human beings fail to receive regular feedback, they tend to rely on those behaviors for which they are always rewarded. Feedback is used in any system to maintain balance. Upon reading the data, Jake observed that most of his problems centered on characteristics for which he had been consistently rewarded.

Strong became intimidating, direct became overbearing, accountable became fear driven, tenacious and determined became rigid and controlling. It wasn't that his strengths were no longer valued, but lacking the ability or desire to moderate them—and given his propensity toward personal power and control—he had become a caricature. Even Jake admitted to this reality.

Most of us strive valiantly to be successful, to become effective, to develop the skills we need that will help us succeed or, at the very least, not fail. But without some caring and supportive feed-back along the way, we, too, will soon be out of balance—overusing the things we've got and minimizing those things less valued that we may need.

The paradox is that for many at fifty, when we need the balance, we may also find ourselves redlined, dead-ended and without the resources to move forward. (That was Jake.) Advancing in the or-ganization in a more demanding role may require less of old ways and more of the skills abandoned on the wayside. There oughta be a law!

Jake was a victim of a system that played him like an instrument and failed to give him the feedback he needed until it was nearly too late. In another organization with less heart, he'd have been gone without a look back or apology. In the eyes of most short-sighted management, the problem would have been Jake because it appeared that he couldn't adapt, not management with their years of support for a narrow range of behaviors.

People's Feelings about Jake

Imagine yourself in a dream walking down a long hallway where you pass everyone you know in your life. And imagine that they, as in Jake's case, are asked to register their three strongest thoughts or feelings about you as a person.

That daunting thought is the beginning of a possible nightmare. Then consider how you would feel if you were to estimate the per-centage of positive, negative, and neutral responses.

Yet that is what people do to us all the time without our know-ing it. They rarely have the opportunity or, perhaps, the *will* to tell us—and that is a huge source of seduction. People know and see al-most everything about us and have feelings about almost every-thing we do: how we walk, talk, play, how we think, and what we say. But, since they don't have permission to tell us, this incredible source of essential information rarely if ever reaches us. Yet we need it desperately if we hope to understand our impact.

In such a difficult exercise, what percentage of positive or neg-ative responses is acceptable? Well, we know we can't please—nor should we—all the people all of the time. And our life goal should not be, as Albert Ellis used to say, to be "liked by every single living human being on the face of the planet."[3] But what would satisfy you? How about 50 percent positive, 40 percent negative, and 10 percent neutral? Or 25 percent positive, 50 percent negative, and 25 percent neutral? Or what about 30 percent positive, 30 percent negative, and 40 percent neutral?

In the first instance, is having 50 percent of people not feeling positive about you satisfactory? Surely not for me, but you may have a greater tolerance for negative opinions. Or what about having more negative than positive opinions—that could be devastating—or don't you care what people think? You are who you are, and if people don't like it they can lump it, right?

It suddenly would become easy to justify, rationalize, and deny the rejecting and negative words. No, I'm not on earth to please everyone, but if I have to get along, depend on others to get a job done, collaborate, or have a satisfactory relationship, I'd better be conscious of how I'm getting in my own way and what's turning others off as a result of my own behaviors.

Many of us can go all the way through our entire educational experience and receive little effective feedback other than grades. This paucity of response inevitably continues in work, and even marriage, where most of us are isolated from information about how we affect others, including our spouses and children. And, finally, what if 40 percent see me as neutral? That could be as threatening as not being liked or even being disliked (the old saying, I'd rather be disliked than ignored).

That brings us to a question often posed by Saul Alinsky, the famous social activist, to his clients: "Do you really want help?" or "Do you really want to know?" Would you? That is the challenge— *having the courage to know.* And then he'd ask it again, *"Do you really want to change?"* He believed the client must first actively desire to change before he would ever be ready to face the enemy, who, more often than not, is himself.

Here we have Jake, who had been going through his life in charge, in control, successful by most standards, and he is asked to take a hard look, to gather data on himself—which he didn't really even want. No, cutting through to the truth of how others see us is not easy. It is tough business even for the most courageous. Don't take it lightly for yourself, and particularly for others.

There was Jake, minding his own business, handsomely paid, acknowledged for years of work well done, suddenly confronted with 23 percent POSITIVE, 60 percent NEGATIVE, and 17 percent NEUTRAL. What is Jake supposed to do?

Certainly there have been jokes about his being tough, mean, tenacious, uncompromising like a bear. But to have words like "angry," "unfriendly," "bully," "rigid," and "inflexible" come flying off the page, or comments like "know-it-all," "here comes the enemy," or "Mr. Trouble" would give anyone pause.

But, you say, he represents an extreme. You chose Jake as an example to make a point. Not so. Of every one hundred manager/ leaders for whom we gather 360-degree feedback, we expect 20 to 35 percent to reflect these scores. After years of "convenience management," and tacitly supporting abuse of other nonproductive and dysfunctional behaviors, Jake symbolizes a problem facing many leaders. Jake and his supervisor—after years of collusion and denial—must own this reality and take responsibility for perpetuating a style that has had destructive consequences.

Bob or others must handle the information skillfully and compassionately so Jake can hear what is said, save face, and begin rehabilitating. If you were to gather the data on yourself, it would be important to share it with someone you trust so you could sort through its implications and determine how to respond for on-the-job behavioral change.

Jake felt the negative word responses focused on "fear" and "distrust." He saw them as symptoms or outcomes of other detrimental behaviors that formed the underlying causes he had to identify, understand, and address. He had already identified strengths that he used excessively, and he saw how they might engender distrust, fear, and intimidation.

When he realized that Bob was not appalled at the data, that he was not going to be dismissed, and that he was going to have the opportunity to change, he accepted the challenge as he always had—with tenacity, goal directness, and determination. He said to Bob, "Well, if we're going to let it all hang out, here goes . . ." and proceeded to be brutally frank in his analysis of his remaining data.

Narrowing the Deficits

The few questions asked generated so much information that it could seem overwhelming. However, there were not nearly as many issues as the variety of negative data might suggest. The challenge was to determine the things Jake could and needed to pay attention to in order to experience success as soon as possible. Usually, a few key attitudes and behaviors cause most of the problems: so a few critical changes can go a long way toward making important improvements.

From the scaled items, as well as the areas of blocks, Jake, responding in the role of the "consultant" reported:

1. Jake apparently failed to communicate effectively at many levels; his style of communicating had to change. He listened poorly to most of his employees. His direct reports tended to find him unapproachable. The fact that three scored a 1 and all but two were under 5 was a serious problem.

   Further, when asked to hypothesize about the relationship between his employees who scored his approachability at 1, 2, or 3 (five altogether) and the two who scored it 8, he imagined that there might be competition, favoritism, and possibly jealousy. Clearly, he was going out of his way to treat people differently and reaping problems as a result.

2. The issue of favoritism was again raised in relation to whether people felt that Jake treated them fairly. Seven of his direct reports, along with one family member, scored him at 3 or below, while one direct report scored him at 8. The same pattern held true in the areas of collaboration, feedback, and delegation.

   All of these behaviors require a positive relationship between Jake and those reporting to him. The consistently low scores suggest poor morale and feelings of impotence among most members of his group. And, predictably, family and colleagues rated him 4 or 5 points higher on almost every item than did his direct reports; Jake treated his peers, family, and superiors more sensitively and respectfully than he did those working closest to him.

3. Additionally, Jake discovered that he had no idea just how deeply people felt about certain issues. For example, he ranked himself high (8) in the area of collaboration, while the median of all the scores was at 4, and his direct reports' ranking was at 2. In talking about this, he said that at meetings he was always seeking people's opinions; apparently, however, he didn't realize that most were unwilling to speak the truth or would defer to him rather than disagree.

   In fact, on eleven of the scaled items Jake rated himself in the highest 25 percent, suggesting that he was generally out of touch with the feelings of most of those around him. Similarly, he scored himself higher than did Bob on twelve of the scaled items. Again, a critical question for Jake was, how could he harbor such delusions and how could he ensure that such discrepancies would not continue?

4. Two scaled items in particular seemed to reflect Jake's leadership abilities. The one with the lowest score (median of 3) related to Jake's willingness to stay calm and patient. He was perceived as overreactive, quick-tempered, and sometimes belligerent; most people feared him. This impatience was tied closely to his apparent inability to handle conflict effectively. It's little wonder most people felt he was difficult to approach. One can imagine staff meetings with Jake providing information but receiving few responses to his requests for questions or information. Typically, the only people to speak out were the one or two who appeared to appreciate him, and he them. Such a climate reduced people's willingness to risk or to disclose personal feelings or ideas that could make them feel vulnerable.

Predictably, Jake indicated that when he observed their protective attitudes, lack of initiative, and increasingly dependent (wait for me to tell them what to do) behaviors, he would feel let down and increasingly less willing to let go and delegate to such nonresponsive individuals. He was in a self-fulfilling, unsatisfactory catch-22. The more he showed his discontent, the more the group withdrew and failed to respond.

5. Finally, on the scaled items, Jake noticed that humor had gotten mixed reviews. He admitted that humor at his level in the organization could be a "little rough." But he had never seen it relative to his scores on other behaviors. He now realized that his sarcastic, cutting humor would only exacerbate the passivity, withdrawal, and self-protection in many of his direct reports. On the other hand, those not likely to be afraid or hurt by his comments, or those who could play the game of old-boy humor with him, saw him as fun to be around. But, as Bob asked, was there an alternative to Jake's type of "humor at someone else's expense?"

Insights from Advice Given

Inevitably, what connects the recipient of 360-degree feedback to his or her data is the direct quotes from the respondents. Unlike the things that block Jake (question 3 of Figure 18, page 225) that are categorized, the items in question 4, in which individuals provide advice they might otherwise be afraid to give, go right to the core.

Given only this opportunity to say it, and given permission to be honest, most individuals speak their true feelings. Those who rated Jake were no exception. The prescriptive messages to him were poignant, pleading, and sometimes brutally frank. The old adage "Don't ask if you don't really want to know" applies double here. What makes the medicine easier to take is that by the time an individual has looked at the first three questions, he pretty well knows what his issues are. Seeing them in quotes only confirms the patterns observed previously.

In this light, Bob asked Jake to select the half-dozen statements that had the greatest impact on him and seemed to capture the essence of the remaining data. Bob also asked him to explain why he chose the items he did:

People resent seeing you treat your boss and peers with loving kindness and those who report to you like pieces of nothing— like the difference between sharecroppers and owners.

The whole idea about favoritism struck home with this comment. Jake told Bob that growing up he had been treated like nothing, and here he was doing it to those he supervised. The appearance of kissing up to his superiors also did not sit well.

———

Relax! Enjoy your job so we can enjoy ours.

Not only did he not think of work as being fun but apparently Jake had never stopped to consider that his ill humor or negative attitude would determine if others enjoyed their work. He had simply lost touch with his impact as a leader. He realized he was known as a person who could have fun outside of work, so why not at work?

He had always thought that you come to work in order to work and save fun for home and family.

———

I and others feel left out in your meetings. It would help if you stopped talking at people and involved them more.

Jake said that he knew meetings were not very pleasant, but he viewed them as minimally important, just something to get through. Most of the meetings he attended were a waste, he said, and "I guess I was just keeping up a bad tradition." He now intended to use meetings to remedy some of what obviously ailed him. Other data indicated the need to build trust, collaborate more, utilize people better, and show a greater fairness.

———

Stop being a bully. Because you're the boss, people can't fight back or even disagree with you. It makes people not want to come to work.

Apparently this affected him greatly. He hated bullies. Yet by not considering the influence of his role and his power, he had unintentionally slipped into one of the easiest of all traps. He admitted that it was easy to shout and intimidate and watch people snap to. That's how he was raised. But it was embarrassing to face that bald truth.

——

Some people are underutilized, and others are used all the time. Try to spread out the work and goodies more evenly.

This statement as well as others hinted at both favoritism and an unwillingness to delegate or to see getting a good assignment as a reward and sign of recognition. His problem with control was confirmed repeatedly by Bob and others at each level. But it was his direct reports whom he had let down. He admitted that his need to control everything might be the most difficult pattern to break and would need Bob's help, but he was willing to try.

——

It appears that you are a kind and giving father. Why not use some of those behaviors on those who work for you?

This comment hit Jake the hardest. He did see himself as a loving father, and the data showed that in most situations, his family ranked him on the scaled items higher than the workers had. He found it interesting that at home he overcompensated for his own noncaring father, but at work he used more of his father's qualities. Perhaps, he thought, that was because at work they seemed to value the macho, tough boss more than the gentle, supportive father. He also joked that he had another "boss" at home to share the demands of parenting.

——

*Stop acting like a marine all the time. It's even going out of
style in the marines.*

Jake laughed when he considered the truth in the statement. First,
there was the new Marine Corps that focused more on relationships and teamwork among the men and women. Second, he admitted that he used a marine style to intimidate people when he
wanted to get something done. In fact, it was one of the things he
had been known and rewarded for. Clearly, it was an old pattern
that would not be easy to change, but he was willing to try.

The Productivity and Morale Question

People love to respond to this question: if you were the boss what
would you do to increase productivity and morale? The question
assumes you want to know and that the individual is placed in a
position of power. It allows him to focus on removing the hurts or
aggravations that he really believes will make a difference. But remember: to ask and then not respond in some measurable fashion
will build even greater disillusionment and mistrust.

Some leaders say that they would never ask that question because then they would be expected to respond to everything others
ask of them. To us, that is not the issue. People simply need to feel
heard and to be responded to in an adult fashion. If something is
not feasible, a leader can say so and say why. If something is a good
idea, the leader can implement it, acknowledge the source of the
idea, and use the accomplishment to recognize and appreciate
people.

Refusing to collect good ideas assumes your workers are petu-
lant children waiting to jump on management if their suggestions
are not implemented. Clearly, the more combative these relations,
the more the expectations will be raised and the greater the need
to take action on at least some ideas. However, most people are reasonable; they appreciate being asked and are pleased when their
ideas are executed. Following are the most important suggestions
Jake chose, along with his rationale.

I'd have a long conversation with each person and try to help him believe we can do more, that we can be more cooperative and less competitive, and agree on how to work together more. As of now everyone does his own thing, and it's everyone for himself.

Jake noted that because the data suggested that he did not know his people well and, in many cases, they didn't trust him, he would have more regular conversations with his direct reports and begin building more personal relationships. This would also address the issue of favoritism and lack of fairness.

———

I'd take a vacation and let people know that on my return there would be a "new day," and I'd begin to treat people at work with a little more respect and dignity.

He believed that he needed to do something dramatic—the idea of a "new day" appealed to him, and he was considering how to accomplish this. Whatever the means, it would require more than platitudes.

———

I'd have a big pizza and beer party as the first in a series of "fun things" we'd do every month to celebrate ourselves as a group.

Jake saw that people who occasionally have fun together feel more committed and very likely care more about work and one another. To do this would reflect a change in his style and send a signal that more changes would be coming. He also realized that it would be uncomfortable at first, and that building trust with himself and within the team would take time.

———

I'd let those working for me have more responsibility and the authority to go with it, so they could do their jobs without always waiting to check everything out.

Powerful evidence suggested that Jake was perceived as being too controlling, that he did more of the "work" of the organization than necessary; if he was going to be a leader, he would have to manage better and build trust through effective delegation. He knew this area would require the most help.

In reviewing the recommendations, Jake believed that the most salient issues were contained in the five he chose for Part 2 of the questionnaire. Between the advice given in question 5, and the feedback he received in question 4, he felt that he had heard the most critical messages.

Action Steps for Jake

At one point, Bob indicated that he and Jake had spent roughly five hours debriefing the data and probing the responses to the questions he had asked Jake to consider. He had new insights about what made Jake tick and felt increasingly committed to his success.

For his part, Jake began to understand how his present situation had evolved and how much of who he was as a leader was rooted in messages and experiences from the past. Although the process was not intended as therapy, by understanding how his strengths (born out of his personal history) meshed with the needs of the organization over a long time, Jake began to understand that the system had changed, but he had not.

Now, could he accommodate the shifting nature of these needs and the expectations of management? Because the data focus had remained on his "behaviors" and not on personality limitations or character flaws, Jake could look at this difficult situation as a problem to be solved rather than as a flash point for anger and resentment.

When asked to develop a list of problems that the data suggested needed solving, Jake identified the following needs:

1. To develop a greater sense of team within his group along with increased trust. This could begin with developing some shared values and ultimately more shared goals.

2. As part of developing trust, to deal with the frustration and anger that appeared to exist toward him and among some team members. This would imply gaining skills as a group in dealing with future conflict.

3. To reduce the perception that favoritism and lack of fairness were involved in how work was distributed and how reward and recognition were earned. This might include looking at a more equitable approach to supervision.

4. To listen better, show more patience, and be less prone to use anger and intimidation as means of control.

5. To develop more creative and collaborative meetings—moving beyond basic show and tell information sharing and using the group to solve problems they all shared.

6. To develop a positive and regular method for generating useful feedback for himself and the team as it moved forward.

The pages of data and hours of work analyzing and interpreting the information yielded six important concerns around which, with Bob's help, serious strategies would be developed. Most objectives centered on the team, their interpersonal relations, and Jake's role as leader and authority.

All goals were achievable; yet all demanded changes on both Jake's part and the group's. Also, as Bob began to support and work with Jake, he, perhaps for the first time, began to understand his own role as supervisor and how, through his absence, he had been a part of Jake's problems.

He had been virtually invisible for years, letting Jake do his thing with little monitoring or criticism. In a sense, no news—or trouble—had been good news. As the 360-degree feedback had revealed, most issues had a common theme of control and its relation to Jake's view of power and responsibility. Had he not gained a very different perspective on these issues, he would not have been willing to consider changing behaviors to become the type of leader management now favored.

Successful Elements of 360-Degree Feedback

Jake had become a troubled employee, nurtured and reinforced by an increasingly dysfunctional organization. The 360-degree feedback data for Jake uncovered issues ignored for years that were symptomatic of a less-than-perfect organization and its impact on a loyal and equally dysfunctional employee. By asking direct, unsophisticated questions agreed to by Jake and his boss, the process of discovery felt both real and emotionally accessible to Jake, who was understandably fearful and suspicious.

In this case, as we've shown earlier, measurement does not have to be complicated or perfect. Furthermore, it is not just for leaders in trouble. It is for managers who want to know their impact fully, to be conscious of the underlying issues they cause that affect their team or organization and, ultimately, their overall performance. Such discovery does not require high-priced outside consultants (although in the case of Jake, an outside perspective might have been useful). It does require a strong commitment from every participant, a willingness to own the data, to share it openly, and to take action in many of the behavioral areas they can control. Our experience over the past twenty-five years suggests that for 360-degree feedback to be effective, the following must occur in an integrated and seamless fashion.

- Each individual seeking personal feedback must have a deep, abiding commitment. If it is seen as obligatory, those responding to the request to share their perspective will be less committed. Similarly, the person seeking feedback must be willing to talk personally with those providing data to show why their help is important and valued.

- The 360-degree feedback process is very personal to those seeking information. When possible, don't use boilerplate questionnaires. Rather, tailor the questions with information unique to the individual being reviewed and most critical to his or her success. Broadly define the desired picture, as in Jake's case, or focus on a specific issue requiring individual feedback as with Jake and Bob.

- We cannot overstate just how scary it can be to provide unfavorable feedback to a peer or boss. Maintain confidentiality to make people who contribute information feel secure. Individual information must pass through the hands of only those who are neutral or totally trusted. Such precautions can make the difference between receiving valid or invalid data. It was true in the case of Jake, and it will be true for anyone seeking confidential data based on suggestions found in this book.

- Receiving feedback from a 360-degree process does not guarantee change. People rarely have the fortitude or discipline to change old habits or patterns by suddenly being made aware of such data. This is a fact and is not meant to be a criticism. Feedback is a single step in a long process that may demand new skills, practice, and structured support. Here progress needs to be monitored and measured whenever possible. Working with a trusted colleague can make the difference between success and failure. Bob's steady support and unwavering honesty helped Jake be honest with himself and provided insights he might not have had otherwise.

- Most people in a work situation know each other well, and an individual's limitations and needed growth areas are no secret. If the 360-degree feedback recipient has the courage to do so, making the data public can lend instant credibility to the process and motivate the individual to succeed in change. An individual who talks about her own areas of desired change is more credible than one who gives participants a summary report of her data. Talking through data with all those affected and showing how they can help will generate support and increase the person's chances for success. Paradoxically, showing vulnerability (not weakness) and seeking support can help a strong person internalize the feedback and strengthen her commitment to change.

- Developing a plan of action framed in *measurable* outcomes with the help of a coach, mentor, or boss can be crucial. Witnessing our own progress by benchmarking our current level of success against old behaviors and our new standards is the gold standard of accountability. The more others are conscious of our progress, the more we can maintain the support we need. In this vein, Kurt Lewin, the father of this approach, would talk about the difficulty of *unfreezing* our old behaviors and then *refreezing* them at a higher, more productive level.[4] Reducing the tendency to revert is at the heart of any successful change effort. Any change takes time to internalize. Good intentions mean little until the change has transformed us.

- Finally, change in the workplace usually takes a crisis or problem to motivate the desired change. In the case of Jake, that reality—until he saw the benefits of change to his life—was that *not changing* would cost him his job. There are few better ways of gaining someone's attention than that realization. Therapeutic change takes on a totally different perspective.

Summary

Jake's case was extreme, although it could be repeated thousands of times. Rewards are one thing, and negative consequences quite another. Creating a contract that *motivates both through rewards and negative consequences* provides a powerful stimulus to spark change.

The potential repercussions if we fail to change are endless; they could include, for example, paying money to a charity, writing a check to a hated political foe, forgoing a scheduled holiday, taking a difficult person to dinner, or giving up a sacred ritual for a time. Consequences must have a negative valence in order to be viable, and we must commit to them if the process is to work. They can provide focus and reinforce our commitment.

Also, having the penalty kick in repeatedly allows us to fail and know we will have to pay again if we fail again. Slipping on the road to change is not the sin; quitting—giving up on the commitment to do what you need to do—is. So we must make it tough on ourselves.

Using 360-degree feedback effectively can have a huge impact on establishing a new reality. Clear, valued information drawn from those we care about is one important example. Further, regular feedback at the end of a meeting that evaluates the quality of the design, the quality of the group's interaction, and the quality of the leader/facilitator's behavior can over time ensure that meetings will gradually improve. But this requires that the information is systematically used to improve future designs. This is the key if the leader is to create a climate of openness and participation, with the focus being both personal and group development.

Everything starts with useful information. Good information engenders trust, especially if the leaders care enough to seek it and then to respond. Making visible course corrections and creating real improvements will build trust and credibility. The notion of continuous improvement was popularized with the advent of the quality movement. But many teachers and advocates in the movement made it difficult and arduous. It can be simple, direct, and ongoing, and it can provide immediate consequences.

The unembellished viewpoint taken here is the antidote to ineffective supervision. Asking hard questions, gathering direct data, and acting on ever-present information are the keys to personal development, which should be an ongoing and relentless part of any management process.

8

Teamwork Matters

The Group Management Questionnaire

I recently took some time to weigh all the things I knew
Versus all the things I didn't know.
It was a useful exercise.
It didn't take very long.
—SY SAFRANSKY

The dilemma of any leader is to obtain the best information available when it is most needed. The reality is that at any given moment we only have the information that people are willing to provide us. With that information our choices will be expanded or diminished. Although we will rarely have all the information we need, seeking the information that matters most can spell the difference between success and failure.

In the case of Pepe Rodriguez when faced with the Texas Rangers, his lack of good information from his "friend" cost him his life. "He's not afraid to die you stinking pigs" was clearly a case of inadequate communication and poor feedback, with a dire result for Pepe. This chapter is about building a reservoir of good information for your team or organization so you have the best metrics available and, as a result, the best choices upon which to act.

261

The Fallacy of a Team-Based Culture

It is difficult to work in a twenty-first-century organization and not hear about teams—production-line teams, marketing teams, sales teams, middle-management teams, and, of course, executive teams to guide all of the other teams. While the literature is replete with examples of how well-trained teams improve both quality and efficiency, the drive toward such team-based cultures was more opportunistic than idealistic. It resulted from the downsizing of U.S. corporations in the 1980s and early 1990s. It was not based, for the most part, on a changing management philosophy and idealism that championed teamwork, cooperation, participative management, and inclusion. Rather, it was the cost saving purge of middle managers to help our lagging economy compete internationally that tipped the scale toward flatter, more lean and mean organizational structures. It required the uncontrolled pressures from abroad, the onset of more global competition, and the supposed efficiencies of the information technology (IT) revolution to prod us to leave the costly hierarchical, top down, command and control, inefficient, dinosaur bureaucracies that had evolved over the past two hundred years.

The results of team-based management range from miraculous to unsatisfactory to downright disastrous. Doing the right thing for the wrong reasons does not always work. In the case of building successful teams, there continue to be myriad problems. For example, all too often some or all of the following exist:

- A disconnect often occurs between some people at the top of an organization and those asked to implement the new team culture. While the reason for creating teams was to increase efficiency and improve communication, this organizational shift also demanded the delegation of real authority—not always welcomed or forthcoming—resulting in an erosion of traditional control and power.

- Many team leaders have little experience or training in their new team-leader role. The result is that dealing with the complexities and idiosyncrasies of a team environment has proven vastly more difficult than had been imagined.

- As might be expected, leaders chosen to lead these teams are often conscripted for reasons other than suitability. Skill, temperament, intuition, and training can make a strong team leader. However, foist on the team someone bred to be controlling, and authoritarianism and adversity will most assuredly follow.

- Additional problems were created by teams having to interact on a regular basis with other teams. Developing interteam relationships and trust is both time consuming and complicated, particularly in those organizations where *internal* competition (between individual employees, departments, office locations, etc.) is as stiff as external competition.

- Teams are a breeding ground for greater conflict, as individual team members vie to present differing opinions. Traditionally, organizations could mitigate some internal conflicts because the hierarchy allowed real power to solve problems. This is no longer the case in more collaborative organizations where lines of authority are often blurred. Instead, resolving team conflicts demands skill, patience, and cooperation—qualities not always easy to learn and never possible to dictate.

- In economic terms, the process of team building is an added expense of time and resources and therefore is not a valued commodity in many organizations. Choosing team members quickly and randomly (or for other reasons unrelated to the task) without giving consideration to the many variables that make a well-planned team can be a recipe for disaster.

Creating a truly team-based organizational culture demands discipline, training, and a consistent philosophy of management mirrored by those at the top. But what if you are a team leader, appointed without training and wishing to avert disaster? What if there is no budget for an exotic team-building course and you are constantly pressured by limited time and demanding expectations? Join the proverbial group—you are not alone.

We agree that today's harried leader needs all the help that he or she can get to build a successful team. Through the Group Management Questionnaire (GMQ), we offer the use of metrics to quell the impending sense of disaster felt by many team leaders. This instrument provides the leader with a vehicle that will create the necessary template to ease the discomfort of team building. Here is an opportunity to improve the climate of the team over time while building team and individual skills through *doing*. This tool is not meant to be a panacea. However, it can bring order to what often feels like chaos. Somewhere along the way to becoming a truly effective team, we recommend training and the opportunity to take blocks of real time for the team to work on the issues that are bound to arise in the process of becoming a team. In the meantime, our approach can be a useful beginning, as it maintains focus on aspects of team development crucial for success.

The Case of Jim Reise

To begin with, Jim is better than your average, ordinary person. He's a "nice guy" who without formal training has found himself being a leader over much of his career, whether he sought it or not. He just plain gets along with people. His best quality is that he's easy to like, and his biggest problem is that he likes to be liked—often giving away his own power in order to maintain the goodwill of the group—sometimes using humor to cover the obvious tensions that are present.

For the past several years he has used his considerable social skills in a staff role in the home office of a twelve-hundred-person company that manufactures a variety of laser products. It is a fast-paced industry, and the work is demanding, because of both a hotly competitive marketplace and the increasing interdependence of the work teams that drive the organization. Two years ago the organization prematurely switched to a team-based management system. The transition has been difficult. During this period, Jim had been working as project assistant to the chief operating officer (COO), partly because he was seen as a good front person for a rather gruff and intimidating boss and partly because, at age thirty-five, he had experience working in most levels of the organization and was familiar with most of the operations and many of the key players.

Recently, the company has been challenged to bring a high-profile product with huge potential to market in sixteen months. The entire effort was to be headed by a new product management team with the ability to monitor and guide the progress of the entire effort. The ten-person team had never worked together before this project. Jim was given the assignment to lead the team. Although he lacked extensive team leadership experience, his abilities to get along with people and to organize were well known. In addition, he brought with him a positive reputation for getting things done. Being well connected to those at the top of the organization was also seen as a definite asset considering the political red tape that had bogged down more than one such high-potential product. Although taking the job would be a loss to the COO and the central staff, this was an opportunity he could not pass up and one that would take him to a new level of respect in this rapidly growing organization. He looked forward to the challenge.

All the members of Jim's new team had some previous success working in high-pressure team environments, some much more than others. All had been selected for this team based on their task specialties and their ability to get the job done. As a group they could be characterized as driven, high achieving, and demanding; motivation would not be the issue. The team was expected to hit the ground running. A demanding set of benchmarks had been established by management, and the team members knew they would be under the scrutiny of the top leaders. They, too, seemed to welcome the challenge.

From the Beginning: Trouble on the Team

The very first meeting showed just how far the group was from being a real team. The team had no shrinking violets, and many of the members were accustomed to running their own shows. At least five of the members seemed to have what Jim would later describe as monumental egos. They professed their expertise not only in relation to their own areas of recognized strength but also in relation to anything anyone else said. To put it mildly, there appeared to be little interest in listening and a whole lot of interest in pontificating. Although there was enthusiasm for the challenge they were undertaking, a battle seemed to be raging for leadership and respect among these highly competent and competitive players. Jim was now beginning to understand how difficult it was for many athletic coaches to develop a winning team from a bunch of stars, even if they had all been proven winners in their past incarnations.

There was a lot of work ahead for the team. They needed to develop a business plan, coordinate communications, and determine how to handle such essentials as performance measurement, decision making, and conflict resolution. But instead of making progress, conflict and chaos seemed to reign. Uncomfortable with the rough beginning, Jim reverted to form. He avoided interpersonal conflicts by calling few large team meetings and attempting to build relations more on a one-to-one level. However, the more he attempted to control things outside of the team meetings, the more individuals kept running into one another. After two months, progress had been embarrassingly slow and morale was deteriorating rapidly. People would buttonhole him and complain about others. Although upper management was not yet alarmed and people were not yet telling their stories outside the team, he could see he was in trouble.

The Value of Metrics in Diagnosing and Refocusing a Team

Not proud, Jim looked for help. He turned to Rachel Henderson, a trusted and acclaimed pro who worked out of the Human Resources Department. Recognizing the kind of pressure he was under, she suggested a strategy that she believed would help Jim and his team focus on the critical issues while at the same time beginning to understand the dimensions of a really effective working team. Knowing that Jim still had the goodwill of the group (based on a number of interviews she conducted), she had Jim complete a simple instrument that would allow her to get his view of the team. Then, after she explained the results and how the instrument was interpreted, he could decide if her idea of using data from the instrument was a means of bringing focus and increasing unity to the group.

Enter the Group Management Questionnaire

Although everyone knew there was a problem (or problems) with the team, no one, including Jim, knew what to do to get highly motivated people on the same page without them killing each other in the process. After all, they all had their own views of the problems, and rarely did the problems have to do with them personally. Blaming and finger-pointing had become the norm. The underground was alive and well, with team members unwilling to deal openly with issues affecting one another. With Jim in retreat, there was no center around which team problem solving could occur. Rachel felt that Jim needed to use this opportunity to take back the reins and reestablish his own authority.

The Group Management Questionnaire

Rachel explained that the Group Management Questionnaire (GMQ) is an easy-to-administer instrument that requires each team member to respond to seventy-two positive statements—all proven to be important to effective teams. Jim was asked to study each statement and determine whether or not it reflected, *on average,* how the team operated. The questionnaire covers eight categories, each one having a huge impact on the team environment. Each category comprises nine related statements, which are interspersed throughout the instrument. Requiring only ten minutes to take and less than two minutes to score an individual questionnaire, the GMQ can easily create an understandable profile of a team's effectiveness. The use of metrics to objectify the opinions of the group could help them to clarify critical issues that were dragging down the team. Also, this instrument provides a means to compare how any individual member sees the team in relation to the perceptions of other members of the team.

Continuing her explanation, Rachel pointed out to Jim that each statement was specific in describing any given team behavior. Thus, rather than being overwhelmed by the whole, it should be relatively easy to focus on particular behaviors that needed adjustment.

Since the team would have opportunity to review and discuss scoring of individual statements, Rachel described how members would then be given latitude to decide whether or not a particular score was acceptable, while also determining the importance of that behavior to the success of their team. Being able to focus the team on a narrow range of behaviors would provide early success, a sense of accomplishment, and diminishment of the notion that they needed to fix everything at once. To help Jim understand, Rachel selected two of the seventy-two items to demonstrate the potential value of this tool to the development of a team.

Item 11 *When conflict arises, the group is willing to deal with it in a timely manner.*

Realizing that conflict resolution is a critical issue in any team effort and that Jim's own conflict aversion was likely handicapping this group of hard driving individuals, Rachel chose this item to help explain how the instrument worked. Looking at conflict from the big picture, Rachel explained that company norms have a huge impact on the behaviors of the team and individual members. She noted that, just as in the larger organization, Jim's team did not deal openly with conflict. Usually, unresolved conflicts were shoved into the informal underground and left to fester. Because these conflicts will not just go away, they ultimately become the source of gossip, drain energy, and create an atmosphere of mistrust among individuals. Developing behaviors to help the team manage conflict, in spite of company norms, would likely be one area for Jim to address.

———

Item 26 Individuals feel free to give honest feedback to other group members regarding what they do well and what they need to improve.

Rachel believed strongly that item 26 is a litmus test for whether a team is working effectively. Given Jim's unwillingness to deal with conflict, their organizational norms, and the early history of his team's apparent dysfunction, Rachel predicted that this item would resonate with Jim and that honest feedback most likely did not exist within his team.

Jim was intrigued and reviewed the instrument as Rachel explained the eight categories related to team effectiveness: Goals, Climate, Conflict, Rewards, Communication, Meeting Design, Leadership, and Supervision.

After discussing each of the categories (see below), Rachel explained to Jim that this instrument could be a vehicle to help him create some team-building priorities. Of interest were those specific areas such as Goals, Rewards, Communication, Leadership, and Supervision in which Jim could have an immediate influence on the team. The questionnaire could also provide a means of benchmarking the team's progress in each of the eight categories, particularly those identified behavioral statements that the team was readily committed to changing. Now Jim had a theoretical template, a lens through which he could organize his thinking about teams and then begin to make headway concerning how team members related to each other and to the team as a whole. For the first time in months, he began to believe that he might just be able to get his arms around this thing called a "team."

The GMQ Categories

Following is the explanation Rachel made to Jim that helped him understand the GMQ and each of its categories, along with a focused interpretation of the team's actual profile.

Category 1: Goals, Purpose, and Direction

Even inexperienced leaders will most likely identify the importance of goals. Why then are goals almost universally an area of needed improvement in team performance? The reason is that many leaders assume that a written goal is sufficient to ensure success. But just writing down the destination does not guarantee one's arrival; a map must be provided and used. Furthermore, leaders need to put goals in a framework or a context from which they can provide direction and team members can perform their subsequent roles. Too often, with time in short supply, leaders have little inclination to create the foundation essential for success in this critical area. Yet unwillingness to invest time at the front end of team development will inevitably result in confusion and disharmony later. The effective team takes the time to build a solid foundation by developing a clear and measurable set of values by which to operate. *The effective team has values that are reflected in its mission and both the vision and long-term direction that the team has determined for its future. It reviews team goals to determine measured progress regularly. It also measures whether or not agreed-upon team values are being reflected in the members' actual behaviors.*

It is easy to give lip service to values. It is much more difficult to live the agreed-upon values that underlie everything the team does. If the team agrees that listening to clients and others is a core value essential to team success, then it must periodically measure those behaviors at both the team and individual levels. If the team's behaviors are measured as ineffective by its critical constituencies, then specific adjustments can and must be made. Most teams have not taken the time to identify their operating values, and it is the rare team that then measures whether it is living up to those values.

Similarly, we also know that a compelling and clear vision can be a motivating factor in team performance, but few teams have taken the time to build and then commit to a time-driven vision of that future. Values, mission, vision, and goals are four essential aspects of the life of any team or organization, and a failure to develop them will almost certainly result in system dysfunction and a negative impact on all aspects of team performance.

Category 2: Team Climate

Of the eight categories measuring team effectiveness, team climate is the most difficult to define. The concepts of clear goals, core values, and a clearly defined vision are relatively easy to understand. But climate is a more nebulous concept that deals with how people feel about the team. The concept is a measure of the cohesion and camaraderie that exist in a team. The question we might ask is, do team members find relationships to be positive and people to be well treated? A team's climate and the resulting level of trust are the outcome of the interaction of a wide variety of behavioral variables. In the long run, improving each behavior can theoretically improve the climate of the team. While a wide range of behaviors can influence the climate of a team, a small number of these variables can act as a litmus test and can provide a relatively good indication of the current climate.

For example, the following are positive perceptions of team members regarding their feelings about communication and relationships with others in the group: *Members feel open, supported, and trusting of one another. They easily share ideas and feelings, and they give feedback and expect it from others. They feel heard and feel that their contributions are valued. As a result, members feel a strong commitment to one another and to the success of the team.*

Because we are dealing here with how people are treated, some of these same variables will show up in several of the other eight categories being outlined in this section. For example, feedback is an essential element of good communication as well as a recognizable element in managing conflict. Nevertheless, it is the combination of these special variables that create what is meant by climate.

In some organizations, team members may sincerely like one another and enjoy being together, and score relatively high on climate, but they may still show strong signs of dysfunction. For example, if the norms of the organization and team are to treat people with respect and avoid conflict at all costs, the measured climate may be high, yet the ability to deal with differences, solve problems, and make decisions may be lacking. On the other hand, when a team scores lower on the climate category than on many of the other categories, the team's overall effectiveness will tend to be lower because both skills and care among the team members may be missing. The result will be that necessary team building will be all the more difficult and require more attention.

Category 3: Conflict

Generally speaking, most people don't like conflict and avoid it if at all possible. We have been raised to believe that conflict is unnatural because it makes us uncomfortable. However, conflict is a natural and an essential part of working together. Frequently, team leaders do not have adequate training in conflict management and do not have the time, skills, or inclination to deal with it; as a result, they avoid, deny, or mishandle conflicts. The consequences are hidden agendas, passive resistance, and frustration that bursts out in unbridled anger at unpredictable times. All of these impede communication and inhibit team progress. A team that is handling conflict effectively uses the following strategies: *The team doesn't hide from conflict but addresses it when it occurs in a timely manner. It actively attempts to reframe the conflicting issues and lend objectivity to the process by gathering relevant data. It maintains a belief among team members that conflict can and will be resolved fairly and equitably. Its members proactively communicate with one another individually and directly to work issues through before raising them in the group or depending on others to intervene. It clearly labels any behaviors such as gossip and backstabbing that undermine honest and open communication as unacceptable.*

Resolving strong differences and moving forward can have a positive influence on a team as members begin to trust that such differences will not cause damage to the team as a whole or to individual members. Dealing effectively with conflict builds confidence. Although some specific skills need to be learned, much of conflict management can be handled if a team is disciplined and willing to establish clear expectations for what is and is not acceptable behavior. By studying the elements that constitute this category, one can get a clear indication of what needs to be addressed.

Category 4: Rewards, Appreciation, and Recognition

Take any group, team, or organization of which you have been a member and consider how many of its members actually felt fairly rewarded, recognized for their contributions, and appreciated for their efforts on a daily basis. From an early age, most of us, whether in school or in our jobs, tend to feel underappreciated and undervalued. This feeling is a predictable source of stress in many organizations, especially for those on driven, hard-charging teams where competition and individual achievement are taken for granted. In a society where acknowledging successes for individuals is downplayed, but where criticism, blame, and faultfinding are common, negativity can eat away at a team's climate and ultimately influence morale and productivity. The effective team is one in which such negative behaviors are replaced by the following positive ones: *The team distributes rewards based on clearly established performance measures that are perceived as fair. Team members feel appreciated for their efforts and recognized for their achievements. The team celebrates accomplishments at both an individual and a team level.*

Many leaders still operate by the old puritanical belief that "a fair day's pay for a fair day's work should be sufficient, so stop complaining." Such leaders don't understand how the individual needs of group members affect both morale and productivity. Lack of appreciation, recognition for the fair value of work, and fairness have been the source of huge discontent in many organizations. Symptoms of a lack of attention to this critical area include the formation of unions, passive resistance, and the loss of good employees to the competition. As in most other areas affecting team performance, half the battle is awareness; the solutions are often not complicated once the issue is identified. The problem with awareness, of course, is that discontent with reward and appreciation issues is usually mumbled about in the underground, as few will raise their concerns directly with the boss.

Category 5: Communication

Problems with communication seem to affect eight of ten organizations that we see. They seem to be part of the human condition. After twenty years of struggling to create a team atmosphere with effective communication, one leader lamented, "It's never done; just when we seem to have it well in hand, something we didn't think of throws another monkey wrench into our communications." More than other aspects of team dynamics, communication is a continual work in progress, and a lack of vigilance will surely come back to bite the leader. Teams need to measure the communications system so problems can be identified before they begin to influence morale and productivity. *Effective teams make information accessible to team members and ensure that it flows easily through the group. They acknowledge issues and address them in a timely fashion. Their communications are characterized by a sense of candor and openness within the team. People feel heard, and feedback is a natural part of the communication process; the feedback loop is normal, rather than extraordinary, and is part of doing business.*

Communication tends to be the most critical element in establishing a positive group climate; therefore, it needs to be continually monitored, addressed, and improved.

Category 6: Group Process and Meeting Design

Meetings consume the majority of the time of individuals in business today, almost regardless of the level of the employee. Such sessions may be required for information sharing, for problem solving, for decision making, or for planning and reviewing resources. Because individuals are spending so much time in meetings, it is important that they be conducted effectively. But few leaders are trained in ways to facilitate a creative, dynamic meeting, and one that fully engages those present. Most team leaders are stuck in old models where rigid traditions, limited experience, and time restraints virtually dictate a disappointing outcome. Rather than a stimulating and challenging exchange that engages those present, a meeting is usually one in which the agenda is rushed and few decisions are made. Even worse, participants leave feeling frustrated and wishing they had been somewhere else. The predictable nature of how such meetings are run, who dominates the discussion, and the boring and uncreative nature of what transpires, often results in a self-fulfilling attitude of passivity, inertia, and even hopelessness among group members.

Turning such meetings into a more productive use of people's time would involve *well-communicated agendas and design strategies that allow full participation of those in attendance. Both task/product and process/maintenance aspects of the meeting would be addressed. Aberrant behaviors would not dominate, and each agenda item would reflect a creative strategy designed to attack the issue at hand in a unique manner. Proper pre- and postmeeting work would also occur, and the monitoring of follow-up activities would ensure accountability. The meetings themselves, including the behavior of the leader, would be routinely evaluated so corrective actions would help in their continuous improvement.*

In a ten-person team meeting that lasts two hours, with a dollar value of each person averaging a hundred dollars an hour, the cost to the organization of the meeting would be at least two thousand dollars. In our experience, meetings rarely have that kind of outcome value. And the dollar amount does not include the cost in terms of morale and lost productivity. Knowing that many meetings are a waste of time, the response of many team leaders is to cut them short, control the agenda tightly, and act as if efficiency drives the meeting. The result is an avoidance of the underlying issues or differences, which if left unresolved, will inevitably block the team's progress later.

Teams can begin to make their meetings more productive by establishing a few standards and measurements. They can establish meeting *process* standards that review and assess, for example, meeting productivity and member utilization. Teams also need to establish the tools and maintain the discipline to measure meeting effectiveness against such standards. By clarifying what an effective meeting looks like and having members as involved as possible, they can make the meetings less frustrating and more concrete so that ultimately people leave the meetings with a sense of accomplishment and a clear direction for future activities.

Category 7: Leadership

Few individuals receive any training on the road to becoming a team leader. Somehow, the assumption is that being a team leader resides in people's genes, or that leaders have experienced and learned from great team leaders in their past. Unfortunately, most members of teams have never even had the opportunity to experience what it is to be on a truly evolved, high performance team. Even fewer have experienced a leader who applied the skills and foresight necessary to achieve such an outcome in a highly intentional and replicable manner. While hundreds of studies and theories posit what an effective leader is, little consensus has resulted. However, we do know some clear management characteristics that successful leaders must have. Successful leaders *establish with team members clear roles that reflect agreed-upon individual and team goals. They provide clear lines of authority and responsibility for both the team as a whole and for individual members of the team. Whenever possible, they allow members of the team to influence decisions that will affect them. In addition, they make an effort to share leadership responsibilities through the effective delegation of challenging work as well as through the functional work of the team itself.* Such behaviors argue against the need for charisma and huge amounts of experience to be successful. Focus and a certain amount of discipline are required, however.

Category 8: Supervision/Performance Management

It can be difficult to differentiate between leader and supervisor, especially in a team situation. Sometimes, one individual has a dual role of leader and supervisor. Other times, the supervisory role is played by a secondary individual (a lower-level manager) or split among many. *Leader* conjures up a vision of one person leading the band, forging ahead into strange territory to meet the challenge at hand by bringing all members into unison. *Supervisor* conjures up one or more captains in the ranks, or committee chairpersons, heading up a smaller division and ensuring that members are marching to the same beat. Regardless, for our purposes, *supervision* means making sure the job gets done according to the established standards and guidelines, in other words, primarily performance management and accountability.

In an effective team, over time members become more accountable both to themselves and to the team as a whole as they manage their performance. This level of accountability is an outcome of a developmental focus, in which individuals have the opportunity to develop their own potential. At this level, both member and whole-team accomplishments can be measured and recognized. Team members may feel vulnerable because of the higher level of scrutiny required to measure performance, and this vulnerability can ultimately push them to become more accountable for their contributions to the team. The team ensures that standards are met through a previously agreed-upon structure of accountability.

Sadly, this expanded notion of accountability is often lost because the team leader or supervisor is more concerned with his or her *own* productivity than with the team's productivity. With a trend toward more value being placed on the leader as a producer—and with rewards following suit—it becomes clear that development of individual members and building the team into a cohesive, high performing unit are often secondary in the eyes of the organization and, consequently, its members.

For the effective team, however, supervision—the essential buttress that supports the team concept—includes *regular, data-based feedback for the team (constituent feedback) and for individual members based on agreed-upon goals and measurable performance outcomes. It also includes a measure of the performance of the team and its members against the values that the group itself established as guiding principles (see Goals). Finally, it incorporates a coaching approach, as regular reviews are conducted with a focus on the individual needs and development of each member.*

Compare such a process of accountability and personal development to the common quick and dirty approach to supervision based on agreed-upon outcomes that are usually *not* behaviorally defined or measurable. In our model, however, product outcomes are balanced by a focus on individual behavioral change based on measurable data feedback and desired positive changes in performance for the team as a whole.

Rachel ended her explanation of the GMQ by reminding Jim that this instrument was not a cure-all. The GMQ would, however, provide him with the framework to improve the quality of team performance over time. She made a distinction between the foundational and process elements of building a team, explaining that the *foundational* elements of goals, rewards, effective communication, leadership, and supervision are supported by such *process* elements as conflict management, feedback, meeting design, and facilitation skills. She said that all of these areas would eventually need to receive attention and would need to work together to promote effective team development. Last, she stressed that bringing these elements together would not happen without improvements in the quality of time utilization for the team.

The GMQ

Although the GMQ (see Exercise 12) focuses on a wide range of leadership behaviors, our primary interest is in the management process within the group context. Our assumption is that your team meets together on a regular basis and plays a functional role within the organization. This questionnaire will help the leader and the members of the team evaluate the team's effectiveness as a unit in relation to various aspects of the group process. A smoothly functioning group that scores high in most of the elements of this instrument will have become an effective team.

EXERCISE 12
The Group Management Questionnaire (GMQ)*

Directions: Following are 72 statements relating to management and team effectiveness. Place an X on top of the corresponding number in the answer grid if you mostly agree that a specific statement is representative of how your group operates. For example, if you *mostly agree* with statement 6, place an X covering the 6. If you *do not agree* that this is reflective of what occurs in the group *most of the time, leave the item blank.*

Respond to all statements. If you are not certain, answer the best you can and move on. Because of the large number of statements, no single item will change the overall picture.

Answer Grid

1	2	3	4	5	6	7	8
9	10	11	12	13	14	15	16
17	18	19	20	21	22	23	24
25	26	27	28	29	30	31	32
33	34	35	36	37	38	39	40
41	42	43	44	45	46	47	48
49	50	51	52	53	54	55	56
57	58	59	60	61	62	63	64
65	66	67	68	69	70	71	72

Total: ___ ___ ___ ___ ___ ___ ___ ___

*We thank Julie Roberts and Pat Sanaghan, who provided both time and expertise in the development of the GMQ. In addition, we were able to use the groundbreaking scoring techniques first developed by Dave Francis and Don Young in their excellent global diagnostic instrument.

EXERCISE 12 cont'd

1. The goals of this group are clear and understood by all its members.

2. People in this group are committed to working collaboratively with the other members of the group.

3. We have the skills and resources within this group to deal with difficult interpersonal issues.

4. The people in this work group are rewarded appropriately for the work they do.

5. Information is openly shared and accessible to all members of this group.

6. Individual opinions are solicited regarding the building of meeting agendas for the group.

7. When possible, leadership responsibilities are shared among the members of this work group.

8. Individuals within the group receive periodic feedback from their supervisor.

9. The actual behaviors used by members within the group are periodically measured against the values agreed to by the group.

10. Individuals feel free to express both what they feel and think within the group.

11. When conflict arises, the group is willing to deal with it in a timely manner.

12. Individuals feel affirmed and appreciated for their efforts and contributions.

13. Members of the group receive necessary information and receive it when they need it.

14. Agendas are communicated prior to any meeting with the group.

15. The leader or facilitator of the group actively solicits feedback regarding his or her performance in that role.

16. Supervision is valued in this organization; we know this because supervisors are provided with the time and incentive to do their supervisory jobs well.

17. The goals of the group are specific and measurable.

EXERCISE 12 cont'd

18. There is a sense of camaraderie and spirit within the group.

19. Providing feedback is often seen as an essential part of conflict resolution.

20. People feel appreciated because all members of the group are informed of one another's accomplishments.

21. Lines of communication are clear within the group.

22. There is consistent monitoring and follow-up on commitments made during meetings of the group.

23. The roles and authority of the various group members are clear.

24. Individuals are provided the time and encouragement necessary to develop new skills and professional interests.

25. Members have a high degree of participation, and thus ownership, in the group's goals.

26. Individuals feel free to give honest feedback to other group members regarding both what they do well and what they need to improve.

27. Most of the group members believe that conflict can be a constructive and necessary aspect of ongoing group development.

28. Both group and individual accomplishments are recognized and celebrated as a natural part of the life of the group.

29. Leaders of the organization respond to the concerns and questions of individual group members in a timely manner.

30. Meetings are evaluated, and the results are used to improve the design and functioning of future meetings.

31. The leader has the ability to assess the different needs of individuals within the group and to intervene appropriately in a constructive and supportive manner based on this information.

32. Individuals receive in-depth performance evaluations that are based on mutually established goals and measurable outcomes.

33. Members have a high degree of commitment to the completion of the goals of the group.

34. Individuals in the group feel heard by one another.

EXERCISE 12 cont'd

35. Differences in style and background are perceived as valuable assets during conflict situations.

36. Rewards are clearly related to the accomplishment of individual goals.

37. Individuals temporarily absent from the group are kept informed and up-to-date.

38. Meetings are designed effectively in advance of the sessions so participants' time is used effectively.

39. The leader is a skilled facilitator with the ability to move the group forward and create changes as needed..

40. Work delegated to individuals challenges them and readies them for greater responsibility.

41. Progress toward group goals is evaluated on a regular basis.

42. Supporting and helping one another are valued as essential behaviors of all members of the team.

43. Members know that when a conflict arises among group members, a fair resolution will be reached.

44. Rewards are perceived as being fairly distributed among group members.

45. Communication between this and other groups is effective.

46. People involved in meetings believe that they contribute to the success of the meeting.

47. Group members believe that they have the opportunity to influence both the tone and direction of the group.

48. Performance reviews are based on self-reports, data from people influenced by the individual, and observations and experiences of the supervisor.

49. The goals of the group are a reflection of the values and the vision of the group.

50. Humor is used positively rather than as a put-down that minimizes others.

51. Seeking data is often a means of creating an objective reality base in conflict situations.

EXERCISE 12 cont'd

52. People in the group tend to feel appreciated for the work they do rather than feeling that they are taken for granted.

53. Written communication is clear and used appropriately (not too much, not too little).

54. Having humor, fun, and celebration in meetings is natural and occurs frequently.

55. Members of the group believe that they have the ability to influence those decisions that affect them.

56. Supervisors take the time to support and coach individuals.

57. The mission of the group is perceived as dynamic and open to the changing needs of the workplace.

58. A high level of trust exists among the members of the group.

59. A key norm in the group is that difficult feedback or information is dealt with up-front rather being allowed to fester.

60. Opportunities for advancement and special perks are seen as open to those qualified.

61. Lines of communication are open and fluid, with information and feedback being continually solicited and used.

62. The group has the ability to adjust meeting agendas to address the changing priorities of the group.

63. Individuals given positions of leadership are supported in clarifying their roles, authority, and expected levels of responsibility.

64. Supervision is developmentally focused; opportunities exist for professional and personal growth.

65. The group's visioning process creates a shared picture of the group's future, its direction, and its priorities.

66. Most often mistakes are treated as sources of learning rather than as signs of failure with blame attached.

67. During conflict the group is often able to break old patterns and reframe the situation and then move to resolution.

68. Simple signs of appreciation and acknowledgment, such as thank you, are common.

EXERCISE 12 cont'd

69. When people have problems with another individual they communicate directly with that person rather than taking their concern underground.

70. Meetings of the group are rarely boring because each agenda item is treated as a unique event and carries with it an appropriate strategy.

71. Leaders are seen diagnosing individuals, their groups, or the larger system to make changes that are necessary for organizational effectiveness.

72. Supervisors are periodically reviewed on their supervisory effectiveness by their direct reports, peers, and bosses.

The analysis of the responses you and the other group members give will spotlight some previously known (though not necessarily addressed) information. In addition, you will undoubtedly gain some new insights that may be useful in moving your group forward. All responses will be anonymous. Clearly, the value of the exercise rests in the willingness of you and other group members to answer as honestly as possible regarding your perspectives of the group. With this valuable information, the group will have the opportunity to deal with the picture created from the data.

A Word about Scoring the GMQ

The GMQ is useful because the statements are so specific you can easily identify specific areas of strength or weakness. In addition, because the eight categories are so relevant to the life of any team, you can assess which areas need a boost or development and then concentrate on that area. Even though the scoring may initially appear complex, it is extraordinarily simple. Taken a step at a time, the results will reveal an enormous amount of information in a short amount of time.

FIGURE 20

Graph of GMQ Data (10 Participants)

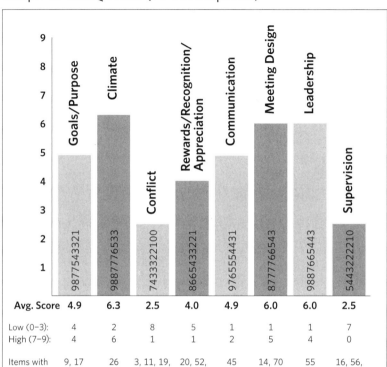

Avg. Score	4.9	6.3	2.5	4.0	4.9	6.0	6.0	2.5
Low (0–3):	4	2	8	5	1	1	1	7
High (7–9):	4	6	1	1	2	5	4	0
Items with low scores	9, 17	26	3, 11, 19, 59, 67	20, 52, 68	45	14, 70	55	16, 56, 72

For this instrument to be of any value in team development, you must look at the average score for each category as well as the items within each category that deserve attention by the team. This will require two separate calculations—one *to average the scores for each category* or column based on the scoring grid and another one *to find the specific items that require attention* as the team moves forward.

To simplify your learning process, we have provided a sample graph representing Jim's ten-person team (see Figure 20). You can create a similar graph for your own team based on the data you generate. We will take you a step at a time through the straightforward process of scoring for this ten-person team. First, we will explain how to view the data for Jim's team and how it was tabulated. Next, we will interpret what the information means for Jim and his team. Finally, we will discuss how Rachel helped Jim interpret and then act on the data in order to help improve his team's effectiveness.

Scoring and Interpreting the GMQ

Following is a brief explanation of how to score and interpret GMQ data in three steps.

Step 1. Score Individual GMQ Respondents

Each of the eight columns of the *answer grid* represents one of the individual categories explained previously. Column 1 has nine items, or statements, under it, all of which relate to Goals, Purpose, and Direction (see items 1, 9, 17, 25, 33, 41, 49, 57, 65 within the GMQ). Column 2 has items in the category of Team Climate, and so on for each of the remaining six columns.

To score an individual's GMQ grid, simply add the number of X's in each column. Each X represents a statement agreed to by the respondent as reflecting something that occurs regularly within the team. The highest score in any column would be 9.

Step 2. Score the Total Group's GMQ Average

As Jim began to determine the scores for his team of ten members, he added the number of X's registered by all of the team members under column 1, which relates to Goals. After adding the total number of X's under all of the column 1's, he then divided the total by the number of those responding (10) and found the team's average score was 4.9. Generally speaking, when groups have not been trained in the skills called for in each of the eight categories, a first attempt at measuring the team's performance will seldom register more than an average of 5 or 6. Thus, the scores in the first column of Jim's ten team members were 1, 3, 7, 8, 3, 5, 4, 9, 7, 2, for an average of 4.9 (these are the numbers in the first column in Jim's grid). So far, so good.

However, as you can easily see, the scores are skewed toward the ends of the scale. Four of the individuals scored quite low (1, 2, 3, 3) while four others scored quite high (7, 7, 8, 9). Apparently there is something causing a split in the scores. Perhaps people are being treated differently or perhaps something else is causing the split. What we do know is that looking only at the average score would tell just half the story. Thus, we need to look at the average as one benchmark and the array of scores as another to determine if there is a pattern that requires further interpretation.

To clarify this, we have arrayed the scores from low to high inside column 1 as represented in the graph of Jim's team from 0 to 3 (low scores) to 7 to 9 (high scores). Jim should be curious as to why this split occurs.

If the average score for a column is *less than 4,* it should be a red flag for the team, and, in this case, for Jim. Our experience suggests that such a low score represents a level of dysfunction that probably needs to be addressed. If the average score of a column is *between 4 and 6,* it deserves attention, although other areas may deserve the attention of the team first. Finally, scores *above 6* place the team in the upper 25 percent of all the teams we have reviewed over the past twenty years. While there may be individual items within the category that need to be addressed, there will undoubtedly be other categories that deserve the team's attention first.

Step 3. Identify Specific Issues That Warrant Attention from the GMQ Assessment

Directly below the arrayed scores are numbers of items from the instrument. These are items where *at least 60 to 70 percent* of those responding to the instrument from Jim's team *failed to register Xs.* Those team members did not feel that the statements described what usually occurred in their team. In column 1 of the graph, the only two items that registered this level of significance were items 9 and 17. By using a cutoff point of 60 to 70 percent, we can be sure that the majority of team members share the perception that the team has a problem. We can say with certainty that the statements referred to in these two items *do not occur* on a regular basis within Jim's group. It is the team's prerogative, however, to determine when and if they will address an item. Like any source of feedback, the GMQ is only a descriptive measure of reality and only Jim or the team decides what needs to be addressed.

Why a 60 to 70 percent cutoff?
If—as in the case of Jim's team—a team has not had training or been provided team building, we suggest a rather high cutoff. In this case, if Jim had used a 50 percent cutoff (that is, half of the team members felt a statement did not reflect what occurs in the team), there would have been many items to address and the result of the diagnostic experience could have been demoralizing. The idea is to identify the items that require immediate attention. For a more experienced team, we would set the cutoff lower so that the team can work toward continuous improvement.

How to undertake a simplified item analysis
The easiest way for Jim to discover which items were problematic (using the 60 to 70 percent cutoff) was to lay the ten grids side by side so that he could easily scan across each of the team members' scored grids. Then, beginning with item 1, Jim glanced across the ten grids and counted the number of spaces left blank for that item. In this case, using the 70 percent cutoff criterion, at least seven spaces for item 1 must have been left blank. In the case of item 1: The goals of this group are clear and are understood by all its members, Jim discovered that five individuals actually placed an X in

that space. Thus, half of the people felt that this behavior occurred at an acceptable level in the group. While not a very high score (one would hope everyone in the group would have a clear understanding of the group's goals), it did not meet the cutoff standard of 60 to 70 percent, or three X's or fewer. However, in the same column relating to Goals, Purpose, and Direction, we noted that two scores did reach the cutoff level. These were items 9 and 17. None of the other items exceeded the cutoff standard. For Jim's team, there were a number of items in other columns that would warrant further consideration given the 60 to 70 percent cutoff.

Rachel's Interpretation for Jim of His Team's GMQ Profile

When Rachel sat down with Jim to help him interpret his team's GMQ scores, they agreed to deal only with items that 60 to 70 percent of the team had left blank, a score that suggested that the team fell short in relation to that particular item. Together they would explore each of the eight categories and the areas of greatest need for improvement. He would then create a set of responses to those items he felt were most important to deal with currently.

Goals, Purpose, and Direction

Although the general purpose of Jim's team was clear—"to get the new product to market within sixteen months"—this long-term goal was not sufficient to motivate team members in the short run. After two months as a team, the 4.9 average score in this category was a symptom of real problems. Any experienced team leader realizes that clear, compelling, reachable goals are often the glue that holds a team together. Assessing this team's score more closely, Rachel and Jim discovered that four of the team members scored the items 0 to 3 while four others scored their responses between 7 and 9. Thus, almost half of the team members believed clear goals and purpose did not exist, while the other half believed these did exist.

Whenever there is such a distinct bifurcation, the team could have some underlying problems that could negatively affect both the morale and motivation of team members. If only half of the group knows their purpose, then the other half is likely wondering "what am I doing here?" With the previously discussed overlap of categories, underlying issues needing further exploration could be in the areas of Communication, Leadership, or Meeting Design, for instance. All of these affect the understanding and internalization of team goals and purpose.

We can get a better understanding of the way these problems are dealt with by looking at the two items in this category that 60 to 70 percent of the team members said were usually not present in the team's behaviors, items 9 and 17.

> *Item 9* The actual behaviors used by members within the group are periodically measured against the values agreed to by the group.

One of the problems that Rachel discovered early in her team assessment was that there were no core operational values that the team had agreed to. With no boundaries or standards defining their own behaviors toward one another, it felt as if anything goes. Such an active, and often aggressive, group of individuals needed to come to grips early on with the principles by which they planned to operate. By establishing agreed-upon ground rules based on a clear set of behavioral values, they would create rules of play. Jim could then use these rules to help control the team meetings and make them more productive. In this instance, an hour of well-designed time could solve many of the issues that had made the team's meetings feel so chaotic and undisciplined.

> *Item 17* The goals of the group are specific and measurable.

As we have discussed, goals are a crucial aspect of team effectiveness. In the case of Jim's team, nearly half of the team members suggested their own goals were unclear. Because goals provide both identity and direction, a lack of clear goals inevitably plays out in the development of dysfunctional behaviors on the part of individuals both inside and outside the team. Because many of the members were highly dependent on one another, problems in one area could easily bleed into other areas. Further, with a lack of effective communication and openness (see Conflict and Communication, categories 3 and 5), frustrations tended to go underground instead of remaining on the surface to be dealt with directly.

Jim needed to have the team build some short-term team-wide goals that demanded cooperation across members. This process would lead to a greater sense of cohesion, team value, success, and confidence.

Team Climate

Team climate is usually the highest-scored single category—especially in a new team. Having gained an understanding of the GMQ over the course of doing hundreds of team assessments and interpreting many different profiles, we have found that this high score can often represent something of an aberration. In the case of Jim's team, the score appears more optimistic than the other data seem to suggest. Individual members probably recognized how good they and their peers were at their jobs and assessed the potential of the group more than its proven ability to act as an unselfish, cohesive, and well-oiled machine. The problematic issues were pinpointed accurately in team members' responses in other categories, all of which related to Climate. Responses in Conflict, Rewards, and Supervision stand in direct contradiction to the score of 6.5 on Climate. Reviewing the numbers leads to the following interpretation: Members of this team valued being supportive and helpful to one another. They also appeared to have a high level of trust with other team members. Still, they didn't feel particularly valued by one another (see Rewards, category 4), and they were nearly incapable of dealing with differences directly (see Conflict, category 3).

Rachel noted that the low score on one item—item 26: Individuals feel free to give honest feedback to other group members regarding both what they do well and what they need to improve—was symptomatic of this situation. This was the only item that reached the cutoff, meaning that 70 percent of the team members believed that honest feedback did not exist within their group. As suggested earlier, the ability to give and receive feedback is the single mechanism that helps a team identify and deal with real problems, make operational adjustments, and provide individuals with specific information to help them become more effective. Without feedback, a group is rudderless, and constructive change will be difficult. When feedback is internalized by the team and flows easily as a natural part of the communication process, gains in both trust and group cohesion can be expected. Strong member relationships are the hard-won prize of a team that has been diligent in dealing with its issues, its unfinished business. If Jim decided to deal only with this single issue, the prospects of the team becoming increasingly effective would improve.

Conflict

For Jim, his team, and his entire company, handling real differences and the conflicts that would arise during this most challenging mission would be one of their most difficult tasks. Overcoming powerful organizational norms that deny or conceal conflict can be exhausting and can have lasting negative repercussions.

Rachel noted that scores on five of the nine items in this category reached the 70 percent level, and eight of the ten members gave the category an average score below 3. Thus, the members were saying that the team had no perceived ground rules or system for dealing with conflict. Certainly, this area needed to be addressed quickly. Following are the five conflict/feedback items that the team gave low scores:

Item 3 We have the skills and resources within this group to deal with difficult interpersonal issues.

_____

Item 11 When conflict arises, the group is willing to deal with it in a timely matter.

_____

Item 19 Providing feedback is often seen as an essential part of conflict resolution.

Item 59 A key norm in the group is that difficult feedback or information is dealt with up-front rather than being allowed to fester.

Item 67 During conflict the group is often able to break old patterns and reframe the situation to move to resolution.

Rachel noted that the team lacked the skills and permission to give feedback. But learning to give feedback is not easy because, regardless of one's skill, it inevitably creates some conflict and tension between giver and receiver. While the task may seem daunting, training team members in the area of feedback strategies and conflict resolution can be accomplished relatively quickly. If members are motivated to alter their norms regarding conflict and feedback, focused training and practice can have a dramatic impact on the team. However, simple awareness and good intentions will never bring about these behaviors. Here Jim needed to take specific actions that would increase skills in the group and provide new avenues for resolving conflict.

Fortunately, Rachel felt that the group represented fertile ground for such an educational experience. She noted that while they were strong-willed and opinionated individuals, they did not appear to be adversarial or antagonistic. First, they would need to learn (through results from the GMQ) the importance of honest feedback, how detrimental the lack of it can be, and the value of learning both feedback and conflict resolution skills to the success of their project.

Rachel believed that strengthening Jim's skills in this arena was critical. As the leader, he needed to support an open, feedback-friendly environment. Only then could group members become more constructive and less critical in their approach to one another. Legitimizing feedback needed to begin with Jim. He could, for example, seek it at the end of every meeting or perhaps solicit feedback on issues important to the team. Efforts to bring difficult issues to the surface, without rancor, would be a first step toward building team communications, member trust, and ultimately the capacity to be an effective group.

Through further analysis, Rachel discovered that the team lacked even rudimentary problem-solving skills. First, she needed to provide Jim with ways to structure group meetings and orchestrate activities for team development in this area. Then he would need to give his team members opportunities to work cooperatively and practice problem-solving strategies. Rachel was particularly enamored with Edward de Bono's work in conflict resolution and problem solving.[1] She explained to Jim how, according to de Bono, easily applied structures could be used to help team members focus their thinking, improve their listening, and use collaborative, non-adversarial decision-making skills. Success in this type of team-based problem solving can help generate greater trust, cohesion, and morale.

Rewards, Appreciation, and Recognition

In many organizations, there is a disparity between what executives think their people want and what the people really want in order to remain committed to both the job and the organization. In many hard-driving and highly competitive organizations those who are out front and leading the charge are being motivated by large rewards, prestige, or status. On the other hand, the majority of individuals, the underlings upon whom the success of the organization is dependent, base their level of loyalty, interest, and personal motivation on the basic elements of appreciation: a personalized thank-you and the occasional recognition for a job well done. Everything else being equal (i.e., competitive salaries and benefits), the human touch and personal recognition are what really drive morale and productivity. Sadly, those very things can easily get lost in the rush of an organization toward success.

In the daily life of Jim's organization, where multiple teams are consumed with their own projects that ultimately drive the success of the entire company, teams are in a hurry, under pressure, under deadlines, and with benchmarks and a hundred crisis points. A review of the GMQ score for the category of Rewards reflected this very scenario. With a score at the 4.0 level, this area was clearly in the danger zone and required attention. Three members of the team were obviously quite unhappy with some of the elements of this category. Prior to looking at the three items that failed to receive 30 percent support, Rachel bet Jim that this area would be easy to correct simply by paying attention to common courtesies. Believing that life was surely more complicated than that, Jim accepted her bet. He was in for a few surprises as they continued their review of the following items that his people felt did not exist in their team.

Item 22 There is consistent monitoring and follow-up on commitments made during meetings of the group.

―――

Item 52 People in the group tend to feel appreciated for the work they do rather than feeling that they are taken for granted.

―――

Item 68 Simple signs of appreciation and acknowledgment such as thank-yous are common.

The first item (number 22) was a real shock to Jim. He had always prided himself on being organized, and he had a reputation for following through. In this case, however, his inability to pull the team together had resulted in some tasks falling between the cracks. He *assumed* people were doing what they had agreed to do without actually monitoring their progress. Later, he held a thirty-minute problem-solving session in which the team developed a manageable system of reminders and accountability checks so that busy people would not forget their commitments. Furthermore, the system helped team members to remember the impact that their own work had on the priorities of others; as a result, they were more likely to give appreciation and recognition to one another. Fortunately, in this case, the GMQ feedback had apparently arrived before resentments became too serious.

The last two items involved common courtesies just as Rachel had predicted. They reflected a view that Jim and others above him in the organization were running too fast. Management was not paying attention to the basic fundamentals of human relationships. And predictably some of the very people who were feeling under-appreciated on Jim's team were treating their own people in a similar manner. The first step for Jim was to raise his own consciousness in this area and then to help his team members grasp the consequences of insensitivity and oversight. While it is difficult to dictate courtesy and gratitude, the team committed itself to the following:

- They would make a more concerted effort to celebrate their own successes as a team as well as those individual contributions that enabled the team to be successful.

- They would slow down and take time in every meeting to acknowledge those who had gone out of their way to be especially helpful.

Jim also committed himself to use the GMQ (every two months for the first six months and then quarterly after that) over the course of the project in order to keep his hand on the pulse of the team. Utilizing this measurement would enable him to determine whether or not members felt that the commitments made were actually being institutionalized.

Communication

In Jim's time-bound, pressurized world of high expectations and deadlines, effective communication was essential. First, communication needed to be timely and accurate. Second, it needed to be honest and candid; those giving it needed to be able to risk displeasure for speaking the truth. Honest communication is crucial, and it is often the first behavior to break down when groups become dysfunctional. Withholding essential information from one another is an insidious affliction and will surely cripple the productivity of a high-potential team from the very beginning (as we've seen with feedback). While not measured as critical, a 4.9 average score is not robust, and indicates that, unless some of the other areas were corrected, communication would continue to deteriorate. The one item that scored below the 70 percent cutoff level (that is, the majority of team members believed this statement was not true of their group) in this category was the following:

Item 45 Communication between this and other groups is effective.

The absence of effective communication between groups in an organization becomes an early warning signal when we remember how and why this team was pulled together. As a new product team, members were selected from across the organization with the intention of ensuring a cross-pollination of ideas. Further, by choosing individuals from varied company departments, management hoped that normal communication dysfunction would be alleviated. Jim needed to have an open forum with his team to discover where the breakdown in intergroup communication had occurred.

The value of the GMQ is evident in this instance. Results of the questionnaire provided team leaders with a warning, a red flag for those areas where trouble may have been brewing. And with Jim paying attention to this red flag, the team could address any communication issues before they became truly dysfunctional and crippled the group.

Meeting Design

As discussed earlier, holding a productive meeting requires much more than just gathering a group of people and letting it happen. It

298 MEASURING WHAT MATTERS

takes solid leadership, planning, time, and creativity to draw the best out of each member. A well-designed meeting provides a rich environment for team building. In real life, however, meetings are usually conducted in a mediocre way, and few participants think about all that goes into a productive meeting. Members of the group attend and expect the same old thing: a boring agenda with most of the items being treated the same. Little time is spent creating a different set of actions based on the uniqueness of each agenda item. Our definition of *meeting design*—taking the time to really think about each task item and creating a unique process accomplishing an outcome that will be valued by the members of the meeting—results in a good use of members' time and of their skills and abilities.

Meeting Design was one of Jim's team's three strongest categories, so it does not appear to need immediate attention. However, we have learned from experience that, as was the case with the Climate category, this score can be deceiving. On the surface, it may appear that everything is fine, especially when motivated team members are accomplishing their tasks. After all, task/project accomplishment is the goal, right? Careful attention is still required here because we desire to build a strong team that will pull the best from its members over the long run. A good meeting design and well-planned agenda can provide opportunity to accomplish that. Rachel believed that the team responses in this category might provide clues that mediocrity was an acceptable standard for Jim's meetings and, more than likely, for the organization as a whole. Mediocre meetings do not provide the fertile ground necessary for team building, and Rachel was concerned that they had already lost opportunities to strengthen the team. Rachel and Jim dug deeper here as they assessed the two items that most members agreed were *not* being met in the team.

Item 14 Agendas are communicated before any meeting with the group.

This item commonly shows up as a low score on many of our surveys, and it is usually given short shrift because more urgent issues force it aside. Infrequent or no communication of agendas prior to a meeting reflects a loose and reactive management approach in which little advance planning occurs. And poor planning can be indicative of a crisis management mentality. The ill-prepared leader does not have a detailed agenda ready with enough lead time to communicate it to attendees. Team members thus miss the chance to research items and come to the meeting prepared with answers.

Item 70 Meetings of the group are rarely boring because each agenda item is treated as a unique event and carries with it an appropriate strategy.

Responses to this item go hand in hand with those of item 14 and in this case confirmed Rachel's hypothesis that Jim was not spending enough time planning the meetings or determining the proper utilization of his team members. Meetings can be boring because people are underutilized and have the sense that "we've been there and done that." All too often, little time is spent by the leader determining how to best utilize the individuals attending and how to make each agenda item come alive. The lack of creativity in meeting design and engagement of the team members keeps people from feeling energized or valued. If Jim wished to create a cohesive team, a first step could be to ensure that each team meeting was carefully designed. This would result in fewer individuals dominating the sessions and more members actively engaging the issues. This way, when individuals left the meeting they would be more likely to feel well utilized and that their time had been well spent. Satisfied members feel better about their individual work, their work as a unit, and each other. This in itself is team building. While this type of meeting planning takes more time, the long-term payoff is substantial in both team productivity and morale. Further, Jim's own status as a leader would increase proportionally.

Leadership

The category of Leadership had a relatively high score, for which Jim could feel good. Four members scored him in the 7 to 9 range. This category is one in which Jim's convivial style and personal motivation paid off. We saw that early on Jim began to spend more time with his team in one-on-one meetings. In that scenario, people got to know and like him, as borne out in the high score they gave this category. However, a further analysis of the scoring indicated that five of the eight GMQ scores were considered less than adequate and three were in the danger zone. One of the statements that members felt was *not* indicative of their team was the following:

> *Item 55* Members of the group believe they have the ability to influence those decisions that affect them.

Interestingly, the perceived inability of members to influence decisions appeared to be a direct result of Jim's one-on-one meetings. Instead of dealing with the chaos of those early group meetings head-on and *helping* the team solve problems and make their own decisions, Jim used the individualized meetings as an escape. By getting involved with members individually, he began to exert his own control over decisions affecting team members. It would have been more beneficial for him to assist them in establishing their own controls and let individual members have more decision-making influence.

Although Jim was liked as a person, as a team leader he was increasingly ineffective, and his score in this category reflected that. Still, the group had not yet started taking their problems out on him personally. But if Jim did not lead the group toward solving their identified problems, he would eventually lose credibility—regardless of how much people liked him.

Supervision/Performance Management

Given the low score in this category, Rachel observed that this is where the Mr. Nice Guys like Jim pay a heavy price. This area represented the team's second lowest score, and Rachel believed it needed to be addressed in the very short run.

She recognized that team leader was a new role for Jim and that it was quite different to build a smoothly functioning team than it was to run interference for a tough COO, the key requirement of his prior position. Not only was he getting used to a new role as team leader, he was also still responsible to his old department. Thus, Jim was carrying a considerable weight. To gain a better understanding of Jim's problems in the supervisory arena, we need to look at the organizational norms to decide where the true culprit lies. Each of the following items was given a negative response by most of Jim's team members:

> *Item 16* Supervision is valued in this organization; we know this because supervisors are provided with the time and incentive to do it well.

> ———

> *Item 56* Supervisors take the time to support and coach individuals.

> ———

> *Item 72* Periodically, supervisors are reviewed on their supervisory effectiveness by their direct reports, peers, and bosses.

In many fast-paced organizations, the focus is on hiring good people who are self-motivated. They are expected to hit the ground running and keep running or be left behind. Often little attention, especially in team environments, is placed on focused supervision or performance management. Employees are often expected to find the answers themselves, learn the jobs on their own, and then just do it. They should not have to be prodded by a team leader acting like a cop. Despite these expectations, nothing is further from the truth. People need training, support, skill development, and team building. They need both supervision and leadership to coach them, to monitor work performance, and, sometimes, to give them a needed prod. Negative responses to all three of the above state-ments reflected an organizational culture that hindered Jim's abil-ity to be an effective team leader and supervisor.

Both Rachel and Jim agreed that he had not provided effective supervision for his team. The fact that seven of the ten members scored him with an average of 0 to 3 reflects a serious problem. Even when Jim pulled back and began putting more time in one-on-one relationships, he was not creating clear goals, measurable performance criteria, or objective developmental feedback to his direct reports. The control that Jim asserted in those individual-ized meetings was off the mark. What was needed was more open-ness among team members and the cultivation of greater trust. For Jim, building close and rather personal relationships was almost beside the point—although it helped to maintain his popularity in tough times. What was necessary was the development of team relationships.

It was crucial that Jim then develop a collaborative role with his team to negotiate clear goals and delineate lines of authority, espe-cially in such a crisis-reactive environment. Teams come together when their members struggle together to resolve touchy issues of authority and when they begin to see the team as more important than any individual. Rachel also believed it would be crucial for Jim to assert himself—not as a top-down and controlling boss but as someone with authority who was focused on building team relationships and clarifying the roles of each member, himself included.

Finally, even though the provision of feedback was not a strong organizational norm, Jim needed to develop the use of this very valuable communications tool, especially in his supervisory role. Feedback from him, and other members of the team, was essential because of the close interaction between most team members. Feedback, as a barometric reading of his supervisory effectiveness, would be very beneficial to Jim. Such a feedback–performance re-view process needed to be part of the team's agenda.

After a thorough discussion of the team profile, Jim and Rachel forged a succinct summary of their findings. This summary helped

Jim focus on a manageable list of mandatory priorities for the short run if the team was to experience a positive turnaround.

Actions for Jim to Take Based on Interpretation of GMQ Scores

Rachel realized that the GMQ was like a puzzle where placing the pieces in the right sequence would determine Jim's success or failure. Given that he couldn't possibly fix everything, he needed to be judicious in choosing his priorities. And, remembering the interplay of variables, he needed to carefully choose those initiatives that would affect multiple areas and give his team the most bang for the buck.

- First, Jim needed to recognize that much of the conflict he and the team experienced was a result of his own leadership and supervision. To reduce the conflict, he needed to clarify several issues, including personal and team goals, lines of authority, members' specific roles, and the issues' relation to one another. This lack of clarity had created confusion and was eating away at the team's ability to trust one another and work effectively together. Once these issues were identified as problem areas, they would become relatively easy to address.

The group needed to focus on naming short-term goals for the team as a whole. Jim would then negotiate specific measurable, criteria-based, and outcome-related goals with each team member. The setting of goals would be predicated on an extensive analysis by team members to determine if the group's resources were being optimally utilized. An effort would begin to familiarize others with individual goals, areas of overlapping responsibilities, and essential cooperation in order to provide further opportunity to build a greater sense of the whole and to begin to diffuse issues of turf brought from previous team experiences.

- The team would set aside time to explore a set of standards (core behavioral values) that would guide members' behavior toward one another and toward others with whom the team interacted. How the team would be accountable to itself in reinforcing these values needed to be part of the discussion and the resulting agreement.

- The team would learn to provide feedback and incorporate it into their behavior and group norms. As Rachel suggested, a relatively brief training session could enable the group to begin assessing and giving feedback about the team's progress in a variety of areas. These areas might include meeting effectiveness, task progress, and accountability (i.e., satisfaction level of their organizational customers regarding the team's progress and overall performance). By bringing feedback out of the organizational closet and beginning to use it as a necessary part of their daily business, the team would begin to model an openness and directness of communication that would spill over into all team activities.

- Jim became aware of the importance of modeling simple courtesies and appreciation to the team, as a whole and to individual members. The team, as part of their understanding of GMQ metrics, would have a frank discussion about changing the norms concerning nonrecognition and the value of celebration so that these could be built into the natural life of their developing team. In any group of ten there are always a few individuals who find such issues not only challenging but also fun, and will volunteer to lead the way.

- Jim agreed to make a commitment to upgrade the quality and overall value of meetings involving his team. Thus, his role expanded to help ensure the full engagement of his team when they met, and to guarantee that agenda items were designed to create a process that utilized the unique qualities of the team members. Such intention would be rewarded with outcomes that would have greater value for the team. Jim would need to take quality time to plan meetings and to involve team members in this process. He would arrange for the value of the meeting, including the role of the facilitator, to be evaluated. And he would use this information to strengthen the next meeting, ensuring a sense of continuous improvement over time.

- Because his experience and skills in the use of problem-solving and decision-making methods were limited, Jim needed to expand his own repertoire and to begin modeling and teaching the team some of these valuable tools and skill sets. He needed to ensure that every time the team came together, they would experience success and an expanding set of skills and methods for doing their work.

- To improve his team leadership skills, Jim had to stop seeking approval and "doing" so much. Interestingly, intense hands-on management was a valued organizational norm in the company. Jim would need to buck the system and, instead of actually doing so much of the work, learn to delegate, enabling others to develop their skills. Jim had to become a facilitator, a coach, and a manager to the team. Because those behaviors were not highly valued within the organization, he would need to learn to deal directly with conflicts that arose. Redefining his role as a strong team leader would take courage and a strong commitment to accomplish his goals.

Summary

Because the statements upon which the GMQ is built are specific and are drawn from a review of best practices in the areas of team development and group management, they provide a well-grounded framework for building a positive team environment. The instrument is both diagnostic and prescriptive in that it offers clues that can themselves be framed as solutions. The benefits include the following:

- It is short, sweet, and easy to take.

- It is even easier to score and to compile as a profile of team behaviors.

- It isolates a range of indices that can provide a variety of insights for leaders and the team.

- It facilitates the building of team priorities.

- It allows a team leader to establish benchmarks in relation to eight categories and in relation to specific items that need attention.

If a team leader is willing to invest the time to learn how to score and how to maximize the various metrics that can be derived from this analysis, he or she will better understand the dynamics of the team's environment. The leader will find that the GMQ can help focus, motivate, measure, and challenge the team in both the short and long term. It can be used as an integral part of the management process that can engage all members of the team in the process of team building and team management. However, like any skill set, it requires consistent use and practice by the leader and the team itself. By focusing on easy-to-use metrics and a set of understandable categories of team performance, the GMQ gives team leaders the opportunity to strengthen their own leadership while at the same time strengthening the cohesion and effectiveness of their teams. Many leaders use the GMQ on a quarterly basis, a practice that provides their teams the opportunity to witness the success of particular initiatives aimed at strengthening either an entire category or particular items identified for improvement.

Performance Matters

Developmental Supervision

We look at art 360 degrees; the only problem is we forget to do that with our lives. —ANDY WARHOL

It is rare to find an organization that does not perceive supervision as an undesirable requirement, a passionless necessity. This historical view is reinforced by current realities, where the focus on short-term, bottom-line objectives provides little room for the supposed luxury of effective supervision. Let's face it, people are rewarded for doing, for producing value-added products—not for coaching others to do their work better, or for holding people accountable for doing what they are paid to do in the first place. These attitudes reflect, in our experience, the prevailing norms in most organizations, whether the organizations fall on the profit or nonprofit sides of the ledger. The problem is that these attitudes obscure huge benefits to be gained by those willing to embrace a longer-term view of work that takes into account what motivates people to be productive, loyal, and dedicated to an organization. Exactly how valuable this long-term approach will be depends, to a large degree, on the selective utilization of data at both the product and developmental levels of supervision.

The issue is, of course, to be selective, choosing the information that will, indeed, matter. As with the preacher who found himself with only one old rather wise parishioner, we are always faced with the question of how much is enough. In the story, the old man was left bored and out of sorts because the minister dumped the whole load on him when a little would have been more than sufficient.

Definition of Terms

Developmental supervision and performance management are two parts of the same whole. Organizations without the capacity to hold people accountable and to reward work accomplished will find it difficult to motivate employees, to measure effectiveness, or to celebrate hard-earned successes. If the process is arbitrary and capricious, trust and morale will suffer. If standards vary across different units, productivity could be adversely affected. If measurement criteria differ among individual supervisors, the very fabric of institutional trust could be undermined.

Similarly, if individuals do not feel personally coached or mentored, and if they have little sense of direction or professional opportunity, organizational loyalty and motivation could suffer.

The blending of performance and personal development is the cornerstone of any successful supervisory program.

"Supervision" can be defined as the process of developing the capacity of individuals to grow personally and professionally in ways that provide them with increased opportunities while continually adding value to the organization. At the same time, they are evaluated in relation to their contributions and rewarded in a manner commensurate with their ability to achieve their agreed-upon goals at the highest possible level.

The underlying belief is that by encouraging individuals to expand their interests, skills, and knowledge, the individuals and the organization will benefit over the long run. By delegating responsibility and authority judiciously, the capacity of the organization will continue to grow, creating further opportunities for others. The key at both the performance and developmental levels is to provide continuous and measurable feedback that objectifies the total process.

Predictable Sources of Resistance to the Process

While many leaders would rationally support a change initiative that would increase supervisory efficiency and effectiveness, a number of issues make such a proposition easy prey to resistance from a wide variety of natural and expected sources. These include the following:

- A leader may have a history in which supervision has been uneven and at best mediocre in its application. Few leaders have ever had a positive experience in this critical area of work.

- The reality in many organizations is that supervision has generally not been rewarded. Individuals have been rewarded for producing work rather than for taking the necessary time to develop others to do work. The result limits an organization's capacity to grow.

- At the top level of organizations, where leaders must be committed to more effective performance management, there are usually widely varying levels of understanding and differing degrees of skill and dedication to quality supervision. Words expressing many of the accepted concepts of modern management often are not reflected in the actual behaviors of these leaders. Since the process of management—outside of bottom-line numbers—is often not evaluated, leaders have little reason to pay attention to supervision as a skill set and area of critical professional competency. Often supervision does not even make it as a measured performance objective.

- For many, supervision is a one-shot experience occurring once a year—something to get out of the way rather than being perceived as core to their success and followed and monitored throughout the year.

- Employees usually do not trust the process because established goals give way to the crisis of the moment without adjustments being made to the goals or expectations that were negotiated previously.

- Similarly, many employees are unwilling to share what they know about morale or productivity with their supervisors because there has been little time spent building trust or openness. Some have a concern that revealing personal limitations or mistakes will be factored "informally" into their performance reviews and might easily influence their salaries or future opportunities.

- While supervision is theoretically tied into an organizational planning cycle, this process itself is not built on sufficient data, candor, and trust. The result is that goal setting at the unit level is dependent on who your supervisor is rather than on a consistent process of even-handed performance management procedures based on an organizational vision and resulting goals.

- There are always those individuals who recognize that they benefit from the lack of consistency and the arbitrary nature of the current supervisory process in an organization. The process is often one that breeds favoritism and a lack of fairness across the organization.

Although such a list can be daunting, the very introduction of a consistent, standardized, and fair supervisory process would go a long way toward reducing the sources of resistance. However, the implementation of any coordinated supervisory program would have to address these quite legitimate concerns. *The effective use of basic metrics is central to overcoming these formidable sources of resistance.*

The Key Question of Commitment

With flatter, leaner, and more responsive organizations, many of the strongest advocates of supervision will be quick to agree that there is little time to supervise. Even the introduction of supposed time-saving technologies has, paradoxically, resulted in more, not less, work, as expectations for responsiveness and quick turn-arounds have increased time demands (and stress levels). Until the early 1980s a high-quality developmental supervision program could be expected to demand 20 to 25 percent of a manager's time. Such a commitment was deemed to be the minimum amount of time essential for a quality program. Times have changed, and with the new environment many organizations are asking a key question:

What is the least amount of time we can utilize to maintain a high-quality supervisory/performance management program for our organization?

There is no indication that the pressure to do more with less will cease anytime in the near future. We must be increasingly inventive in the ways we allocate time and resources to the supervisory process. We assume that most leaders—given a span of control of from six to twelve employees—give considerably less than 10 percent of their time to the performance management process, and many organizations want to keep it that way. For us, the issue isn't time but rather the discipline of how such supervisory time is allocated and how well metrics are adapted to support it. Few managers we have worked with would suggest that 10 percent for supervising their direct reports is not a fair use of their time. Taking the cold numbers, that gives the average supervisor 260 hours a year with which to work with his or her direct reports. Two hundred and sixty hours—impossible, you say. True, if supervision is undervalued, if it is not part of the rewards system, and if it remains the last priority on a manager's chaotic schedule, that number will not work. For many leaders, supervision is relegated to a short time each spring, just prior to the end of the fiscal year, when performance evaluations are due. *The result is often a superficial, unproductive goal-setting session that feels force-fed rather than a thoughtful, reflective session that allows time for evaluation and personal development.*

The Numbers

In the following pages we will address how to rework this picture into one where supervision is a manageable and highly valued part of an employee's work life. Because making supervision and performance management a priority and building a schedule that maximizes its effectiveness is of theoretic importance, let's revisit the numbers and determine the requirements for an ideal performance process for a manager and her eight reports. Later we will investigate exactly how to commit the expenditure of time. First, see Table 10 for our proposed allocation of a supervisor's time.

TABLE 10
Proposed Allocation of a Supervisor's Time

- Meetings with each of eight direct reports for one hour twice a month to review individual progress, to strategize, and to coach. *192 hours*

- Two-hour team meetings every other week with eight direct reports to plan, strategize, problem solve, and review progress. *52 hours*

- Three-hour Supervisory Dialogues with each of eight direct reports once a year. *24 hours*

- One hour follow-up sessions to the eight dialogues four months later. *8 hours*

- A two-day team-building and planning/goal-setting retreat with the team. *20 hours*

Estimated time for supervisory management processes over the course of a business year. *296 hours*

The estimated 296 hours for related supervisory work represents 11 percent of total work time during a year. Because individual performance is the key to any successful organization and is tied directly to holding employees accountable to their goals and other commitments, the question is, is an 11 percent commitment of the supervisor's time a valuable investment in the success of his or her direct reports and of the team? What we do know is that unless organizations institutionalize a committed, disciplined, and metrics-based performance management process, they will end up with the kind of arbitrary, inconsistent, and ineffective process all too familiar in many organizations.

Supervisory excellence is built on a foundation of regular meetings in which work is monitored and individuals are coached and supported in their efforts to improve their performance while developing personal and professional skills. This demands measuring what truly matters for each individual.

The Heart of Performance Management

Supervision is all about helping people become successful in doing their work. It should be about coaching, not blame, about supporting and developing more than criticizing and reprimand. The Supervisory Dialogue is the centerpiece of a program in which individuals feel supported in their efforts to improve, change, and grow. *Historically, supervision has been either a passive or a reactive process. This program is a developmental process* in which employees have the opportunity to track their own progress, both in terms of their actual performance and their particular chosen areas of development.

By its nature, the Supervisory Dialogue is a collaborative process, with each supervisor working closely with direct reports and using a wide variety of data to help gain a full picture of each individual's work reality. A ten-question dialogue provides the substance of the review process in relation to both goal setting and personal development. During the Dialogue employees have the opportunity to review their own progress by answering the ten questions. They are also asked to consider what their supervisor might say in relation to each of the same questions. Their responses are then compared with the supervisor's own responses to the same questions. The Dialogue results from the exploration of the agreements or discrepancies between these various points of view. It allows each person's perceptions and expectations to be clarified so that over time the discrepancies decrease while the communication and understanding increase. Over a number of years, supervisors can discern patterns, measure progress, and monitor and reduce identified areas of concern.

A Discipline

The Supervisory Dialogue represents a commitment by both employee and supervisor to work toward the systematic and measured improvement of the employee's effectiveness. Whereas most supervision focuses on measured outcomes and successes and failures, here fully two-thirds of the questions relate to the process of work and the direct or indirect influences on the ability of each individual to accomplish his or her agreed-upon goals. By focusing on these questions, and by being accountable to the process itself, progress is almost guaranteed. Although the ten questions provide focus, the actual success of the Dialogue depends on the supervisor's commitment to the process itself, as evidenced by a willingness to take the necessary time, to listen, and to provide the feedback, support, and guidance necessary to move the individual forward.

Rationale

The purpose of the ten questions is to create, in a relatively short time, an enormous amount of information so you, as supervisor, can understand each employee's feelings, attitudes, and performance. The questions can help you understand the employee's personal and professional dreams, how she would like to reach them, whether anything is holding her back, and how you, as her supervisor, might be personally helpful in her development. This process provides a structured dialogue that will help to build your relationship with each individual. Many managers take the time to build little more than superficial relationships with their direct reports, and many don't know how to go about building a relationship even if they would like to. Many feel that building a more personal relationship is inappropriate, since it might reduce the capacity of the boss to be objective and dispassionate in his evaluation of those reporting to him. Nothing could be further from the truth. The issue is how to develop a trusting and personal relationship by developing an evaluation process that is fair, objective, and consistent across individuals. We assume that a personal and open supervisory relationship is the key to building trust, and trust is an essential element in the creation of an effective supervisory team. When people feel fairly treated, they bring that sense of support and openness to the team. The Dialogue is a formative experience that is common to each of the team members. Done well, it can build trust cumulatively among individuals and with the team as a whole.

The nature of the ten questions, and the fact that both the supervisor and the employee are responding to them immediately, reduces the inclination of one person or the other not to be candid. We have found that the responses of the boss and the employee are usually very similar. Because both are aware that they are working from a relatively similar experience and that their responses will provide a reality test for which neither would like to be too far off track, they are usually on common ground. Employees often do know more about their own experience and have a greater sense of their own reality. But where there are shortcomings, the last thing they will want is to be perceived as not being conscious of their own imperfections. The time is right for them to be self-critical and candid. The boss has an interest in being perceived as aware, realistic, and on top of the situation. Putting employees in the shoes of their boss provides the potential for a powerful reality check that is

316 MEASURING WHAT MATTERS

useful for both parties. As the supervisor, you need to know how direct reports see you and your perceptions of their job, their performance, and your grasp of their strengths and limitations. Employees can discover how personal projections or untested assumptions can influence their behavior.

The kind of data gathering proposed for the Dialogue is generally described as "subjective," yet it is an incredibly important source of information for the two parties involved. Because of the pressure on both the boss and the employee to be truthful and candid, the way the data evolve is as important as the information itself. As is often noted, perception is reality, and the perceptions of the boss and the employee form the foundation of their relationship. If each is not clear on the other's perceptions, both will be vulnerable to miscommunication and potential dysfunction.

Creating the Substance of the Dialogue

Discrepancies between your answers and those of your direct report provide the seedbed for conversation and negotiation. For example, if you see your direct report as having been particularly successful in one area that he does not mention, you have an opportunity to praise him and to discuss why he did not see this as a success or achievement. Similarly, you may overlook something important to the employee, or his perception of his success on a project may be different from yours. You should attempt to get behind the words and to learn how individuals really think and feel about their work. What is important in the Dialogue is the degree of understanding that the question format can accomplish. Along the way, the employee will get to know a great deal about you based on how willing you are to be open, to share your feelings and your values in relation to what is being discussed. At the end of the three-hour Dialogue meeting, the result should be an increase in trust, clarification of expectations and concerns, and the establishment of clear priorities and a positive atmosphere supporting real negotiations. Before exploring the Dialogue in detail, we will discuss the pre-Dialogue work essential for its success.

The Pre-Dialogue Orientation

You will want to prepare your direct reports for the Supervisory Dialogue. This usually requires conducting a fifteen- to thirty-minute meeting with each direct report or with the team a week or so before the evaluation session. This pre-Dialogue meeting sets the tone for the entire three-hour Dialogue. It also presents an opportunity to outline expectations, answer specific questions, and explore the expected level and quality of responses to various questions. Knowing what to expect reduces apprehensions for employees. Affirm that the process is about development as much as it is about evaluation and measured goals. Make sure that all employees know that the meeting will last at least three hours and that they will want to prepare themselves by answering the ten questions twice in writing—first, as they perceive themselves and, second, as they perceive that you, their supervisor, perceive them. Make clear that the dialogue is just that—a discussion about performance and areas of strength and areas of needed development. Writing the answers is meant to provide focus as well as clarity.

We have found that having employees write out their responses helps them determine clearly whether there are differences in how they see themselves versus how they believe you will respond. Having them see things through the eyes of their boss is an essential part of the process, because to be out of sync can have a dramatic effect on employees' priorities, expectations, standards, and other factors usually assumed and often not discussed. Their goal is not to guess correctly but rather to gain a clear understanding of whether everyone is on the same page and, if not, where differences lie that could spell problems. Both differences and similarities often stimulate further discussion.

If individuals arrive for the Dialogue unprepared, *do not conduct the interview*. This is equally true for you as supervisor. Credibility and trust can be undermined if it is obvious that your responses are being generated as the Dialogue unfolds and that you have given little thought to the serious nature of the process.

During this pre-Dialogue meeting, you will find it useful to review the employee's job description as a framework for further discussion and later role clarification. You need to lay the groundwork for the Dialogue, and doing that begins with the job description.

Ideally, you should conduct the Dialogue, Exercise 13, at a comfortable off-site location where you can have refreshments at hand and maintain an atmosphere of informality and comfort. It is not helpful to have it in the boss's office—a neutral environment can somewhat diminish issues of status and authority. As a kickoff for the year-long supervisory cycle, the Dialogue is the foundation for everything that follows. The employee should receive a set of the questions in Exercise 13, but the rationale immediately following Exercise 13 will make more sense to you and will provide a greater understanding of specific questions, the Dialogue in general, and your role in it.

Understanding the Rationale for the Ten Questions

Following is an overview of the ten questions and why they are asked. The questions reflect a comprehensive approach that attempts to address the needs and interests of both the employee and the supervisor. Understanding the rationale for each question is central to placing the Dialogue in the proper supervisory context.

Question 1

What are your five or six greatest accomplishments or successes of the past year? Please be specific and explain why each is important to you and to the organization.

Question 2

What are the three or four things you like best about working here?

EXERCISE 13
The Supervisory Dialogue

Directions: Please consider the following questions and respond to them from two points of view. First, being as candid as possible, answer each question from your own perspective and provide specific examples. Second, answer each question as you believe your supervisor will respond based on his or her perceptions of both your work during the past year and your goals for the next year. Please write out your responses in preparation for the Dialogue meeting.

1. What are your five or six greatest accomplishments or successes of the past year? Please be specific and explain why each is important to you and to the organization.

   _____

   _____

   _____

   _____

   _____

   _____

2. What are the three or four things you like best about working here?

   _____

   _____

   _____

   _____

3. What are the three or four things you like least about working here? How does each hinder your ability to be as successful or as satisfied as you might be?

   _____

   _____

   _____

   _____

   _____

4. What are three or four things you failed to accomplish over the course of the past year that you believe you should have accomplished? For each, consider why this occurred and what you might have done differently had you had the opportunity.

   _____

   _____

   _____

   _____

   _____

EXERCISE 13 cont'd

5. What are the five or six most important goals or projects that would be a measure of success for you during the coming year and why? (One of these should include supervision if you have supervisory responsibilities.) How much time do you believe each of these goals will take? Over what period of time will they be completed?

_____

_____

_____

_____

_____

_____

6. Considering each of the goals identified in question 5, what specific behaviorally based criteria could be used to measure your success? In other words, how will you know when you have accomplished each goal? Are the criteria measurable? Observable?

_____

_____

_____

_____

_____

_____

7. What are potential blocks that could inhibit your ability to accomplish these goals and limit your success over the next year? These could be a lack of knowledge or skills, a lack of support or guidance, political realities, or any of a number of other factors. Again, please be specific.

_____

_____

_____

_____

_____

_____

8. What strategies—such as being coached, taking a special class or an internship, seeking out special resources, or even reading— might help to reduce these potential blocks to your success?

_____

_____

_____

_____

EXERCISE 13 cont'd

9. Where would you like to be professionally five years from now? How can the organization help you reach your dream? How can I, as your supervisor, help you?

_____

_____

_____

_____

_____

_____

10. What do we need to do to strengthen our relationship? How do we increase our trust and ability to work effectively together? What can I do to be more helpful? Are there specific things I can do to support you in specific goals or projects you are undertaking? When and how often should we be meeting to help ensure your success this year?

_____

_____

_____

_____

_____

_____

Question 3

What are the three or four things you like least about working here? How does each hinder your ability to be as successful or as satisfied as you might be?

Together questions 1, 2, and 3 allow an individual to talk about his successes, his likes, and his dislikes while working within the organization. They could easily take an hour to cover. Because most people are not accustomed to talk at this level with their boss, you may need to probe beneath the initial responses to gain the level of understanding that is so essential. These questions provide a doorway into the individual's fears, expectations, needs, and dreams.

They also hold clues to the individual's values and aspirations. They are designed to open and explore the relationship; by pointing to areas in which the person isn't happy, and doing what you can to help out, over time you will increase your credibility and further build trust. As the supervisor, your most important role is to *help the employee be successful*. However, this is not the time in the Dialogue to solve problems. Rather, it is a time to listen, and to explore differences or similarities in your perceptions without judgment.

The ten questions are rarely a part of most performance reviews. They provide an opportunity to build trust at the beginning of the Dialogue based on your ability to listen and to show understanding and empathy through your responses. Even when your own responses differ from the individual's, the exchange can broaden the relationship. Over several years, patterns are more easily perceived. You will also have many opportunities to help resolve problems and to support the individual during the course of the year based on what you learn here.

For example, if your views of success differ from the individual's, the difference might point to a need to be more conscious of the kinds of success he has defined and to pay more attention during the course of the year. Or the difference might be because of a miscommunication on your part so that the individual simply does not realize what is important to you. While you are not after conformity to your views, it is important that your views are clearly understood.

Question 4

What are three or four things you failed to accomplish over the course of the past year that you believe you should have accomplished? For each, consider why this occurred and what you might have done differently had you had the opportunity.

This question is designed to help each individual own her problems or failures with the least amount of defensiveness possible. What puts most people on the defensive is being told that they are wrong, or feeling that they are being blamed or criticized. However, even if the failure is very real, using this process, the individual being evaluated will say most of what needs to be said. Because she realizes that you have specific areas in which you believe she failed to accomplish previous goals and have noted them in your assessment, she is left with a choice. She can fake it and not acknowledge the obvious. Or she can step up to the plate and own the problems that certainly exist because of the failure to resolve them during the course of the past year.

The result, in our experience, is 80 percent agreement between the boss and the direct report on problem areas she has identified. Suddenly, rather than finger-pointing and blame, there is agreement and the opportunity to explore the issues that might have gotten in the way of success. The issues could be a shortage of resources, a lack of necessary training, unrealistic expectations, or myriad other factors. Such a problem-solving focus opens the door for you to work together to gain a more complete understanding and to determine what might be done differently in the future. The places where you disagree are opportunities for discussion and clarification. Why didn't she see something you identified as a problem? Or why didn't you identify something on her list? It is a time for candid talk and clearing the deck for the coming year.

Critical to this discussion is the unfinished business that can still be corrected and what you and this person can do to make that happen. Is the issue more or less a problem now than it was before, and will it deserve priority status during the coming year? (See questions 5 and 6.) If so, how should it be handled differently? There may not be sufficient time during the Dialogue to provide a complete assessment, discussion, and closure for each issue. If necessary allocate further time at a later date—particularly if goals for the coming year are influenced by what occurred previously.

Question 5

What are the five or six most important goals or projects that would be a measure of success for you during the coming year and why? (One of these should include supervision if you have supervisory responsibilities.) How much time do you believe each of these goals will take? Over what period of time will they be completed?

Question 5 focuses on the individual's areas of responsibility during the coming year in relation to desired projects, goals, objectives, and outcomes. Consideration of this question, along with some of the previous questions, gives the review meaning and helps in the development of the individual's work responsibilities. Your role is to make certain that both you and the employee understand as clearly as possible what your priorities are in relation to what he believes he should be doing. Explore your similarities and discrepancies in thinking in depth. Ideally, this discussion represents a true negotiation of how the individual will utilize his time and skill in light of the organization's needs.

In most cases, if the organization's goals and those of the unit have been clearly defined, the individual's goals and the organization's or unit's goals will be closely aligned. Clearly, there may be a problem if your perception of the individual's goals differs dramatically from his own and from what he believes you will expect. Again, as in all of the other questions, it is important that your direct report answer both for himself and for how he believes you will respond. Your role is not to capitulate to capricious interests of the person, but he may know something that you don't, or he may have an interest that was not considered, one that will motivate him and benefit the organization.

If the individual has supervisory responsibilities, those responsibilities should be one of his legitimate five or six project goals for the year. Because time is a crucial resource and reflects what is valued, look at how much time is to be spent on each of the individual's roles and actual goals, including the goal of supervision. If supervision is not a legitimately measured performance goal, it will rarely become an important priority in the work life of the individual or, consequently, of his direct reports. The Supervisory Review (see Exercise 14, page 339) provides the behavioral data for measuring the degree to which individual supervisors are taking their responsibilities seriously and are applying the skills necessary to be effective.

Finally, keep in mind that the problems identified in question 4 may still exist. Question 5 provides the opportunity to address them if they are still sufficiently important to be a major goals. Questions 7 and 8 may add insight as well, because they provide feedback and strategies for dealing with specific issues of skills or leadership behavior. At this point, however, it is essential not just to acknowledge past failure or a remaining current need but what things must change in order to improve chances of success. You must determine exactly what changes must occur for the effort to be successful. That is why it is so important to be realistic in your agreed-upon goal expectations and the time allotted for their success. Here is where the negotiation involves identifying a set of goals and responsibilities that can result in success. *All too often the employee develops an unrealistic set of goals to please you and, as a result, guarantees failure in the future.* Your role is to be sure that success is possible and that personal enthusiasm on the part of the direct report has not clouded reality or might impinge unfairly on his family life. Similarly, the negotiation surrounding question 5 allows the opportunity to stretch an employee's view of success, to challenge him, and to encourage greater responsibilities or effort.

Question 6

Considering each of the goals identified in question 5, what specific behaviorally based criteria could be used to measure your success? In other words, how will you know when you have accomplished each goal? Are the criteria measurable? Observable?

Question 6 is based on the assumption that we can and should measure agreed-upon work outcomes. You need to be certain that the outcomes are clear and agreed to up-front and that the criteria of success have been fairly negotiated. Given that effective supervision is a goal, one example of measures you can establish is based on the Supervisory Review (see Exercise 14 on page 339), which can be distributed to each of the individual's direct reports to provide feedback regarding his ability to supervise.

Often a brief follow-up session is required after the Supervisory Dialogue because the final list of agreed-upon goals is the result of a negotiation between you and your employee. In addition, the criteria often need some strengthening, especially if the employee has had little training or practice in the use of criteria-based goal setting. Part of the reason the supervisory process works is that both progress and a final evaluation can be compared to what you originally agreed on. The end result should be a brief written contract, signed by both you and the individual, outlining the agreed-upon goals and the accompanying criteria used to measure success. Formalizing the agreement raises its value and gives you something you can return to at various times over the course of the year, if necessary, in order to clarify expectations.

Question 7

What are potential blocks that could inhibit your ability to accomplish these goals and limit your success over the next year? These could be a lack of knowledge or skills, a lack of support or guidance, political realities, or any of a number of other factors.

Question 7 is critical to the entire supervisory process. To help your direct reports be successful, together you must examine the potential blocks to their success. This is your opportunity to provide them personal feedback based on past performance about what you see as possible obstacles (see also question 4). Such feedback can relate to specific behaviors that may inhibit their success because of inadequate skills, issues of attitude, or the quality of their work.

Here is where coaching and support for an individual's personal development is most pertinent. It is also the area that is most often avoided by supervisors. Again, by asking each individual to identify what he perceives as factors blocking his success and to identify what he thinks you might say, you begin an important thought process in advance of the Dialogue itself. The perceptions of the boss and employee are usually not that far apart because neither party wants to appear insensitive to the realities of the situation. Most employees realize their limitations. This process provides an atmosphere in which the ownership of such limitations is not threatening and in which developing alternatives is legitimate and supported.

Question 8

What strategies—such as being coached, taking a special class or an internship, seeking out special resources, or even reading—might help to reduce these potential blocks to your success?

This question provides the opportunity to explore the strategic actions that will help the person to overcome the blocks identified in question 7. Be creative. Suggest helpful opportunities for the individual's development. The possibilities include opportunities for observing an expert, creating an internship, and taking special courses or workshops.

When issues identified in question 7 pose a threat to the person's success or ability to do the job successfully, then together you need to work out a strategy to make change possible. Clearly define the initiative and incorporate it as a goal to be included with those established in question 5. Making it a goal legitimizes sufficient time and focus to ensure the kinds of change needed. And by defining criteria, you can benchmark the individual's progress over time. Of course, you can decide on other strategies that are not tied in to measurable criteria. Nevertheless, commitments to action, beyond good intentions, make this question vital to the personal development and growth of the individual.

Question 9

Where would you like to be professionally five years from now? How can the organization help you reach your dream? How can I, as your supervisor, help you?

This question helps individuals focus on the personal and professional choices available to them for their futures. One way to maintain people's motivation is to help them establish clear career paths and enable them to make continuous progress along those paths. Ultimately, the process should increase individuals' skills and sense of worth. Not everyone has to be ambitious with a high-level need for achievement, education, or status. However, in today's rapidly changing world of technology and work, all employees must be prepared, minimally, to ask questions about what they need to do to keep pace and to be ready to handle the changing demands of the organization. Most workers at all levels are interested in the possibilities for future promotions, job opportunities, and shifts in responsibility. Those who want to advance will need a plan and a commitment to study or prepare for building skills. This process provides a place and time to begin exploring such possibilities.

If supervisors work to delegate, to promote, and to prepare people for greater challenges, the benefits will accrue, to the individual and, ultimately, to the organization. Even if individuals leave the organization for greater challenges, their leaving will open opportunities for other deserving people from within. Furthermore, the organization will become known as a place that develops its people and provides opportunities for individuals to take increasing responsibilities and to grow, both personally and professionally. This process provides another opportunity to develop the level of personal relationship and trust that can only result from exploring the options and getting to know the lives of your employees.

Question 10

What do we need to do to strengthen our relationship? How do we increase our trust and ability to work effectively together? What can I do to be more helpful?

The focus of this question is on how to improve the supervisory relationship and to increase the value of supervision for each individual. Each person has different needs and deserves the opportunity to shape the supervisory process in a manner that best suits his needs. Some will require more hands-on coaching while for others there will be extended periods when only reviewing projects or delegated responsibilities is needed. Since it is often difficult for the employee to be candid about supervision, you may need to do some encouraging and modeling to bring the discussion to a meaningful level.

Conclusion

The commitment to leadership development and individual growth is designed to create a more competent and committed workforce. If you educate, train, and support individuals in their growth and development, the result will be a loyal and dedicated group of workers who will be more likely to commit themselves to the organization and to its values, its customers, and the services it provides.

Underlying Pressures to Reassess Our Supervisory Assumptions

In most goal-directed organizations, employees must remain current, adaptable, and responsive to the changing needs of the organization. Not only this, but individuals deserve and require ongoing feedback in relation to their contributions and to their individual effectiveness. Rewards and recognition should, in turn, be ongoing and reflect changes in success and overall performance.

We can assume that even though most employees are not necessarily committed to the institution for the duration, they are likely to remain in one place of work for five or even ten years. Such a moderate commitment to an organization can more likely be secured if employees have opportunities for personal and professional development and if they get recognition and rewards commensurate with their achievement levels and skills.[1] Increasingly, when supervision does occur in many organizations, it is ritualized with a standardized format and is squeezed into the least amount of time possible. It makes use of checklists and goal-setting formulas and takes a minimalist approach to the entire process. Unless there is a problem that demands attention, supervision is likely to be increasingly ceremonial and less and less substantive.

Such a pro forma approach to supervision is characterized by undifferentiated reviews and salary increases. Since to differentiate on the basis of performance demands evidence and attention to actual achievements, one way to reduce overt conflict is to reduce the differences among the salaries of individuals at the same level. When most people are given nearly the same salaries, and fewer dollars are allocated to those achieving true excellence, there is less room for argument, an outcome often welcomed in conflict-averse organizations. In the absence of easily defined differences, such as in sales and marketing, the trend is to create simplistic boilerplate approaches to supervision that act to save time and reduce the potential for conflict. The outcome can be a slow slide into organizational mediocrity over time, with the disillusionment of some high-performing employees who resent the lack of recognition for their extra effort and both the quality and quantity of their contributions. In the long run, the price paid in falling morale and productivity can be large indeed.

> **To differentiate salaries on the basis of individual performance in a fair and equitable fashion requires skill, time, discipline, and valid data. Without these ingredients morale and personal motivation will decline and, ultimately, so will productivity.**

The Three-Year Supervisory Cycle

Paying equal attention to every employee every year can be draining, repetitive, and inefficient. Although goal setting and the monitoring of individual progress need to take place on a yearly basis, other aspects of the supervisory process can be distributed over time. A supervisor can work developmentally with dedicated employees over a longer period. Obviously, she will have to monitor those individuals with problems or those on probation on a more regular basis.

The following proposal assumes that a supervisor will commit 11 percent of her time on average to the evaluation and development of the individuals who report directly to her.

Stage I Supervision: Each Employee Every Year

At the heart of the supervisory process is the Supervisory Dialogue. It consists of a three-hour review of each individual's goals, personal development accomplishments, and blocks to success and an exploration of measurable, criteria-based goals for the coming year. In addition, direct reports will evaluate their supervisor's effectiveness on a yearly basis. The interview-based format of the Supervisory Dialogue allows for responses and comparisons of both the employee's and the supervisor's views on each of ten questions. The agreements and discrepancies stemming from this dialogue provide the foundation for further discussions throughout the year, with the opportunity to evaluate progress against the various agreements reached. The Dialogue, while focused on the ten questions, can and should be far-reaching as an effort to explore what is working and not working for the employee in his work life.

We continue with our model supervisor who has a span of control of eight individuals and follows his Dialogue with a one-hour follow-up session six months later to focus specifically on progress, problems, and successes relating to the Dialogue. This meeting is in addition to biweekly supervisory meetings, as suggested previously.

What we propose here is a dimension of supervision that requires an entirely new level of effectiveness for only a small increase in the expenditure of a supervisor's time. While the Dialogue and follow-up sessions focus to some degree on personal and professional development (see questions 2, 3, 4, 7, 8, 9), justice can be done only with more quality data and with an increase in time allocated for thorough discussion and planning.

Stage II Supervision: One-Third of the Employees Each Year

Most supervisors have limited opportunities to witness their employees at work, especially as the ranks of middle managers have been thinned and workloads of all supervisors have increased. Although supervisor observation is critical to any effective reporting process, that process can be dramatically improved by the inclusion, on a periodic basis, of a modified 360-feedback reporting process. The additional data from such a process can focus on specific skills, leadership behaviors, or attitudes central to the individual's success. The process itself can be individualized, or standardized across the organization.

Typically, an uncomplicated and direct approach to such an assessment is preferable. Twenty-five behaviorally based scaled items and four or five open-ended questions can provide a substantial indication of how each person being reviewed is perceived by those he influences on the job. Of course, a number of preconditions must be present to ensure the quality process essential for success. These include the following:

1. Each supervisor must be trained in how to review the data with the employee and how to provide the developmental planning and monitoring necessary to ensure success. The training would ideally include observation and feedback during one of the supervisor's actual Dialogues to be certain that she has the empathy and listening skills essential for this level of supervision. (For an example, see Jake's case study in Chapter 7.)

2. The employee must be protected from threat, intimidation, or the possibility of retribution based on the 360-degree report. This developmental aspect of the individual's supervision should be separate from the goal-directed criteria used to determine salary and promotion.

3. Each manager's supervisory skills should be reviewed to ensure that the manager has the sensitivity and positive relationship with his or her direct reports to ensure the success of this aspect of the supervisory process.

4. To attain the most accurate picture of the individual employee, a well-monitored process must be in place that stan-

dardizes how data are collected for individuals and ensures anonymity and confidentiality.

In most situations, individuals receiving their data will be helped to develop specific action steps to improve their ability to be effective on the job. Normally, there would be no relation between performance goals and the personal development goals and action steps derived from the 360-degree data. In some instances, however, the data would be strong enough to suggest that one or more of the individual's measurable performance goals developed as part of his yearly Supervisory Dialogue would relate directly to the 360-degree feedback data. The relevant part of the feedback data would then become part of the regular performance review and be one of the conditions reviewed in relation to his overall success, including salary.

We have found that the additional data analysis, problem solving, and counseling may require as much as an additional half day of work with each of the three individuals engaged in the Stage II Supervision—a small investment of time given the obvious benefits to be gained. Clearly, the purpose of this process is to help each individual strengthen identified behaviors or skill areas that are limiting his effectiveness.

Stage III Supervision: Monitoring Phase for One-Third of the Employees

On a scheduled three-year cycle, the employees who experience the 360-degree feedback in year two are then monitored during the following year. The supervisor focuses on the Supervisory Dialogue as well as the action commitments based on the 360-degree data from the previous year. The data from the 360-degree feedback can supplement the normal Dialogue process. This allows a convenient vehicle for benchmarking specific behaviors or issues drawn from the 360-degree information. Such monitoring and follow-up to Stage II takes small amounts of time and can usually be included in the individual's yearly Supervisory Dialogue.

334 MEASURING WHAT MATTERS

Developmentally, the three-year cycle provides time to focus on work behaviors, future plans, and yearly goals. Acting as coach, mentor, and evaluator, the supervisor should become a consistent source of support and accountability for the individual at both the performance goals and developmental levels.

Exempt and Nonexempt Differences in the Supervisory Process

Every employee deserves quality supervision. However, when managing others is not part of the equation, and when the work tends to be more focused, technical, and routine, a different approach to supervision can be taken. If we take the ten-question Supervisory Dialogue as the foundation of supervision for all employees, then it would be logical for employees not focused on management or special projects to skip questions 4, 5, and 6, which are focused on criteria-based goals. This would reduce the estimated time for the Dialogue by nearly an hour and would not require the same in-depth follow-up sessions demanded with more project-focused work.

Furthermore, 360-degree feedback conducted in the second stage of the three-stage supervisory cycle is most beneficial for individuals working across units and with external customers. However, it is relatively easy to develop feedback instruments reflecting the uniqueness of any individual's role. For example, an assistant to a management team member, who engages a broad range of personalities across the organization during the course of a year, may wish to have a review that contains specific questions that provide feedback reflecting the peculiar nature of his or her role. A sampling of the assistant's many constituencies can easily provide this information. Clearly, the feedback is only as useful to individuals as it is relevant to their roles and responsibilities. For them, it too depends on *what matters for their success.*

Nevertheless, the more routine, the more predictable, and the more consistent the work of any individual, the less the need for broad-ranging feedback or project-based goals. With simpler needs, the nature of supervision can be simplified. To maintain standards across the organization, the feedback instruments for a particular type of role may be standardized with supervisors and the employees themselves trained in the specific nature of the expected standards.

Why Performance Management Often Fails

Even the best-intentioned and well-organized efforts at performance management sometimes fail. There are two primary reasons. First, all too often, the boss uses the goals and the criteria of success more as a means of threat and intimidation than as a vehicle for counsel and support. While criteria-based goals do provide for accountability, the idea should be to create opportunities for success and not to establish a case for reprimand or criticism. How often do leaders render the supervisory process useless by pushing employees toward unreachable goals so that success is rarely achieved—all in the name of motivation? Their goal is to squeeze every last piece of work out of the employee. In contrast, the Dialogue allows a context for both performance and personal development based on a comprehensive view of the individual and the job itself. Holding written goals over people's heads to drive them to greater performance will inevitably result in mistrust and generally will work only in the short term.

A second reason such criteria-based performance often fails has to do with the reality of new business. In any given year, new challenges and goals, new priorities are bound to arise. The problem is not that these changes occur but that what has been previously negotiated is taken for granted and new tasks and goals are simply added to the old list with nothing being removed. The result is a guessing game for employees as they attempt to determine which goals are most important and which should be put aside. In all probability, the new added goals have not been included as part of the criteria-based evaluation. In order for the total performance evaluation process not to lose credibility the performance criteria need to be adjusted.

Assume that a person's performance criteria negotiated during the Supervisory Dialogue represent 100 percent–plus of her time and commitment. If a new and important project arrives on the scene, one that will take perhaps 10 to 20 percent of the person's time, new criteria should be agreed upon and new time expectations and priorities should be established. Only by removing something from the original list—taking an item off the individual's plate—will the performance management process maintain its integrity. While there is always room for emergencies, the failure to renegotiate the criteria in good faith will result in future negotiations being manipulated. All too often individuals will attempt to protect themselves by negotiating down so they are not left vulnerable by not being able to complete the goals upon which they had agreed. They assume that the process lacks integrity and, with no room made for changing demands, they need to protect themselves.

Data Supporting the Three Stages of Performance Management

The kinds of information generated for each of the supervisory stages must not become ritualized and lacking in meaning. The information must be limited so that those receiving it do not become overwhelmed. Similarly, if highly complex and unnecessarily elaborate, the individual data will be too difficult to organize and monitor, and too expensive to maintain. With this in mind, the following explanations focus on categories of information that would seem relevant across a variety of organizations and reflect the kinds of information that will be most useful and sustainable over time. Determining a sampling of behaviors that are consistent with a particular organization's values, as well as its ideal qualities of supervision and leadership, is essential if the process is to be useful. Following are suggestions for the categories to be included:

1. The ten questions of the Supervisory Dialogue are asked on a yearly basis and are completed by both the supervisor and the employee. The employee also estimates what he or she believes the supervisor would say. If either the expectations or the assessment of the supervisor diverge from those of the employee, the Dialogue provides a unique opportunity to resolve differences before the discrepancies result in problems during the year.

2. The yearly definition of reachable, measurable, and criteria-based goals (questions 5 and 6 of the Dialogue) form the basis for measuring actual performance. The goals themselves become the source of critical questions for each evaluation—to what degree was the individual able to accomplish the tasks implied in the goal statements?

3. A brief scaled-item questionnaire is given anonymously by all supervisors to their direct reports on a yearly basis with the results to be reviewed at the time of the Supervisory Dialogue with their supervisors. This is essential if supervision is to be taken seriously. It also assumes that one of the measurable performance-based goals of each manager's Dialogue includes supervision. Without supervision being perceived as being as important as any other goal, there is no reason for it to be given priority over competing tasks.

4. The scaled items included in Stage II of the supervisory cycle should include three types: behaviors reflecting agreed-upon organizational values, behaviors relating to generic leadership behaviors thought to be relevant across job roles, and additional behaviors unique to an individual's role and job responsibilities and believed to be essential to a particular individual's success.

5. The Stage II open-ended questions should be generic and useful to individuals regardless of their specific organizational roles; questions appropriate for understanding a particular individual's role can be added if needed.

Exercises 14 and 15 were developed to support the Three-Stage Supervisory Cycle. They consider executive leadership skills and attributes and competencies drawn from a wide range of resources. They have been designed to keep costs, complexities, and redundancies to a minimum while still being comprehensive and representative of the skills and behaviors most often recognized as crucial to effective leadership and management.

Steps to Ensure Successful Performance Management

In spite of the apparent rationality of this approach and its minimal demands on a supervisor's time, several things must occur if such an effort is to be successfully institutionalized. Going through the motions of supervision is very different from having it become part of the very fabric of how business is accomplished. The eight items below represent bottom-line demands that such a program requires of management if they and staff are to reap the benefits of such a thorough, and ultimately valuable, supervisory process:

1. Performance management must be built into the rewards system with qualitative and quantitative data used to establish agreed-upon standards and consequences. Special awards for excellence should help legitimize the process in the eyes of supervisors.

2. A certain commitment and discipline must be modeled from the very top. Unless such a commitment is perceived by everyone, even the best-organized and best-intentioned program is doomed to typical supervisory mediocrity and inconsistency.

3. People respond to real consequences (both positive and negative), and the consequences need to be both visible and immediate in relation to both the administration of this program and the effectiveness of the supervisors responsible for its implementation.

EXERCISE 14
The Supervisory Review

Please rate _____

on the quality of the supervision you have received during the past year. Score each question on a 10-point scale based on whether you have experienced the behavior regularly (8–10), occasionally (5–7), or rarely (1–4).

____ 1. Your supervisor helps you define your areas of responsibility and authority.

____ 2. Your supervisor has delegated responsibilities to you that have given you the opportunity to learn, grow, and increase your skills.

____ 3. You and your supervisor have developed a relationship in which timely help and support are easily accessible to you.

____ 4. You experience the supervisory process as one in which your professional development is important and encouraged.

____ 5. Recognition and rewards are distributed fairly, based on your performance and contribution and that of others in the organization.

____ 6. The goals and objectives that determine your success, along with agreed-upon criteria of success, are fairly negotiated.

____ 7. You meet regularly with your supervisor to discuss your work progress and issues critical to your success.

____ 8. Your supervisor has observed you sufficiently on the job to have a sound grasp of your role, skills, and needed areas of development.

____ 9. Your supervisor has helped you create strategies for improving your performance in the areas of development you have identified.

____ 10. Your supervisor provides you clear and timely information relating to your own job role.

    1. Please identify your supervisor's *three greatest strengths* as a supervisor. Be as specific as possible.

        _____

    2. What *three pieces of advice* would you give your supervisor to help improve the quality of his or her supervision?

        _____

The Leadership Effectiveness Survey

Part 1. Leadership/Organizational Behaviors

Directions: For each of the following, please rate _____ according to your experience of him/her in the organization. Place a score on the line to the left, using a ten-point scale: 8, 9, or 10 reflects outstanding performance or a high level of skill; 5, 6, or 7 represents a moderate level of effectiveness; below 5 is less than satisfactory.

___ 1. Is well organized, well prepared.

___ 2. Utilizes own time and that of others effectively.

___ 3. Leads from a set of clear goals and a future vision.

___ 4. Works to involve others—a true collaborator.

___ 5. Assesses problems effectively—a good diagnostician.

___ 6. Is decisive and willing to make decisions in a timely fashion.

___ 7. Designs meetings effectively—they are creative, value-added, engaging, productive.

___ 8. Communicates ideas and information in a clear and understandable fashion.

___ 9. Will take charge of a situation and act—is recognized as a problem solver.

___10. Continually seeks to improve self and others (seeks out best practices, new training opportunities).

___11. Supports fun and humor as an essential part of the workplace.

___12. Shows a strong understanding of the intellectual and technical aspects of the job.

___13. Builds strong relationships among employees and attempts to create a real sense of team.

___14. Handles conflict effectively and in a timely fashion.

___15. Is an effective listener—people feel heard.

___16. Produces work at a consistently high level of quality.

___17. Solicits and acts on feedback from others.

___18. Is willing to provide others with meaningful and timely feedback.

___19. Acts in a fair and impartial manner.

___20. Acknowledges own mistakes and is nondefensive.

EXERCISE 15 cont'd

___21. Is consistently honest, trustworthy, and ethical in behaviors to others.

___22. Is approachable and emotionally accessible to others.

___23. Shows appreciation for the work of others—makes it easy to recognize others' good works.

___24. Is recognized as a planner—based on data, establishes priorities, plans implementations, then monitors progress.

___25. Has a customer focus (either internal or external) and assesses customer needs and levels of satisfaction on a regular basis.

Part 2. Open-Ended Questions as Performance Measures

Directions: Please consider this individual in relation to the following questions and provide specific information—with examples when possible—that describes the person's performance as you experience him or her.

1. What three strengths does this person exhibit that should be maintained?

    _____

    _____

    _____

2. What three specific behaviors would you have this individual change in order to improve his or her effectiveness?

    _____

    _____

    _____

3. If you were in this person's position of leadership, what recommendations would you make to improve the morale and/or productivity of the unit?

    _____

    _____

    _____

4. What pieces of advice do you believe this individual needs to hear that others, for whatever reason, might be reluctant to tell him or her?

    _____

    _____

    _____

4. The basic elements of the program must be clearly defined in a written paper, in which new and old employees can gain understanding of any particular aspect of the program. The program would be supported by an individual at the executive level with a personal goal and the responsibility and authority for its effective implementation.

5. The quality control of the program must be legitimized through a department that has the authority to mobilize the support and resources necessary to ensure that the program standards are maintained. The responsibilities would include the coordination of training as well as the provision of coaching for supervisors and counseling for staff. This includes monitoring of the 360-degree feedback process.

6. Since supervision as outlined here depends on its perception as a developmental process, the ability of the supervisor to build trust among his or her direct reports is essential. If trust cannot be achieved, the process itself will be of limited value. The ability to build trust should become a standard for all supervisors. Plainly, supervision is not meant for everyone, regardless of a person's achievements in other areas.

7. Both supervisors and direct reports will need training to understand the nature of each aspect of the supervisory process, including the expectations of Stages I, II, and III as well as the implementation of the Dialogue. Included in the training would be practice and feedback.

8. Because the interview aspect of the Supervisory Dialogue is so critical to the process, every supervisor should be observed periodically as a measure of quality control. The understanding and agreement of confidentiality with the person being interviewed would be required.

Summary

Institutional change depends on creating an acceptable structure to contain the change initiative. It then demands the commitment and discipline necessary to move the idea forward. In addition, the initiative must be sustained through the application of real rewards and consequences as part of its implementation. Finally, it requires the sincere interest of those for whom the process is designed. If any of these givens are missing, success will not be forthcoming. With them, the team or organization can be assured of valuable dividends in the areas of performance, including higher levels of morale, greater trust, and, quite possibly, greater productivity. In the end, it is the metrics and creative means of gathering and utilizing the data that will spell the difference between success and failure. See the Appendix, "Building Effective Goals and Measurement Criteria," for further discussion and examples of defining and measuring goals.

10

Profit Matters

The PEI-Genesis Story

*I went to the woods because I wished to live deliberately,
to front only the essential facts of life, and to see if I could not
learn what it had to teach, and not, when I came to die,
discover that I had not lived.* —HENRY DAVID THOREAU

We position this story of PEI-Genesis as the final chapter because it is a living example of how an organization can measure what matters for successful results. PEI-Genesis is an actual functioning, breathing company. As such, it gives hope to those companies that currently feel they are adrift, like the manager in the hot air balloon in the story in Chapter 1, not knowing where they are or where they are going.

This could be the story of any of ten thousand manufacturing organizations in this country: a company having fewer than five hundred employees, filling a small technical niche in a competitive field, and attempting to compete in an international economy where labor efficiency is everything. Its leadership prides itself on using the best management practices, paying fair wages, and constantly exploring new ways to improve the company's productivity and its service to its customers.

The leaders had always generated a wide variety of data, but the facts were disconnected, and when used they were often inconsistent.

When it came to asking what really mattered, the leadership finally agreed it was two things:

- **Production cycle time:** How long it takes to produce one item of product from start to finish. Lower cycle time translates directly to lower costs and higher profits.

- **Employee Absenteeism:** Affects productivity, morale, and cycle time.

By addressing these two critical issues, the leaders believed they could project a potential turnaround that would take the company from being a barely competitive organization to one in which dramatically improved cost savings and customer service would move them to a new level in their field. Addressing these issues would force them to look at all aspects of the production process and also at underlying factors influencing morale and, ultimately, productivity.

On the surface, the product is relatively simple; it is a valve that is tooled to certain specifications, with quality control being essential. Their unique problem was that every client had slightly different requirements—different specifications, so that each order was tailor-made to that client. Now that's a problem!

Their South Bend plant was seen as key to a major production turnaround. The employees had a healthy suspicion of management, and South Bend was traditionally a union town with an adversarial relationship with management built on years of mistrust, tough bargaining, and strikes—lots of them. If you worked in manufacturing, nearly everyone had lived through a no-holds-barred strike at one time or another. Skepticism was in their blood, flowed through their veins, and fed the quite understandable suspicion. The cynicism people would carry with them to every meeting was likely to flavor conversations both at work and away from the plant. "How will they exploit us this time?" was the real question underlying every discussion.

In a way, this attitude was unfair, because this management team, located in the New York–Washington business corridor, had acquired the plant with the belief that good old midwestern values would include such things as trust and goodwill along with the expected work ethic. In the minds of management, it was easterners they would expect of such skepticism, not homegrown midwesterners. Not only this, but they came in peace and truly wanted to create a positive work environment.

But history counts, organizational cultures are real, and this new management was not going to be trusted just because their intentions sounded admirable. Not only this, but management was perceived as a bunch of interlopers who would not understand them, or even care to. Why should the employees not feel that way? There had been a history of wrongs that they believed would not be addressed—because they never had been. The result was business as usual—doing no more or less than was expected, maintaining the us-versus-them climate that had existed for years.

With their past frustrations, would they, could they, change their attitudes and, ultimately, their behavior? Could they become a responsive, open, collaborative, and trusting workforce with such a history of antagonism and doubt? It was clear that one could not demonstrate trust and fairness with words and pep talks. But it had to begin somewhere.

Changing Minds and Attitudes— One Person at a Time

Steve, the president, is a straightforward sort of guy. He tries to say what he means with not a lot of fluff—just the truth as much as he is able to express. And he was frustrated at the failure of previous efforts that had been undertaken with good intentions. But regardless of efforts at training and collecting data and pep talks, nothing had seemed to work. The production cycle continued to barely budge, and rates of absenteeism and other indicators of morale were below expectations.

He called everyone to a meeting. He was characteristically brief and to the point. He was at his wits' end and needed people's help. He asked, "What is wrong? What do you need that I can provide that will break this logjam of mistrust?" For a few minutes there was cold silence. But he was committed to being patient, to really listening, to getting under the stones of resistance, and to forging some modicum of trust. One hand went up rather reluctantly. "What about the lack of picnic tables for lunch?" Another asked about a "smoking bench," and still another complained about taxes being taken out of their bonuses. He didn't have answers, but the questions were reasonable and deserved to be answered. He would look into each one. There were other issues, but none that seemed as if they should generate the levels of resistance that he and the other leaders had experienced. While real, these issues were, of course, tests of his listening, of his willingness to act; they were tests of his will and whether people should even bother beginning to trust.

But for Steve and his management group it was a beginning. They had begun by *taking the pulse of the employees,* listening with their hearts and minds to what was underlying the resistance. For them a face-to-face meeting was critical, without the distance created by a questionnaire. But what happened afterward, the follow-up, was just as critical. Seeds of hope had been planted, and comments were heard, like "In all our years we've never had such a meeting." Basically, employees had to be shown that management really cared. Steve committed himself to sitting down with anyone who desired his time. It was a beginning.

There were other meetings, other efforts to meet employees' very reasonable needs. And the questions became more direct, less convoluted, less cautious. With Steve's accessibility and candor, the suspicion began to melt away, suspicion that there was some underlying agenda, that there would be a price to pay for the conversation and the benefits that were being gained a bit at a time. But the drawbacks never came.

And Steve was rather blasphemous. At one of these initial meetings, he said quite pointedly that he was not really their boss. Whether they succeeded or not was not up to him. The real boss was the clients, all *their* clients. The sole determinant of their future, of their security, and, ultimately, their earnings was the clients' satisfaction with the quality of the product and the service they experienced. After weeks of such meetings, Steve began to get their attention. The employees began to imagine that perhaps, just perhaps, Steve was different, and that they could be different. It became clear that Steve could not mandate that people show up for work, that they not be late, or that cycle time be reduced. It was theirs/ours, all of ours—that was the new story.

As trust and interest built, employees had the opportunity to become part of voluntary work teams, teams dedicated to discussing problems of efficiency and recommending solutions to issues that influenced all of their success. They discussed questions like how to reduce absenteeism (only 2 percent had perfect attendance and 10 percent of employees were absent every day), and how to share some of the wealth if they could increase their productivity and their efficiencies. Eventually there were eight different groups exploring a wide array of problems that needed solutions. They were built on the basis of goodwill and without professional facilitators or costly training. Each of the eight working groups had the ability to formulate new questions as well as to generate some answers.

Over time, management continued to listen, to engage, and to negotiate with the employees in good faith the solutions that reflected good business. The turnaround was dramatic and rapid. It turns out that the employees had been hungry for the opportunity to succeed, to build quality products and to support good, cooperative management. And during the process, they began to feel proud of the opportunities they provided themselves, and of the increasing morale and their increased productivity. Now when talking to their friends, they could point with pride to what made them so different, the exception, the improbable. They began to experience the real meaning of transparency, of candor and data-based feedback. They constructed many of their own work rules.

The teams brought in customers to talk about what the customers really needed and how the company could improve the product to better meet those needs. They talked to one another, and they talked regularly to the organizational leadership. The results were stunning.

Management's goal was to drive the production cycle time for the 130 people working on the floor down from 14 days to 5 in one month. In fact, the employees dropped it to a 3-day cycle in 90 days; currently it's 1.1 days. The employees are in every sense the home of best practices in their area of work. And a formula was agreed to that rewarded workers for the ever-improving productivity cycle with real dollars in their pockets, rewards that could literally be followed on a daily basis.

On the subject of absenteeism, the employees decided that it was important not to threaten but to reward people for being present, for excellence in attendance just as in everything else they were attempting to stand for. But it was also clear that the workers weren't only about money. Recognition was, in some cases, equally important. Employees and management agreed that perfect attendance would be rewarded with a dinner cooked and prepared by the bosses every month—an excuse to celebrate and break down the walls that had for so long separated management from those upon whom success was dependent. Perfect attendance over a year went from just over 2 percent to a current average of 60–70 percent.

Both management and leaders have learned that motivation and morale are connected at the hip and that numbers and measured performance can be the seedbed for high morale and, ultimately, for high productivity. Being creative and thinking outside of the box is essential so that routine does not lead to monotony and discipline does not get replaced by self-satisfaction, in the process driving out motivation. Currently there are both functional and cross-functional teams operating in the South Bend plant. Many of these teams have no management presence. One recently successfully instituted a drug-free policy supported by employee testing.

The central concept is that data are not used to "catch" people or to police their activities. Rather, they are used to support a climate of inquiry, rooted in teams and a cooperative, interdependent view of organizational life.

New Territory

PEI-Genesis measures almost everything. But the company has a number of measures that matter most, and everyone knows them. If cycle time is low and quality measures are high, everything else will tend to work. This was one of the essential lessons that Steve and his leadership team acknowledge. Other lessons were that they need to act authentically and to reward good works as promptly as possible. Most of all, they learned that measured excellence should be rewarded, never resented, and that sharing the rewards of good work will, in the long run, create more business, and even more rewards, for everyone. Some leaders resent the fact that people tend to work harder when they are rewarded for extra effort. Their belief is that if people are paid a fair wage, they should work at their full potential all the time. Such naïveté goes against everything that experience has taught us about personal motivation, human conditioning, and reinforcement theory.

Steve had no book to follow as he entered a collaborative world of management that was grounded in trust, openness, and kindness. His intuition suggested that he had to engage people on two levels. First was the level of equality in a world of inequality that created prejudices on both sides of the management-worker divide. Second was the level of accountability and rewards and how they came together in the realm of numbers and measurement. These numbers and the transparency of their use in turn reinforced trust and openness.

Used only as tools, or sometimes as weapons and threats, metrics will never succeed, but used in positive relationships the results are much different. At PEI-Genesis the marriage of metrics and rewards resulted in huge leaps in efficiencies, reducing the number of employees required to do the same work by 20 percent and doubling worker efficiencies. Most of all, the combination has helped employees achieve a more secure future, a happier place of work, and the knowledge that the pride that drives their work is real, deserved, and measured every day.

The process takes time—time to listen deeply, time to translate information into ideas, time to continually look for better answers. It is ongoing and demanding and requires great discipline. But, most of all, it demands that everyone, whether on the production or management side, tell the truth and be prepared to receive the feedback that occurs routinely every day. This in turn unleashes the creativity of the employees as they, together with management, attempt to resolve the blocks to their own future.

The Idea of Fairness

For an organization to last over time, to continue achieving in an increasingly competitive world, it has to have a good product that is in demand and is of dependable quality, and a workforce that is efficient and reliable. Steve had toyed with the notion of going public, of becoming really big. But he feared two things. One was that he would fall prey to the quick fix, bottom-line profit-driven mentality in which time spent building relationships was not valued. Also not valued were sharing potential profits with the employees upon whose backs they were generated and taking workers away from production time to serve as production consultants. Treated fairly, the workers had given Steve and others something to measure that had resulted in a self-fulfilling prophecy of increased efficiency, productivity, and higher morale, along with all that goes with them. It was not about being nice—although that matters—it was about good business and the will and rigor to stay the course and live the values that feed the best in people. Ultimately it was about providing greater value to the customer, to the employees, and to the owners. The marriage of all three can be seen vividly in the PEI-Genesis example.

So, What Have We Learned?

Steve's lessons, framed in relation to manufacturing and a production line, were not far off from Lupe's lessons in her retail-oriented college bookstore (from the First Bookstore case study in Part 1). In neither case was success dependent on advanced degrees, special courses in psychometrics, or computer analyses. They both, however, needed a willingness to ask hard questions and then to go out and deal with the truth. Knowing the truth and framing it in meaningful numbers provide both leaders and workers with choices and opportunities. If the numbers are going in the wrong direction, leaders can change course, get creative, problem-solve, and involve those who are coming up short in ways that give them a real stake in their own success. Then they can reward them for their successes.

Questions for Leaders

Following are sixteen tough-minded questions that will demand good information and your courage as the leader to both deal with them and to make needed changes if success is to be sustained over time. The questions are at the heart of measuring what matters. There are others, of course, but these will put you well ahead of the game.

1. Do you have a purposeful, systematic means of obtaining *balanced feedback* from the three critical constituencies— customers, employees and owners—in your part of the organization?

More than anything, this question frames all of the others. It represents a way of thinking, an aggressive commitment to inquiry from the three critical stakeholders in the life of any organization.

———

2. Does your organization have a clear purpose, or mission, explaining clearly what it is, what it does, and what differentiates it from its competition?

This is the beginning point of effective organizational decision making, providing focus and direction. Each subunit or team's mission should be a clear reflection of this overall system purpose. Each team, in turn, should have its own mission.

———

3. Do you have the means of measuring specifically what each of the three organizational constituencies *value* and expect from their relationship with you?

Value is at the heart of understanding each of these groups—what drives them, what they need, and what stake each has in the life of the organization based on their desired outcomes.

———

4. Are you able to measure the gap between what the three constituencies say they value and how satisfied they are in what they receive?

The discrepancy between expectations and reality provides the opportunity for improvement. This is not to suggest that everything that is valued can be accomplished. However, the greater the congruence between needs and achievement, the greater the satisfaction of each constituent group.

———

5. Do the work teams within the organization know and understand their *owners*—those to whom they are ultimately accountable?

Understanding that owners are part of the system and not adversaries is a crucial element in promoting goodwill and harmony within any organization.

———

6. Is there a clear alignment between organizational purpose and the distribution of internal resources?

This alignment provides the opportunity for determining focused roles and responsibilities as well as the possibilities for greater efficiencies within the various operations.

––––

7. Do the work teams or units have the capacity for measuring both the efficiency and productivity of the organizational *processes* that are most fundamental to their success?

Measurement is at the core of a team's capacity to change, to evolve into a more effective performing unit. It implies the means to observe and determine the effectiveness of the group in relation to some internal or external standards.

––––

8. Is there an organizational mechanism in place that allows teams to analyze the data from the process review as well as to problem-solve the issues resulting from the analysis?

Process reviews focus on the means of refining how work occurs within the team in pursuit of its own mission and particular goals. Data provide the key to unlocking resistance to change, overcoming dysfunctional habits, and moving toward greater effectiveness.

––––

9. Is there an effort to compare the methods used within teams to external best practices and to internal standards provided by the teams' own efforts at improvement?

Many organizations and their functional teams are locked into their own parochial views of work and the processes they use. Long-standing organizational habits, or norms, are particularly difficult to overcome in insular organizations, where work patterns are seldom questioned because of reputations or the specialized nature of their work.

_____

10. Is there a deep knowledge of the competition? What are its similarities and differences with your organization? What are its strengths and limitations?

You will find it useful to look internally and identify effective and ineffective patterns of work and to compare current work to best practices in similar and related fields. Being conscious of the competition can often be the difference between long-term success and failure—especially in affecting the willingness to upgrade and change.

_____

11. What are the core operational values that support how your people work and how they treat one another? Are the values measured periodically at both the team and organizational levels?

Core values are usually placed on a placard and then forgotten. Lupe used the core values (speaking the truth, excellence, respect, and integrity) as complementary to the organization's vision and mission. Without being measured and built into the daily life of the organization, they will fail. Thus, their measurement is crucial to system accountability as well as to action-oriented responses.

_____

12. Has the vision of where the teams are going over the next three to six years been mapped out in terms of measurable goals and benchmarks?

Organizational and unit or team visions allow success to be measured in terms of progress toward specific long-range goals. Such specific visions can be prime motivators in system and team change. Given measures of a team's current reality and projected future, they support the periodic review of what is valued by various stakeholders and how this is changing and is likely to change over time. This can be a simple or complex process, but it should be done.

———

13. Is there an instrument (such as the GMQ—see Chapter 8) for measuring how well a team is functioning as a team—how effectively the members work together?

Dysfunction within a team can occur as a result of ineffective work procedures or *process*. It can also occur because of the inability of a team's members to get along with one another through lack of trust, support, communication, collaboration, or the willingness to deal with the conflicts that are bound to arise. This type of team maintenance should be tracked and monitored on a regular basis or it will surely influence how work is accomplished.

———

14. Are your employees monitored on a periodic basis to determine their morale, attitudes toward work, and their satisfaction with work as a part of their lives?

Unhappy workers will inevitably influence both the quality and quantity of work they provide. Simple measures can allow team leaders insight into the changing dynamics of both individuals and their teams. Since many workers put on a positive face to leadership, it is important to provide them the opportunity to speak candidly, with confidentiality ensured.

———

15. Are individuals evaluated on a regular basis in relation to both their individual goal achievement and their own personal development?

After hiring good workers, the next most essential role of management is to ensure that personnel are both meeting their goals and being allowed to develop over time to maximize their own potentials. The future of any team or organization lies in fulfilling this role.

———

16. Is supervision (the act of performance management) taken seriously and measured periodically in relation to its impact on both productivity and morale, as seen through the eyes of those receiving the service—the workers themselves?

The quality of supervision is usually as effective as is the supervision of the supervisors themselves. Unless periodic reviews are conducted and the results are related to how supervisors are rewarded, the supervisory process will almost certainly deteriorate over time, and be accompanied by the inevitable decline in morale, productivity, and efficiency.

With so many critical areas of measurement, which are the most important?

Ideally, you need to pay attention to all sixteen areas reflecting the key areas of leadership and management in modern teams and organizations. As we have shown, none have to be done in ways that are hugely time consuming or complicated. But they all require some time and attention. They need to be institutionalized so they become a part of the way business is accomplished on a daily basis. But if you are a start-up or have not engaged many of these ideas previously, it is important to choose a few areas that will provide the most benefit for your particular unit.

Summary

PEI-Genesis was doing considerable measurement in many areas. But the progress it had to make on its bottom-line efficiencies was tied to creating a communications vehicle so the workers—upon whom everything depended—finally felt heard and appreciated. This vehicle took the form of informal conversations with Steve, the CEO. The conversations were his approach to data gathering. As a result, they focused on the production cycle and on absenteeism. Both of these initiatives relied heavily on employee support and could not be mandated. The result was that measurements began to be used in more fruitful ways, because the workers helped define success, helped shape the measures, and set the standards increasingly built on pride of work and the growing reputation of what was becoming *their own company.*

As we have said many times during the course of this book, measurement will be successful if it is conducted in a humane, caring, and supportive manner. True, it can provide numbers, and ultimately may increase efficiencies in all aspects of work. But the consequences—productive change, recognition for good work, and a more positive work environment—begin with the attitudes and values of those seeking the various measurements in the first place. Done well, measurement reflects the best of what we know about participative management and collaboration and their marriage with technology.

Appendix

Building Effective Goals and Measurement Criteria

It has become increasingly evident that there is a great distance between having the skills necessary to conduct a successful Supervisory Dialogue and being able to apply those skills. Well-intentioned supervisors agree on the nature of an employee's goals and, generally, how to measure them. However, the breakdown often comes later during a year-end review or during the course of a midyear review session. Typically, the original agreement will have lacked sufficient specificity. This makes it difficult to determine how well the person has actually performed. Here we provide some clear examples of what we mean by performance goals and the criteria necessary to measure them. We begin with the assumption that *if you can define a goal, you can measure it.*

The Game of Unclear Goals and Ill-Defined Criteria

Let's face it, most people do not like to be measured in terms of specific outcomes. Hazy and ill-defined goals provide wiggle room. The less specific, the less threatening. Further, as people move higher in most organizations, they tend to find goals, objectives, and related criteria to be less defined. Often the assumption is that people are skilled and motivated and will do what they verbally agree to do. The truth is that people vary greatly in what it takes to motivate them or hold them accountable. By demanding clearly defined, criterion-based goals, the supervisor levels the playing field and sets a tone of professionalism that cannot be attained otherwise.

So, why then would supervisors not jump at the opportunity to engage in such a positive process? By working with an employee to define clear performance outcomes along with their measures, supervisors have to understand the capabilities of the individual, the nature of the work/project, and the kind of effort it would take to complete the work at a high standard. Many leaders do not have the patience or are not willing to take the up-front time to consider each major project an employee undertakes. Also, by playing it loose, by keeping expectations less well defined, it is easier to slip in additional projects or make additional demands of the employee. As strange as it seems, clearly defining work expectations takes away power from the supervisor—the power to be arbitrary and unfairly critical.

The greatest protection an employee can have against being unfairly treated is a clearly defined job role, along with clear, outcome-based measures of success. Conversely, the greatest protection the employer can have against poor work performance is the establishment of clearly defined goals and the agreed-upon criteria of success.

The reality is that in a litigious, critical, and sometimes unfair world, both the boss and the employee are more secure if clear, unambiguous, descriptive goals exist. They must be supported by measurable criteria that detail unequivocally what success is. For employees, goals of this nature, with accompanying criteria, provide standards against which their own performance can be measured. The more descriptive the better. Reaching an agreed-upon outcome is difficult to deny when the performance can be weighed against predetermined standards of success.

For the employer, knowing how well employees attain agreed-upon goals and their behaviorally based criteria can aid in distributing rewards and recognition, in providing timely and specific coaching, or, in extreme cases, in taking other steps—such as termination—when other measures have been of no avail. Clear goals and measurable criteria go hand in hand with gaining the documentation necessary to take such actions. Whatever the case, the details create objectivity and provide a climate of fairness based on something other than subjective judgments and gut feelings.

Work at the front end of the supervisory process can pay huge dividends to both parties at the other end when accountability is evaluated. Good employees welcome clear standards. The development of criterion-based goals allows them to pace themselves and celebrate their own successes. Too often good, driven employees need unambiguous boundaries to help them focus and not abuse their own tendency to overwork, to lack balance, and, eventually, to burn out. Part of an effective supervisor's role is to help such individuals, and providing clear, measurable, time-bounded goals can help enormously.

Performance management often fails when the employer is not encouraged to renegotiate new goals and criteria after substantial new work and additional responsibilities arrive on the scene. The result can be an exhausted, frustrated, and unappreciated employee for whom complaining would be a breach of loyalty or simply a negative act in their own eyes or, perhaps, the eyes of their boss.

Too often, the boss, anxious to meet the demands made by his or her own supervisor, or perhaps a board, piles additional work on the employee most easily influenced (often the individual who complains least and is most capable). The result is that both morale and the quality of performance decline. Worse yet, what appeared on the surface to be an objective, goal-based process of performance management becomes subjective and arbitrary. Employees find themselves distributing their time according to how they believe success will be measured. This leaves them increasingly vulnerable and dependent on the whims of the boss. Almost certainly, employees learn from the experience and negotiate "down" the next time goals are being established. The tendency then will be to commit to as little as possible so that when the additional work is thrown their way without regard to previously contracted goals, they will not feel punished for negotiating a full plate of goals in the first place.

The integrity of the ten-question Supervisory Dialogue depends on the credibility of the original goal negotiation process. Goals can change during the course of a year, but then outcomes and expectations must also change to reflect these new realities; a new contract must be agreed upon.

As we know, emergencies happen, and most workers will attempt to adapt to such extraordinary situations without complaint. The problem arises when the exception becomes the norm and the original goal negotiations become a farce. The integrity of the supervisory process itself and the trust upon which all effective supervision is based are then lost.

Establishing Clear, Descriptive, Measurable, Outcome-Based Goals

The saying goes, if you can't see it, taste it, smell it, and measure it, it's not worth much and you shouldn't trust it. The point is that employees at all levels need to know when they have succeeded at accomplishing a goal as well as when an agreed-upon standard has been attained. If I am a dedicated supervisor, I will do the best I can to create the most objective evaluation process possible. The closer I come to that end, the more I will benefit both myself and my employee. After all, the goal and criteria of success guide the efforts of each employee and become sources of motivation, satisfaction, and measurable accomplishment.

Outcome-based goals, such as those we discuss here, are defined by what must be accomplished and, if possible, at what level of specificity, efficiency, or quality. Both the supervisor and the employee define the individual's goals and the criteria separately because there are many ways to frame a goal and many ways to measure its success. Defining and then negotiating the best definition of success helps determine how well individuals understand the task, how motivated they will be to complete it, and how good they feel once it is achieved. Following are some of the terms relevant to this part of the Supervisory Dialogue.

Outcome or product based. The *outcome* or *product* is what we are attempting to accomplish: dollars earned, attitudes shifted, paper written, conflict resolved, building completed, course taught. These provide clear evidence that what was agreed to was accomplished.

Descriptive. The more we can *describe* the outcome, the less chance there is for confusion. Being *descriptive* and *specific* are the two pillars of effective feedback. Any good evaluation process includes a descriptive picture of what has been accomplished. The more specific the better. Being descriptive removes critical or judgmental language from the process. It allows us to stick to the facts and reduces the tendency for people to become defensive or have to justify themselves. What is, is.

Measurable. If we can quantify what it is we are attempting to accomplish, we can remove a great deal of subjectivity from the evaluation equation. To increase earnings by so much, raise standards by a third, implement something by a particular date, or measurably improve my ability to listen—such measures make it much easier to determine how successful a person is.

Any particular goal or the criteria for measuring the successful accomplishment of the goal will utilize these and other terms to varying degrees. There is no set formula. What we do know is that establishing an effective goal and the accompanying measurable criteria for determining how effective the individual has been is crucial to any successful performance review.

The usual assumption is that the kinds of goals outlined here demand a considerable amount of the employee's attention, over and above normal day-to-day activities. It is these goals, however, that provide the individual with challenge, opportunities for personal growth, and the chance to contribute significantly to the forward movement of the organization. The one exception is the goal of supervision. As we discuss in Example 9 (page 371), without measured accountability in this area, supervision will predictably be undervalued and underutilized. Without consequences, other ways of expending our energy and time will matter more to us.

Examples of Effective Goals and Measurable Criteria

Sometimes the measurement of a goal's effectiveness is embedded in the goal itself. In other instances, the measurable criteria provide critical benchmarks or more specific outcomes. For each of the following goals, we offer a rationale for presenting it.

Example 1: To hire a new director and two new associate directors by the first of the year.

Additional performance measures: A group hiring model will be utilized; the final candidates will be measured against common criteria by means of their performance in behavioral vignettes and questions given to each of the finalists.

Explanation: In this case the goal itself is unambiguous. The supervisor and the employee agree that a particular hiring strategy will be utilized. The assumption is that the employee is skilled in this process. Otherwise, learning this skill set could be one of the employee's agreed-upon commitments in question 8 of the Supervisory Dialogue—strategies for overcoming blocks to their effectiveness in the coming year.

Example 2: To develop a strategic partnership with _____ corporation in order to maximize our resources and reduce our costs within ____ unit.

Additional performance measures: By June I will have laid out an agreed-upon strategy for this initiative with our executive council. By September I will be in negotiations either with _____ or _____. By November executive council members will have the proposed contractual relationship in hand for their deliberation and decision. Our goal is to begin the alliance by the first of the year; we realize success could be influenced by our future partner. Based on our estimates of the potential for savings, our aim is to save _____ by the following June.

Explanation: Clearly, this goal is predicated on substantial pre-work and discussion. Again, as in the first goal, it is assumed that the individual has an understanding of the complexities of creating such a strategic alliance. Otherwise the use of a consultant would be legitimate. A less aggressive goal might be to explore the pros and cons of such an alliance, including potential partners. Often the more specific and concrete a goal is, as in this case, the more motivating it becomes. The negotiation by the employee is in being sure there are sufficient resources and knowledge available to allow success.

Example 3: To reorganize the _____ office to increase efficiencies and better utilize our current resources.

Additional performance measures: By this time next year, operational expenses will be reduced by a full 15 percent; at the same time, service in the department will be measurably increased. This will be measured by a 10 percent reduction in unsolicited client complaints and a 10 percent increase in client satisfaction, as measured in our annual client survey.

Explanation: None of these measures appears difficult to obtain and could be easily developed even if there was no precedent. The idea is never to create busy work or create roadblocks for the employee. Rather, the intent is to provide clarity and focus through the specifics of the performance measures.

Example 4: To create and implement a prototype course in distance learning that connects our national offices with a low-cost training program in _____.

Additional performance measures: The technology investment will remain below $25,000 based on information from our research of other organizations. The content of the training program will be developed in house, with an estimated expenditure of no more than $10,000 on a consultant specialist to help us format the program. Our aim is to air the first one-hour module by March 1, with successive modules to be aired at two-week intervals over a ten-week period.

Explanation: An effective goal should be more than a wish list and not based on conjecture. While a goal can be exploratory in nature, most goals are the result of a specifically identified need and where there is sufficient knowledge to include some important specifics. This is just such a case. The distance learning project has been explored at some depth, best practices in related fields have been studied, and the current goal allows the employee to mobilize the resources necessary to ensure forward movement.

Example 5: To oversee the development of a systemwide strategic planning initiative that will help us increase our competitive advantage over similar institutions. More specifically, the year-long effort will examine resource allocation and measured return on investment, as well as best practices in the areas of marketing and client retention, and will involve futurists to help us expand our own views in these critical areas.

Additional performance measures: Key to the success of this initiative will be the creation of a highly credible steering group to guide the process and determine critical time lines, consultant resources, and levels of stakeholder involvement. This group will be convened by September 15. By November 1, a complete schedule of events and levels of projected participation will be available, along with the projected cost of the entire planning process (agreed to be less than $125,000).

Explanation: Many goals represent a work in progress and cannot be detailed beyond a certain point. Even so, as in this case, the employee has an interim deadline. It would be at that time that a renegotiation of the individual's own goals might be in order, depending on the demands resulting from the work of the steering committee.

Example 6: To display a high level of competence in the utilization of effective design strategies during all meetings of an hour or more.

Additional performance measures: Each such meeting will be evaluated, minimally, in relation to what worked and what failed, as well as to make recommendations for improvement. Both task and process goals will be outlined in advance of each meeting with design strategies linked to them. Review of the evaluations will be utilized to determine overall success and general level of effectiveness.

Explanation: In this case, a senior management team had agreed that most meetings had been a waste of time. Often the wrong people attended meetings and the resources at the meeting were generally underutilized. It was agreed that for a period of two years, key leaders, after being trained in the use of design strategies to increase meeting performance, would be evaluated on a regular basis. The leadership group would reconvene periodically to explore how to continue developing their skills and to clinic the design strategies of other members. There was a sincere commitment by these leaders to use performance measures as a means of stimulating change in the organizational culture regarding meetings.

Example 7: To improve the ability to listen, so that those I influence feel their ideas are being heard.

Example 8: To show a measurable increase in my openness to receive feedback.

Additional performance measures: At two points in the fiscal calendar year (September and February), I will benchmark my progress in these two areas using data from my recent 360-degree feedback as the baseline against which to compare my current performance. A brief, anonymous, scaled item questionnaire will be developed and distributed to from ten to fifteen of my direct reports and others with whom I deal on a regular basis. HR will help me develop the instrument, gather the data, and organize it for my review. I will then share it with my supervisor. Following are several examples of the kinds of items I plan to include in this brief instrument.

1. The degree to which _____ is an effective listener.

1	2	3	4	5	6	7	8	9	10
Not at all				Somewhat					Completely

2. The degree you feel heard by _____.

1	2	3	4	5	6	7	8	9	10
Not at all				Somewhat					Completely

3. The degree to which she or he openly solicits feedback in a work setting.

1	2	3	4	5	6	7	8	9	10
Not at all				Somewhat					Completely

4. As you currently experience _____ as a leader, what several pieces of advice can you provide him which will help him further improve his listening skills?

   _____

   _____

   _____

Explanation: In this case, the person had discovered through his 360-degree data feedback that he needed to make considerable improvement in these two areas of communication. Motivated to improve in the short term, he had identified these two areas on question 7 of his Leadership Dialogue as areas that might block his success in reaching his other leadership goals. He then suggested in question 8 during the same review that such a questionnaire could be utilized to benchmark his progress.

When individual behaviors are shown to be blocking a leader's ability to succeed, as in this case, it is a logical use of the Supervisory Dialogue to help structure such change as a legitimate part of his performance review. It also gives the supervisor the opportunity to model such a risk-taking strategy for employees. Such a developing culture of openness and trust must necessarily be modeled at the top. In our experience, it is not the ability to measure a particular outcome or, in this example, behavior that is the problem. Rather, it is the courage to publicly own the problem and to move toward needed change with accountability being open to public view. It is assumed that, as in the case of the 360-degree data, the results are shared by the leader with those most influenced, such as the individual's direct reports.

Example 9: To perform my supervisory functions at a level of excellence as agreed to by our leadership group and detailed in the Supervisory Evaluation Instrument.

Additional performance measures: The Supervisory Evaluation Instrument will be distributed anonymously to all of my direct reports a month prior to my year-end review. In addition to the ten scaled items, it will include three open-ended questions agreed to by the leadership group. These will be tabulated by HR, analyzed by me, and utilized as part of my Leadership Dialogue with the supervisor. This goal will have a weight equal to any of my other key leadership goals.

Explanation: As in example 6, this goal is meant to focus the organization's leaders on the importance of supervision. It is intended to create the necessary leverage to alter norms that give little importance to the supervisory process. Building these into the evaluation process of each leader with supervisory responsibility will dramatically increase the chance that improvement on a system level will, in fact, occur. Key to this is the gathering of data around agreed-upon criteria of effective supervision. It is also assumed that each supervisor has had the necessary training to be successful. Knowing, however, that the discipline of supervising had often been superseded by other demands on the supervisor's time, this goal was established to increase quality and commitment.

Examples of Questions for Evaluating Supervisory Effectiveness

With this organization, ten specific behaviors were identified as core to their definition of effective supervision. Behaviorally

---

Directions: Please place a check on the line to show your perception of this supervisor's level of competence regarding the specific behaviors listed. Each of these items corresponds to a standard to which we have committed as an organization to move toward. Each supervisor will be evaluated regularly as part of the yearly review.

---

1. Clearly defines his or her limits of authority.

    1   2   3   4   5   6   7   8   9   10
    Not at all   Somewhat   Completely

2. Jointly works with you to determine the criteria of success upon which your own performance will be measured.

    1   2   3   4   5   6   7   8   9   10
    Not at all   Somewhat   Completely

3. Actively helps you focus on your own career development and the opportunities available to you both within and outside our organization.

    1   2   3   4   5   6   7   8   9   10
    Not at all   Somewhat   Completely

4. Solicits information from you and those you affect on your job concerning your own effectiveness.

    1   2   3   4   5   6   7   8   9   10
    Not at all   Somewhat   Completely

5. What are this person's greatest strengths as a supervisor?

    _____

    _____

    _____

6. What advice would help increase his or her effectiveness? Please be specific.

    _____

    _____

    _____

defined, the items lend themselves nicely to a scaled item review. They are similar to the behaviors used in examples 7 and 8 above. In addition, with this review being provided for each supervisor, it is easy to use the results, without the names of the individual supervisors, to benchmark how the organization is doing as a whole in the areas of supervisory improvement. A number of examples of these criteria are shown on page 372.

Summary

How well individuals set their sights on particular goals and achieve agreed-upon results can say more than anything about their on-the-job performance. Removing the arbitrariness from the process of evaluation provides security for both the employer and the employee. Most goals can be measurable in concrete and observable terms. Such measures can focus strictly on the product side of goal achievement or, equally important, may include measures of how effective the individual was in carrying out the steps toward the ultimate outcome. Such process measures are not difficult to develop and often provide the clues concerning issues of motivation and leadership potential.

Selecting from four to seven goals of importance to the individual and to the organization can provide a profoundly rich picture of how the individual goes about his or her business. The evaluation data represent the seeds for each person's individual growth and development. The information enables the supervisor to work closely with direct reports to actualize their potential. In addition, while routine, day-to-day work can be assessed, what will differentiate people is their work on specific goals felt to be important both to them and their supervisor. Here is the playing field upon which merit pay can be determined in a fair and equitable manner, since it is criterion based and includes a broad band of behavior and achievement.

Notes

Chapter 1

1. Kenneth Blanchard and Spencer Johnson, *The One Minute Manager* (New York: Berkley, 1981); Thomas J. Peters and Robert H. Waterman, *In Search of Excellence* (New York: Warner Books, 1982).
2. Stephen R. Covey, *7 Habits of Highly Effective People* (New York: Fireside, 1989). For the Pareto Principle, see Joseph M. Juran and A. Blanton Godfrey, 5th ed., *Juran's Quality Handbook* (New York: McGraw-Hill, 1998).
3. Joan Magretta with Nan Stone, *What Management Is* (New York: The Free Press, 2002). See Peter F. Drucker, *The Essential Drucker* (New York: HarperCollins, 2001).
4. Harvey Mackay, *Swim with the Sharks without Being Eaten Alive* (New York: Ballantine, 1988).

Chapter 2

1. Harold Geneen, *Managing* (Garden City, NY: Doubleday, 1984).
2. Stephen R. Covey, *The Eighth Habit: From Effectiveness to Greatness* (New York: The Free Press, 2004).
3. Arthur R. Tenner and Irving J. DeToro, *Process Redesign: The Implementation Guide for Managers* (Reading, MA: Addison-Wesley, 1997).

Chapter 3

1. Wayne Rice, *Still More Hot Illustrations for Youth Talks* (Grand Rapids, MI: Zondervan Publishing, 1999).
2. Karl Albrecht, *The Only Thing That Really Matters: Bringing the Power of the Customer into the Center of Your Business* (New York: HarperCollins, 1992).
3. Andrew Neely, Chris Adams, and Mike Kennerly, *The Performance Prism: The Scorecard for Measuring and Managing Business Success* (Upper Saddle River, NJ: Prentice Hall, 2002); William H. Davidow and Bro Uttal, *Total Customer Service: The Ultimate Weapon* (New York: Harper Perennial, 1990).
4. Neely, Adams, and Kennerly, *The Performance Prism;* Davidow and Uttal, *Total Customer Service.*

5. Leonard Berry, *Discovering the Soul of Service* (New York: The Free Press, 1999).
6. Jan Carlzon, *Moments of Truth* (Cambridge, MA: Ballinger, 1987).

Chapter 4

1. Chuck Jones, "Truth or Consequences," *New Horizons Community Church*, http://www.horizonsnet.org/sermons/tc09.html (accessed June 8, 2005).
2. Marcus Buckingham and Curt Coffman, *First, Break All the Rules: What the World's Greatest Managers Do Differently* (New York: Simon and Schuster, 1999), p. 57.

Chapter 5

1. Wayne Rice, *Hot Illustrations for Youth Talks* (El Cajon, CA: Youth Specialties, 1994).
2. Wayne Rice, *More Hot Illustrations for Youth Talks* (El Cajon, CA: Youth Specialities, 1995).

Chapter 6

1. Some of the material in this chapter first appeared under the title "Building Trust: a Key Factor in the Process of Institutional Change" in the following publication: Pat Sanaghan and Rod Napier, *Intentional Design and the Process of Change* (Washington, DC: NACUBO Press, 2002).

Chapter 7

1. Ever since 360-degree feedback caught the imagination of upper management, it has attracted an army of consultants and organizations dedicated to helping and offering one-of-a-kind data, support, data interpretation, and strategic problem solving. The price for this management ticket can be extraordinarily high; such organizations differentiate themselves by offering increasingly stylized approaches, sophisticated and complex data, and related information. However, you can undertake 90 percent of the data gathering and related methods with easy-to-follow guidelines. Once again, the key is measuring what truly matters.

Overcoming ineffective behavior assumes that individuals interested in improving their performance could replicate what we did for Jake. The same principles could be utilized in a team approach as well. Outside help may be desirable, but it is not necessary to be successful.

2. Three hundred sixty–degree feedback is often used strictly as a critical piece in the process of leadership development with no relation to compensation, advancement opportunities, or, as in Jake's case, specific problems. In fact, it is being used increasingly as a normal part of the supervisory cycle, separated from quantitative goals and performance-related requirements.

3. Albert Ellis, *Overcoming Destructive Beliefs* (Amherst, NY: Prometheus Books, 2001).

4. Kurt Lewin, *Field Theory in Social Science* (New York: Harper and Row, 1951).

Chapter 8

1. Edward de Bono, *Six Thinking Hats* (Boston: Back Bay Books, 1999).

Chapter 9

1. Marcus Buckingham and Curt Coffman, in their book *First, Break All the Rules: What the World's Greatest Managers Do Differently* (New York: Simon and Schuster, 1999), revealed in dramatic fashion how even minimal attention to personal development had a direct correlation with both increased profits and reduced turnover; their conclusions were based on a study of more than one hundred thousand employees in twenty-four companies.

Index

absenteeism, 346–347, 350
accountability, 194, 277
affection, 199
Albrecht, Karl, 80
assurance, 88
attention: focused, 24; informal, 8–9; measured, 9–11
authority, 193

benchmarking, 6
benchmarks, 76
Blanchard, Ken, 8
board of directors, 29–30

Carlzon, Jan, 92
change: feedback and, 197–198; implementation of, 182; internalizing of, 182; motivators of, 259; summary of, 342–343; 360-degree feedback and, 258; winning, 15–16
clearly defined goals, 192, 290–291, 362–365
clearly defined purpose, 50
communication: absence of, 297; in Group Management Questionnaire, 274; measurement of, 274; organizational climate affected by, 274; problems with, 190; trust affected by, 194
comparison, 10–11
competition, 356
confidentiality, 257
conflict: avoidance of, 272; in Group Management Questionnaire, 272–273; resolution of,

196, 268–269; strategies for, 272; in teams, 263
connecting strategy, 34–35
consultant reviews, 76
content knowledge, 191–192
continuous process improvement, 33
contributions, owner, 21, 47, 50, 78
core behavioral values, 304
core values, 89, 356
Cornell, Ezra, 27
corporate fitness, 142–143
Covey, Stephen, 9, 133, 171
criteria-based goals, 335
customer(s): as stakeholders, 12–13, 17, 24; ask the experts about, 88; asking of, 88–89; assessment of, 22, 127; case study of, 79–80, 98–124; choices for, 80; contributions by, 21; core values expected by, 89; cycle of service, 92–93; definition of, 17, 82; employee interactions with, 130; expectations of, 18–19, 22, 96, 173; external, 83–84; feedback, 82, 137; identifying of, 82–86, 100–101, 125; importance of, 173; input from, 88–90; internal, 83; loyalty of, 89; prioritizing of, 84; retention of, 81; summary of, 125–127; understanding of, 132; value exchange with, 81, 87; value for, 19, 22, 104, 176; work team values and expectations of, 84, 87–89, 97, 125–127

customer contributions: corporate purpose and, 95–97, 127; description of, 95; resources to organization, 97

customer perceptions: assessment of, 94; management of, 92; summary of, 126

Customer Relationship Management, 17–18

customer relationships: managing of, 80–81; resources used for, 81

customer satisfaction: assessment of, 91–92; description of, 81; surveys of, 91–92

customer service: dimensions of, 88; economics of, 80–81; importance of, 81

cycle of service, 92–93

data analysis, 228

data gathering: about stakeholders, 182; myths regarding, 187

descriptive goals, 365

developmental supervision, 308–309

differentiating value, 89

directive mission, 34

downsizing, 262

Drucker, Peter, 11

Edmond, V. Raymond, 17

Einstein, Albert, 9

emotional fitness, 144

empathy, 88

employee(s): absenteeism by, 346–347, 350; affection for, 199; appreciation for, 273, 294; as stakeholders, 12–13, 17, 24; assessment of, 143–148; career

aspirations for, 327–328; case study of, 148–169; change by, 142; circumstances and, 133; company/team value and expectations, 142–143, 169–170; contributions by, 21; corporate fit for, 143–144; customer interactions with, 130; definition of, 17; expectations for, 143–144, 170, 322; expectations of company/teams by, 136–141; failures by, 322–323; feedback from, 144; identifying of, 131–134, 169; importance of, 130–131, 174; individual differences among, 132–133; job description for, 145; lack of appreciation for, 273, 294; learning about, 131–134; monitoring of, 357; monitoring phase for, 333–334; morale of, 195; objectives for, 145; organization relationships with, 168; perceptions of, 131; performance reviews, 146; power of, 130–131; productivity indicators for, 145; responsibility areas for, 324; rewards and recognition effects on, 193; role clarity for, 192–193; self-motivated, 301; summary of, 169–170; survey of, 141; talents of, 142–143; two-way assessments, 146; value exchange, 135, 137; values, 136–141, 176, 322; work outcomes for, 325–326

employee contribution: company/team value and expectations, 142–143, 169–170; summary of, 170

employee satisfaction, 135
exchange of value: with customers,
    81, 87; description of, 22–23, 76;
    with employees, 135, 137; fos-
    tering of, 182; with owners, 76
Executive Role Counseling, 219
expectations: customer, 18–19, 22,
    96, 173; employee, 143–144, 170,
    322; stakeholder, 18–20; work
    teams, 18–20, 82–84, 89–95, 97,
    126–127, 136–141
external comparisons: description
    of, 44–45; sources for, 76
external customers, 83–84

favoritism, 193
feedback: change and, 197–198;
    confidentiality regarding, 257;
    customer, 82, 137; employee,
    144; importance of, 302; orga-
    nizational climate for, 269; pro-
    viding of, 304; stakeholder, 182;
    360-degree. *See* 360-degree
    feedback; trust and, 197–198
First Bookstore case study: cus-
    tomers, 98–124; employees,
    148–169; owners, 51–75; stake-
    holders, 177–182

Geneen, Harold, 32
goals: clearly defined, 192,
    290–291, 362–365; criteria-
    based, 335; descriptive, 365;
    effective, 366–371; in Group
    Management Questionnaire,
    270; measurable, 365–371; out-
    come-based, 364–365; product-
    based, 364–365; summary of,
    373; unclear, 361–364

Group Management Question-
    naire: actions based on,
    303–305; Communication cate-
    gory of, 274, 296–297; Conflict
    category of, 272–273, 292–294;
    description of, 264, 267–270;
    focus of, 278; Goals, Purpose,
    and Direction category of,
    270–271; Group Process and
    Meeting Design category of,
    274–276, 289–291; interpreta-
    tion of, 289–303; item analysis,
    288–289; Leadership category
    of, 276, 300; Meeting Design
    category, 274–276, 297–299;
    Rewards, Appreciation, and
    Recognition category of, 273–274,
    294–296; sample, 278–284;
    scoring of, 284–289; summary
    of, 305–306; Supervision/
    Performance Management
    category of, 276–278, 300–303;
    Team Climate category of,
    271–272, 291–292

Holmes, Oliver Wendell, 9–10

individuality, 133
Industrial Revolution, 5–6
inertia, law of, 180–181
informal attention, 8–9
internal customers, 83

job description, 145
job role, 362
Juran, Joseph, 9

key processes: case study, 67–75;
    documenting of, 43, 48;

key processes, *cont'd*
evaluation of, 43–46, 49; external
comparisons of, 44–45; identification of, 42–43, 48; improvement in, 46–47, 49; measure of,
43–46
knowledge: content, 191–192;
product, 191–192

law of inertia, 180–181
leaders: commitment by, 338; effectiveness of, 190; information
gathering for, 261; planning by,
188; questions for, 353–358;
supervisor vs., 276–277
leadership: behaviors necessary
for, 221; development assessment for, 222–225, 232–241;
effectiveness survey, 340–341;
in Group Management Ques-
tionnaire, 276, 300; improvements in, 305
Lewin, Kurt, 259
listening skills, 196–197

Mackay, Harvey, 17
maintenance factors, 19–20
management: case study of,
213–215; definition of, 132;
measuring what matters and,
209; process of, 182; structure of,
192–194; team-based, 262–263;
trust affected by, 192–194; trust
building in, 209–210
measurable goals, 365–371
measured accountability, 194
measured attention, 9–11
measurement(s): of effectiveness,
22–23; errors in, 4; insight

gained from, 10–11; of key
processes, 44; for owners, 21;
summary of, 23–24
measures: comparison of, 10; insight gained from, 10–11; for
key processes, 43–46; purpose
expressed in, 4; wise, 9–11
meetings, 274–276, 297–299, 304–305
mental fitness, 144
mission statement: description of,
34; sample, 61
moment of truth, 92–94
morale, 195, 253–255
Myers-Briggs Type Indicator®
personality inventory, 133

natural work teams, 51
nominal technique, 197

objectives, 145
operational values, 290
organizations: affection for, 199;
authority in, 193; collaborative
climate in, 195–196; compart-
mentalization in, 32; customer
contributions to, 95–97; customer-
driven, 89; employee relationship with, 168; founders of, 28;
founding of, 27–28; lines of
authority in, 193, 276; as living
organisms, 7; maintenance
skills and behaviors in, 195–199;
people in, 7–8; process skills
and behaviors in, 195–199;
processes in, 5–7; productivity
in, 14; purpose of, 4–5, 38–39;
role clarity in, 192–193; stakeholders and, 12–13; success of,
24; supportive atmosphere in,

196; trust in. *See* trust; value in, 24
outcome-based goals, 364–365
outsourcing, 76
owners: as stakeholders, 12–13, 17, 24; case study of, 51–75; contributions by, 21, 47, 50, 78; definition of, 17, 77; founders as, 28; identification of, 28–30; importance of, 173; measurements for, 21; process performance valuation by, 32–33, 37, 41–42, 48; purpose alignment valuation by, 31–32; responses offered by, 50; summary of, 76–78; understanding of, 354; value for, 176; work team expectations, 31–33, 47, 77

Pareto Principle, 9, 41
peer reviews, 76
PEI-Genesis case study, 345–359
people, 7–8
people process adviser, 181
perceived performance, 139
perceptions: customer. *See* customer perceptions; employee, 131
performance audit, 172
performance dialogues, 147
performance management: data in support of, 336–338; failure of, 335–336, 363; steps to ensure success in, 338, 342
performance outcomes, 362
performance reviews, 146
personal relationships, 17
Peters, Tom, 8
physical fitness, 144

planning, 188
prescriptive vision, 34
process: definition of, 5, 41–42; evaluation of, 41, 77–78; importance of, 5–7; improvement in, 46–47; ineffective, 357; key types of. *See* key processes; methodologies for improving, 6; poor, 41; purpose accomplished through, 5; resistance to, 309–310; review of, 78; work and, 33
process certifications, 76
process performance: case study of, 66–75; description of, 21, 32–33; valuation of, 48; in work teams, 32–33, 37, 41–42, 48
Process Reengineering, 41
process review, 355
product knowledge, 191–192
product-based goals, 364–365
productivity: indicators of, 145; ways to increase, 253
purpose: alignment with internal resources, 355; clearly defined, 50; customer contributions and, 95–97, 127; definition of, 77; implementation of, 174; importance of, 4–5, 353–354; in measures, 4; process and, 5
purpose alignment: assessment of, 34–35, 36–40; case study of, 63–64, 66; description of, 21, 31–32; owner's value of, 31–32; stakeholder alignment for, 35; structural alignment and, 36–37

relationship building, 315, 328
reliability, 88, 126

respect, 198
responsiveness, 88
retaliation, 226
rewards: in Group Management
Questionnaire, 273–274; importance of, 193
risk taking, 198
role clarity, 192–193
Rosenbluth, Hal, 129–130

self-motivation, 301
shared values, 35
site visits, 76
spiritual fitness, 144
stakeholder(s): aligning of, 12–13,
15, 174–176; case study of, 177–182;
contributions by, 21–22; customers. *See* customer(s); data
gathering about, 182; employees.
See employee(s); expectations
of, 18–20; feedback from, 182;
identification of, 17–18; metrics
for assessing, 22; owners. *See*
owners; perceptions of, 20;
purpose alignment and, 35;
satisfaction of, 18–20; trust
among, 173–174; work teams
and, 18–20
stakeholder value: description of,
11–12; exchange model for,
14–22; work team application
of, 14
strategy, 34–35
strengths assessment, 243–244
supervision: assumptions,
329–330; commitment to,
311–312; coordinated program
of, 310; definition of, 308; description of, 142; developmen-

tal, 308–309; effectiveness
evaluations, 371–373; exempt
differences, 334–335; in Group
Management Questionnaire,
277–278, 300–303; nonexempt
differences, 334–335; pro forma
approach to, 329; purpose of,
313; quality of, 358; responsibilities, 324; rewarding of, 309;
time allocation to, 312–313
supervisors: assessment of, 145;
description of, 136–137; incom-
petence of, 215–217; leaders vs.,
276–277; relationship building
by, 315, 328; supervisory cycle
for, 330–335; time allocation,
312–313
supervisory cycle, 330–335
Supervisory Dialogue: data gathering, 316; definition of, 313;
employee's participation in,
315; format of, 313–314; overview of, 337–338; performance
data gained through, 336; pre-
dialogue orientation, 317–318;
questions in, 318–329; rationale
for, 314–316, 318–329; substance
of, 316
supervisory review, 339

talents, 142
tangibles, 88
team(s). *See* work teams
team members, 87, 277
team-based culture, 262
team-based management, 262–263
360-degree feedback: analysis of,
228; assumptions of, 219–220;
case study of, 220–224, 226–232,

241–256; change and, 258; commitment necessary for, 257; confidentiality and, 257; data summary for, 232–241; description of, 217–219; elements necessary for effective use of, 257–259; groundwork for, 224, 226; interpretation of, 228; origins of, 219–220; personal nature of, 257–258; summary of, 260
total quality management, 6, 41
trust: affection and, 199; as outcome, 190–199; building of, 188–189, 195; clearly defined goals and, 192; collaborative climate and, 195–196; communication effects on, 194; conflict resolution and, 196, 272–273; content knowledge and, 191–192; data gathering approaches, 187; establishment of, 188–189; failure to build, 188; feedback skills and, 197–198; importance of, 189; lines of authority and, 193, 276; listening skills and, 196–197; management application of, 209–210; management structure and discipline effects on, 192–194; measured account ability and, 194; measurement of, 200–208; participation and, 195–196; in planning process, 188–189; product knowledge and, 191–192; relative nature of, 199–200; respect and, 198; rewards and recognition effects on, 193; risk taking and, 198; stakeholders, 173–174; support-

ive atmosphere and, 196; view of, 189–190
Trust Survey: description of, 201; example of, 203–208; follow-up to, 208; scoring of, 201–203
two-way assessments, 146

value(s): assessment of, 25; creation of, 11–12, 23; for customers, 19; in Group Management Questionnaire, 270; importance of, 354; as input, 11; as output, 11; of owners of work teams, 31–33; shared, 35; for stakeholders, 11–12, 19; as standards of behavior, 24
value exchange: with customers, 81, 87; description of, 22–23, 76; with employees, 135, 137; fostering of, 182; with owners, 76
value-added products, 307
vision statement: description of, 34; sample, 61

White, Andrew Dickson, 27
winning change, 15–16
wise measures, 9–11
work flow, 43
work outcomes, 325–326
work teams: asking of, 84, 87; assessment of, 33–47, 89–95, 182; case study of, 51–75, 264–267; climate of, 271–272, 291–292; conflict in, 263; customer values and expectations of, 82–84, 89–95, 97, 126–127; description of, 14; effectiveness of, 22–23; employee values and expectations of, 136–141; expectations

work teams, *cont'd*
  of employees, 142–143; expectations of owners, 47, 77; foundational elements of building, 278; function of, 24; interteam relationships, 263; key processes in. *See* key processes; meetings, 274–276; members of, 87, 277; metrics used to diagnose and refocus, 266–267; owners of, 28–30, 47, 77; process performance in, 32–33, 37, 41–42; purpose alignment in, 31–32, 34–35, 40; self-assessments by, 20–21; stakeholder alignment in, 174–176; stakeholders expectations and value regarding, 18–20

workflow process adviser, 181
workflow processes, 6